T0235996

AGILE TESTING: HOW TO SUCCEED IN AN EXTREME TESTING ENVIRONMENT

In an IT world in which there are differently sized projects, with different applications, differently skilled practitioners, and onsite, offsite, and offshore development teams, it is impossible for there to be a one-size-fits-all agile development and testing approach. This book provides practical guidance for professionals, practitioners, and researchers faced with creating and rolling out their own agile testing processes. In addition to descriptions of the prominent agile methods, the book provides twenty real-world case studies of practitioners using agile methods and draws upon their experiences to populate your own agile method; whether yours is a small, medium, large, offsite, or even offshore project, this book provides personalized guidance on the agile best practices from which to choose to create your own effective and efficient agile method.

John Watkins has more than thirty years of experience in the field of software development, with some twenty-five years in the field of software testing. During his career, John has been involved at all levels and phases of testing and has provided high-level test process consultancy, training, and mentoring to numerous blue chip companies.

He is both a Chartered IT Professional and a Fellow of the British Computer Society, where he is an active member of the Specialist Group in Software Testing (SIGiST), previously serving on committees of the Intellect Testing Group (representing the U.K. technology industry) and the SmallTalk User Group.

He is author of *Testing IT: An Off-the-Shelf Software Testing Process* (Cambridge University Press, 2001) and currently works for IBM's software group.

AGILE TESTING

How to Succeed in an Extreme Testing Environment

JOHN WATKINS

CAMBRIDGE
UNIVERSITY PRESS

Shaftesbury Road, Cambridge CB2 8EA, United Kingdom

One Liberty Plaza, 20th Floor, New York, NY 10006, USA

477 Williamstown Road, Port Melbourne, VIC 3207, Australia

314–321, 3rd Floor, Plot 3, Splendor Forum, Jasola District Centre, New Delhi – 110025, India

103 Penang Road, #05–06/07, Visioncrest Commercial, Singapore 238467

Cambridge University Press is part of Cambridge University Press & Assessment, a department of the University of Cambridge.

We share the University's mission to contribute to society through the pursuit of education, learning and research at the highest international levels of excellence.

www.cambridge.org
Information on this title: www.cambridge.org/9780521726870

First published 2009

A catalogue record for this publication is available from the British Library

Library of Congress Cataloging-in-Publication data
Watkins, John (John Edward)
Agile testing : how to succeed in an extreme testing environment / John Watkins.
    p.   cm.
Includes bibliographical references and index.
ISBN 978-0-521-19181-4 (hb) – ISBN 978-0-521-72687-0 (pbk. : alk. paper)
1. Agile software development.   2. Computer software – Testing.   I. Title.
QA76.76.D47W384   2009
005.1 – dc22   2009011362

ISBN   978-0-521-19181-4   Hardback
ISBN   978-0-521-72687-0   Paperback

"To my Father, My Methodical Role-Model"

Contents

Foreword

Bob Bartlett, CIO, SQS

It is fascinating to see that so many members of our global software development and implementation community are at last agreeing violently on the principles behind agile. It is gratifying to see developers and testers working side-by-side aiming for the same goals and supporting each other. If you didn't know what agile was but could see productive, disciplined, and self-organizing teams engaged in developing working software prioritized by business value, you would know that whatever they are doing must be right. Testers in particular have benefited from greater pride in their work as they are accepted as equal partners in the software development team.

Agile development and testing is a thirty-year-old overnight success; in fact, most of the younger developers and testers who so enthusiastically promote this new way of developing software had almost certainly not been born when the likes of Barry Boehm and James Martin first began to develop the Rapid Application Development (RAD) method!

Agile certainly seems to be being promoted as the latest silver bullet for all software development problems; the topic is included at pretty much any software event, user group, or standards group you attend, and much of the IT literature is full of agile references. For example, I recently hosted a conference on Software and Systems Quality and invited as a keynote speaker a senior development manager from IBM, who spoke of the corporate-wide initiative – spearheaded by the Chairman – to implement agile methods and processes groupwide. He reported (with good evidence) that product teams have adopted an agile development method in order to be responsive to customer needs and deliver software on time and to budget, with much higher quality – measured by incredibly low rates of postrelease faults.

This is not to say that agile doesn't have its detractors; many traditional IT development practitioners will tell you agile only works for small, simple, and well-bounded software development projects, where the customer and development team are co-located and staffed by experienced and capable practitioners. Why wouldn't a project succeed under such circumstances? So what happens if the customer or some of the team are offsite (or even offshore)? What happens if the application is large, complex, and carries significant technological risk? What if you can't afford to staff your development project with highly experienced, capable, motivated, and very expensive agile experts?

These are certainly some of the major challenges that agile must meet if it is going to be widely accepted, adopted, and used successfully. But in an IT world where there is no universal one-size-fits-all software development process, how can agile be successfully applied to small, medium, large, and offsite/offshore projects? How can agile be used to address complex, difficult, or special-needs IT projects? How can IT practitioners of varying experience and ability adopt and use agile best practices effectively?

There is certainly a risk that such a megatrend as agile becomes overhyped and overexploited commercially. However, the enthusiasm to share experiences and the availability of free and open tools and information is building the community belief and commitment. I have observed many times how intuitively people adopt the agile principles and practices – particularly testers, who embrace their new-found ability to contribute from the outset and "design in" quality on projects. The enthusiasm is contagious and the results of agile teams as seen in systems and software products show what can be produced when there is a dynamic and flexible approach to achieving well-understood goals relentlessly prioritized by business value.

This book is the product of a number of people who felt confident and committed enough to document their experiences in the hopes that others would share their positive results and success. Each case study tells a different success story and at first you may feel overwhelmed with good ideas and ways to develop software. Just bringing these stories together makes for a worthy and valuable book. I am pleased to see that the whole story is told from many perspectives, not just the testing side.

I have known John Watkins for about ten years now. During that time, I have seen and listened to him evangelize about testing and have supported events he has organized, such as the Rational Industry Testing Forum and the Rational Testing User Group – both of which I have spoken at. His passion for effective and professional testing has been constant, as has his commitment to the industry.

John has spoken several times at Software Quality Systems (SQS) events that I have organized, as well as at numerous industry-wide events. John was an invited keynote and session speaker at the Scandinavian *Ohjelmistotestaus* testing conferences, and spoke at the Software Quality Assurance Management (SQAM) testing conference in Prague. He has also been active in the British Computer Society (BCS) (having made Fellow in 1997) and the Object Oriented (OO) and Specialist Group in Software Testing (SIGiST) special interest groups (where he has spoken many times, sat on testing discussion panels, chaired "birds of a feather" sessions, and so forth). He helped me tremendously in setting up and running the Intellect Testing Group, where I was grateful to have him on the management committee and to have his participation by writing and presenting on test process.

John has done a tremendous job to elicit the contributions in this book, but he provides an even greater service by finding the common threads and practices and explaining why twenty-three different people shared in success. I am sure John feels proud that so many people can share in the creation of this book and the contribution to the "My Agile" process he describes.

Acknowledgments

I would very much like to thank the following people for their advice, assistance, and encouragement in the writing of this book:

Scott Ambler, Christine Mitchell-Brown, David Burgin, Dawn Davidsen, Abby Davies, Dorothy Graham, Andrew Griffiths, Dr Jon Hall, Karen Harrison, Elisabeth Hendrickson, Ivar Jacobson, Anthony J Kesterton, Nick Luft, Frank Malone, Simon Mills, Simon Norrington, Jean-Paul Quenet, Andrew Roach, Manish Sharma, Jamie Smith, Ian Spence, Julie Watkins, and Nigel Williams.

I would also like to thank the following people for their invaluable contribution in providing the agile case studies:

Stephen K. Allott, Managing Director of ElectroMind

Colin Cassidy, Software Architect for Prolifics Ltd

Dass Chana, Computer Science Student

Nick Denning, Chief Executive Officer of Diegesis

David Evans, Director of Methodology at SQS Ltd

Isabel Evans, Principal Consultant at the Testing Solutions Group Ltd

Tom Gilb, independent testing practitioner and author

Greg Hodgkinson, Process Practice Manager, Prolifics Ltd

Trond Johansen, Head of R & D Norway, Confirmit AS

Peter Kingston, Consulting Test Manager

Howard Knowles, Managing Director of Improvix Ltd

Dr Peter May, Technology Consultant, Deloitte

Michael G. Norman, Chief Executive Officer of Scapa Technologies Ltd

Joanna Nowakowska, Rodan Systems S.A.

Martin Phillips, Test Lead, IBM Software Group

Graham Thomas, independent testing consultant

Nick Sewell, European Managing Director of Ivar Jacobson Consulting Ltd

Professor Lucjan Stapp, Warsaw University of Technology

Geoff Thompson, Services Director for Experimentus

Jon Tilt, Chief Test Architect ESB Products, IBM Software Group

Richard Warden, Director of Software Futures Ltd

James Wilson, Chief Executive Officer of Trinem

I would also like to give particular thanks to Bob Bartlett for his excellent foreword; he is a well-recognized testing industry figure, someone I have great personal respect for, and someone I have had the pleasure of working with on numerous occasions, and I am very grateful for his assistance in providing the foreword to this book.

And last, but certainly not least, I would like to express my appreciation for the insight and experience of my technical reviewer Duncan Brigginshaw, and for the constant "encouragement" and guidance from my editor Heather Bergman and her assistant David Jou of Cambridge University Press.

1 Introduction

> If you try to make the software foolproof,
> they will just invent a better fool!
>
> **Dorothy Graham**

1.1 Why Agile?

In today's highly competitive IT business, companies experience massive pressures to be as effective and efficient as possible in developing and delivering successful software solutions. If you don't find strategies to reduce the cost of software development, your competitors will, allowing them to undercut your prices, to offer to develop and deliver products faster, and ultimately to steal business from you.

Often in the past, testing was an afterthought; now it is increasingly seen as the essential activity in software development and delivery. However, poor or ineffective testing can be just as bad as no testing and may cost significant time, effort, and money, but ultimately fail to improve software quality, with the result that your customers are the ones who find and report the defects in your software!

If testing is the right thing to do, how can you ensure that you are doing testing right?

If you ask managers involved in producing software whether they follow industry best practices in their development and testing activities, almost all of them will confidently assure you that they do. The reality is often far less clear; even where a large formal process documenting best development and testing practice has been introduced into an organization, it is very likely that different members of the team will apply their own testing techniques, employ a variety of different documentation (such as their own copies of test plans and test scripts), and use different approaches for assessing and reporting testing progress on different projects. Even the language is likely to be different, with staff using a variety of terms for the same thing, as well as using the same terms for different things!

Just how much time, effort, and money does this testing chaos cost your organization? Can you estimate just how much risk a project carries in terms of late delivery, with poor testing resulting in the release of poor-quality software? To put this in perspective, the U.S. National Institute of Standards and Technology recently reported that, for every $1 million spent on software implementations, businesses typically incur more than $210,000 (or between a fifth and a quarter of the overall budget) of additional costs caused by problems associated with impact of postimplementation faults [1].

The most common reason that companies put up with this situation is that they take a short-term view of the projects they run; it is much better to just get on with it and "make progress" than to take a more enlightened, but longer-term, view to actually address and fix the problems.

Many organizations are now adopting some form of formal test process as the solution to these problems. In this context, a process provides a means of documenting and delivering industry best practice in software development and testing to all of the staff in the organization. The process defines who should do what and when, with standard roles and responsibilities for project staff, and guidance on the correct way of completing their tasks. The process also provides standard reusable templates for things like test plans, test scripts, and testing summary reports and may even address issues of process improvement [2].

Although there have been numerous attempts to produce an "industry standard" software testing process (e.g., the Software Process Engineering Metamodel [3]), many practitioners and organizations express concerns about the complexity of such processes. Typical objections include:

▶ "The process is too big" – there is just too much information involved and it takes too long to rollout, adopt, and maintain.

▶ "That's not the way we do things here" – every organization is different and there is no one-size-fits-all process.

▶ "The process is too prescriptive" – a formal process stifles the creativity and intuition of bright and imaginative developers and testers.

▶ "The process is too expensive" – if we are trying to reduce the cost of software development, why would we spend lots of money on somebody else's best practices?

Interestingly, even where individuals and organizations say they have no process, this is unlikely to be true – testers may invent it on the fly each morning when they start work, but each tester will follow some consistent approach to how he or she performs their testing. It is possible for this "approach" to be successful if you are one of those talented supertesters or you work in an organization that only hires "miracle QA" staff. For the rest of us, we need to rely on documented best practices to provide guidance on the who, the what, and the when of testing, and to provide reusable templates for the things we create, use, or deliver as part of our testing activities.

So, here is the challenge: how is it possible to produce good-quality software, on time and to budget, without forcing a large, unwieldy, and complex process on the developers and testers, but still providing them with sufficient guidance and best practices to enable them to be effective and efficient at their jobs? To restate this question, what is the minimum subset of industry best practice that can be used while still delivering quality software?

This book provides practical guidance to answer this question by means of real-world case studies, and will help you to select, adopt, and use a personally customized set of agile best practices that will enable you and your colleagues to deliver quality testing in as effective and efficient a manner as possible.

1.2 Suggestions on How to Read This Book

This book is divided into three main sections (plus the appendices), each of which are closely linked, but each of which can be read and applied separately.

Part 1 of the book provides a review of both the traditional or "classic" view of software testing process and examples of agile approaches:

▶ If you are interested in reviewing the early history of software development and testing process, Chapter 2 (Old-School Development and Testing) begins by reviewing the traditional or "classic" view of process. This chapter explores the good and the bad aspects of classic test process, and provides a useful baseline for the rest of the book to build on.

▶ If you are interested in understanding the development of agile approaches to software development and testing, Chapter 3 (Agile Development and Testing) provides an overview of the principal agile approaches that have been used to develop software, with particular emphasis on the testing aspects of the method described.

▶ Although Chapter 3 provides a high-level overview of the principal agile approaches, if you require a deeper understanding of these methods then refer to Appendices A through D. You may find this to be of particular benefit in preparation for reading the agile case studies in Part 2 of the book.

Part 2 of the book contains twenty case studies, which provide real-world examples of how different organizations and individual practitioners have worked in an agile development and testing framework or have implemented their own agile testing approaches. Each chapter reviews the specific testing requirements faced by the testers, provides a summary of the agile solution they adopted, describes the overall success of the approach, and provides a discussion of which specific aspects of the approach worked well, and which aspects might be improved or omitted in future testing projects.

Part 3 of this book provides an analysis of the agile case studies presented in Part 2 and draws upon the material from Part 1 to make a series of proposals about what components might be used to generate your own successful agile testing process:

▶ If you would like some guidance on agile best practices from a practitioner perspective, Chapter 24 (Analysis of the Case Studies) examines in detail the agile case studies presented in Part 2, identifying particularly successful agile techniques, common themes (such as successful reusable templates), as well as those testing approaches that were not successful and which may need to be treated with caution.

▶ If you are interested in guidance on how to set up your own agile development and testing process, Chapter 25 (My Agile Process) draws on the information provided in the case studies and their analysis to make a series of proposals for how you might set up and run a practical, effective, and efficient agile testing process.

▶ If you would like some guidance on how to introduce your agile testing method into your own organization, Chapter 26 (The Roll-out and Adoption of My Agile Process) provides a series of tried and tested best practices describing how you can roll out the process and drive its successful use and adoption.

The Appendices

If you would like to find more detail on the agile methods described briefly in Chapter 3, Appendices A through D provide further description of each of the key agile approaches covered in Chapter 3, with particular emphasis on the software quality aspects of each approach. You may find value in reading these appendices in preparation for reading the case studies presented in Part 2 of this book.

Appendices E through G provide a set of reusable testing templates that can be used as a resource to be reused in your own agile process (these templates are also available in electronic format from the Cambridge University Press Web site at http://www.cup.agiletemplates.com), including

▶ an agile test script template,
▶ an agile test result record form template, and
▶ an agile test summary report template.

Appendix H contains a checklist of agile best practices that shows which practices are particularly appropriate for the different styles and sizes of agile project described in Chapter 25. This checklist can be used as a summary of the practices and as an *aide memoire* to assist you in populating your own agile process.

References cited in the text are fully expanded in the References section at the back of the book.

PART ONE

REVIEW OF OLD-SCHOOL AND AGILE APPROACHES

> Fact of the matter is, there is no hip world, there is no straight world. There's a world, you see, which has people in it who believe in a variety of different things. Everybody believes in something and everybody, by virtue of the fact that they believe in something, use that something to support their own existence.
>
> **Frank Zappa**

This section of the book provides a review of both the traditional or "classic" view of software testing process and agile approaches.

The chapters in this section are:

▶ Chapter 2 – Old-School Development and Testing, which begins by reviewing the traditional or "classic" view of software testing process. This chapter will explore the good and bad aspects of classic test process, and provides a useful baseline for the rest of the book to build on

▶ Chapter 3 – Agile Development and Testing, which provides a review of the most prominent agile approaches that have been used to develop software, with particular emphasis on the testing aspects of the method described. If additional information on a particular approach is needed, more complete details of each method are provided in Appendices A to D.

2 Old-School Development and Testing

Testing is never completed, it's simply abandoned!

Simon Mills

2.1 Introduction

This chapter discusses what software development and testing process is, reviews the historical development of process, and concludes by providing a review of the elements of a traditional or "classic" software testing process, providing a useful baseline for the rest of the book to build on.

2.2 So, What Is Process?

A process seeks to identify and reuse common elements of some particular approach to achieving a task, and to apply those common elements to other, related tasks. Without these common reusable elements, a process will struggle to provide an effective and efficient means of achieving those tasks, and find it difficult to achieve acceptance and use by other practitioners working in that field.

Test process is no different; we have many different tasks that need to be achieved to deliver effective and efficient testing, and at a variety of different levels of testing from component/unit/developer testing, through integration/module testing, on into systems testing, and through to acceptance testing [4].

Even before testing process was "invented", good testers have done things in a particular way to achieve good results – such as the best way to find the most defects, to complete testing more quickly or more cheaply, to save time by reusing things they had produced in earlier testing projects (such as a template for a test plan or a test script), or to ensure consistent nomenclature (such as common terms for testing phases).

Such enlightened practitioners were even known to share such best practices with their colleagues, passing on or swapping reusable templates, publishing papers on testing techniques, or mentoring other staff on test management approaches, for example.

As the IT industry matured, with customers demanding increasingly complex systems, of ever higher quality, in shorter timescales and with lower cost, the

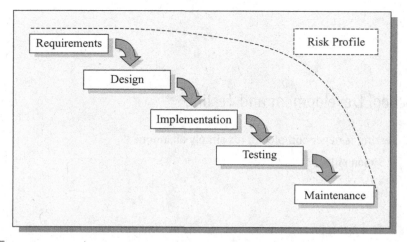

2.1   The Waterfall Phases and Risk Profile (dotted line).

resulting commercial pressures forced those organizations developing software to seek methods to ensure their software development was as effective and efficient as possible. If they did not find the means to deliver software faster, cheaper, and with better quality, their competitors would.

Successive waves of new technologies, such as procedural programming, fourth-generation languages, and object orientation, all promised to ensure reductions in the occurrence of defects, to accelerate development times, and to reduce the cost of development. Interestingly, it was observed that it was still possible to write poor-quality software that failed to achieve its purpose and performed poorly or included defects, no matter what technologies were used!

As with so many instances of a new technology failing to solve a particular problem, the issue actually turns out to be a people problem. Human beings need guidance, they need to build upon the knowledge and experiences of others, they need to understand what works and what doesn't work, and they need to avoid wasting time reinventing things that other practitioners have already successfully produced and used. Project chaos, where each project and practitioner uses different techniques, employs different terminology, or uses (or worse, reinvents from scratch) different documentation, was increasingly considered to be unacceptable.

The following sections review a number of the early approaches to software development and testing that sought to avoid such project chaos.

2.3   Waterfall

One of the earliest approaches to software development is the waterfall approach. A paper published by Winston W. Royce in the 1970s [5] described a sequential software development model containing a number of phases, each of which must be completed before the next begins. Figure 2.1 shows the classic interpretation of the phases in a waterfall project.

From a quality perspective, the waterfall approach has been often criticized because testing begins late in the project; as a consequence, a high degree of project risk (that is, failure of the software to meet customer expectations, to be delivered with acceptable levels of defects, or to perform adequately) is retained until late into the project. With the resultant reworking and retesting caused by the late detection of defects, waterfall projects were also likely to incur additional effort, miss their delivery dates, and exceed their budgets.

The waterfall approach has also been criticized for its lack of responsiveness to customer requests for changes to the system being developed. Historically, it was typical for all of the requirements to be captured at the start of the project and to be set in stone throughout the rest of the development. A frequent result of this approach was that by the time the software had been delivered (sometimes months or even years later), it no longer matched the needs of the customer, which had almost certainly changed by then.

Because of increasing dissatisfaction with the rigid structure of waterfall projects, other solutions were investigated that would be more flexible in terms of addressing changing requirements.

2.4 Spiral

Many attempts were made to address the shortcomings of the waterfall approach, such as the spiral model of software development defined by Barry Boehm in 1988 [6]. Intended for use in large, complex, and costly projects, and intended to address the issues of meeting customer requirements, this incremental development process relied heavily on the development and testing of a series of software prototypes of the final system. The typical steps involved in a spiral model–driven project are as follows:

1. In discussion with the customer, the requirements for the system are defined and documented in as much detail as possible.
2. An initial design is created based on the requirements.
3. A sequence of increasingly complete prototypes are constructed from the design in order to
   ▷ test the strengths and weaknesses of the prototypes, and to highlight any risks;
   ▷ assist in refining the requirements by obtaining customer feedback; and
   ▷ assist in refining the planning and design.
4. The risks identified by testing the prototypes are reviewed with the customer, who can make a decision whether to halt or continue the project.
5. Steps 2 through 4 are repeated until the customer is satisfied that the refined prototype reflects the functionality of the desired system, and the final system is then developed on this basis.
6. The completed system is thoroughly tested (including formal acceptance testing) and delivered to the customer.

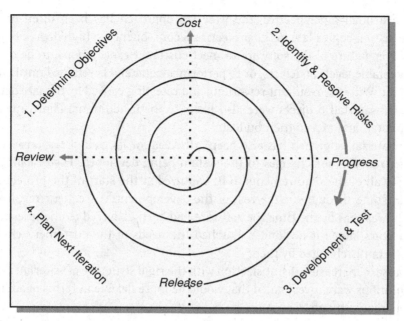

2.2 Graphical Overview of the Spiral Model.

7. Where appropriate, ongoing maintenance and test are performed to prevent potential failures and to maximize system availability.

Figure 2.2 provides a graphical overview of a typical interpretation of the spiral model.

Although considered to be an improvement over the waterfall approach in terms of delivering systems that more closely match the customer's requirements, and for delivering higher-quality software (achieved in large part by the spiral model, which encourages early and continued testing of the prototypes), issues existed regarding the difficulty of estimating effort, timescales, and cost of delivery; the nondeterministic nature of the cycle of prototype development and testing meant that it was difficult to bound the duration and effort involved in delivering the final product.

2.5 Iterative

Iterative models of software development evolved to address issues raised by both waterfall and spiral approaches, with the goal of breaking large monolithic development projects into smaller, more easily managed iterations. Each iteration would produce a tangible deliverable (typically some executable element of the system under development).

The Objectory method [7] provides a good example of such an approach. In 1987, while assisting telecommunications company Ericsson AB with its software development efforts, and concerned with the shortcomings of earlier methods, Ivar Jacobson brought together a number of the development concepts he had been thinking about, such as use cases [8], object-oriented design [9], and iterative development, to create a new approach to developing successful object-oriented applications.

The Objectory method supported innovative techniques for requirements analysis, visual modeling of the domain, and an iterative approach to managing the execution of the project. In essence, Objectory would break down a project that might have been run in a large and inflexible waterfall manner into smaller, more easily understood, implemented, and tested iterations.

Such an approach brought a number of important benefits for software quality:

▶ Testing could begin much earlier in the project (from the first iteration), enabling defects to be identified and fixed in a timely manner, with the result that timescales were not impacted, and that the effort and cost of fixing and retesting defects were kept low.[1]

▶ Testing would continue throughout the project (within each iteration), ensuring that new defects were found and fixed in a timely manner, that newly added system functionality did not adversely affect the existing software quality, and verifying that defects found in earlier iterations did not reappear in the most recent iteration.

▶ The valuable visual metaphor provided by use cases and visual modeling enabled the developers and the customer to more easily understand the intention of the system functionality – in effect the customer, analyst, designer, and tester share a common language and understanding of the system.

▶ Testers discovered that the scenarios described by the use cases could very easily be used to design and implement effective test cases[2] – the actors (people or other systems) identified in the use cases and their interactions with the system under development, mapped easily onto the steps and verifications needed to develop the test scripts.

The Objectory process was organized around three phases:

1. The *requirements phase* – which involves the construction of three models that describe in a simple, natural-language manner what the system should do:
   ▷ The *use case model* – which documents the interactions between the actors and the system, which are typically captured using use case diagrams and natural-language descriptions.
   ▷ The *domain model* – which documents the entities within the system, their properties, and their relationships.

---

[1] It is generally considered that for each phase of the project during which you fail to find a bug, the cost of fixing it increases by a factor of 10 [4]. In practice, my experience is that this is a conservative estimate.

[2] A test case represents the design for a test. A test case is implemented by means of a test script.

▷ The *user interface descriptions* – which document the various interfaces between the actors and the system.

2. The *analysis phase* – which involves the construction of two models that are a refinement of the information captured during the previous phase:

   ▷ The *analysis model* – which is a refinement of the domain model produced in the previous phase and which documents behavioral information, control objects (linked to use cases), and entity and interface objects.

   ▷ The *subsystem descriptions* – which partition the system around closely coupled and similarly behaving objects.

3. The *construction phase* – which refines the models produced in the analysis phase. During this phase the following models are generated:

   ▷ *Block models* – which represent the functional modules of the system.

   ▷ *Block interfaces* – which specify the public operations performed by the modules.

   ▷ *Block specifications* – which are optional descriptions of block behavior using finite state machines [10].

In its time, Objectory was considered to be a very successful software development method, and many of its key principles, such as use case analysis and design, continue to be widely used today.

In 1991, after having worked closely with the Objectory process for several years, Ericsson AB purchased a major stake in Ivar Jacobson's company (Objectory Systems), changing its name to Objectory AB.

In 1995, Objectory AB merged with the Rational Software Corporation, and shortly thereafter, the Rational Objectory Process version 4.0 was published, which incorporated elements of Grady Booch's object-oriented analysis and design method [11] and Jim Rumbaugh's object modeling technique (OMT [12]). Much of the procedural side of the Objectory method (such as use case modeling) was incorporated into the Rational Objectory Process, with the addition of many notational and diagramming elements from the OMT and Booch methods.

Ultimately, through an incremental process of extension and enhancement, the Rational Objectory Process evolved into the Rational Unified Process (RUP) version 5.0, which incorporated modeling and design extensions addressing business engineering, plus best practice guidance on configuration and change management, data engineering, and user interface design.

The release of version 7 of RUP provides extensive best-practice guidance on traditional and agile software development and testing methods, such as the ability to optionally select an "extreme programming" style of development (see Appendix B), as well as the means of customizing the RUP framework to support the user's own specific agile approaches.

The RUP is covered in further detail in Chapter 3, along with a number of other agile approaches.

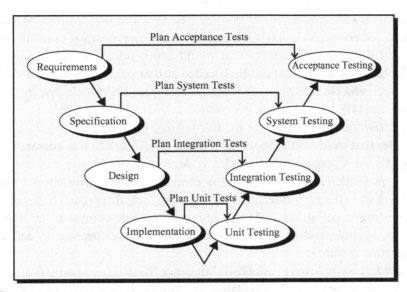

2.3 The V-Model; Waterfall Phases and Associated Testing Phases.

2.6 Traditional Elements of Test Process

The final section of this chapter reviews the typical elements of a traditional testing process, focusing in detail on the relationship between the classic model of testing and the development approaches described in the earlier sections.

Many traditional views of software testing are based on the V-model [4], which itself is largely based on the waterfall view of software development. The V-model approach to organizing testing has also been applied to spiral and other models of software development, producing a number of variants, such as the W-model [13]. Figure 2.3 shows a typical interpretation of the V-model.

The V-model provides a powerful means of assisting testing practitioners to move testing earlier into the software development life cycle, and to encourage more frequent testing.

A major tenet of the V-model is that testing can begin as early as the requirements acquisition phase – with the test manager reviewing the requirements to determine the resources needed for testing, and with the test analyst or designer reviewing the requirements to determine testability and identify errors in the requirements (such as omissions, contradictions, duplications, and items that need further clarification).

As a generalization, we can identify four basic test levels or phases associated with the V-model approach to testing:[3]

1. *Unit test* (also known as developer or component testing) is typically conducted by the developer to ensure that their code meets its requirements, and is the

---

3 However, in practice we might also include other variations of the testing phases, such as systems integration testing (often employed where the application under test has a requirement to interact with a number of other independent systems), user acceptance testing, and operations acceptance testing.

lowest level of testing normally identified. Historically, unit testing was a manual process (often involving a test harness or some other means of simulating other planned software components that would communicate with the component under test, but which had not been coded at that point). Today, unit testing is usually conducted using one of the many developer testing tools that are available (see, e.g., [14]).

2. *Integration test* (also known as module testing) is used to demonstrate that the modules that make up the application under test, interface and interact together correctly. As a general rule (but clearly dependent on the size and importance of the project), integration testing is conducted by the developers under the supervision of the project leader. Where a more formal approach to development and testing is being followed, possibly on a large or commercially important project, an independent tester or test team could be involved in conducting integration testing.

3. *System test* is employed to establish confidence that the (now completed) application under test will pass its acceptance test. During system testing, the functional and structural stability of the system is examined, as well as the nonfunctional aspects of the application under test, such as performance and reliability. Typically, although again dependent on the size and importance of the project, system testing is conducted by an independent testing team. Often, a customer or user representative will be invited to witness the system test.

4. *Acceptance test* (also known as user acceptance test or UAT) is used to ensure that the application under test meets its business requirements, and to provide confidence that the system works correctly and is usable before being formally handed over to the end users. Typically, UAT will be conducted by nominated user representatives (sometimes with the assistance of an independent testing representative or team).

The role of *regression testing* is also worth noting; its purpose is to provide confidence that the application under test still functions correctly following a new build or new release of the software (perhaps caused by requests from the customer for modifications or enhancements to the software, or a change to the environment in which the software runs, such as a new release of the underlying operating system).

Within each of the test levels or phases, we can identify a number of common elements that they all share. In each testing phase the following must be addressed:

► *Overview of test phase* – providing information on the purpose of the testing phase, its goals, and its characteristics. Information should also be provided relating this testing phase to the appropriate development phase within the V-model and to the adjacent testing phases.

► *Test phase approach and test data requirements* – describing the overall approach to the testing used in this phase (such as white box or black box testing; see [4]), and addressing the format, content, and origin of the data required to successfully test the software.

▶ *Test planning and resources* – providing the plan used to drive the testing conducted during this phase, its timescales, milestones, dependencies, risks, and deliverables, as well as information on the resources needed to complete the testing successfully (including both the staff and the physical resources, such as computer equipment).

▶ *Roles and responsibilities* – specifying the staff required to fulfill the various roles within this phase (such as test team leader, test analyst, or tester) and their specific responsibilities (e.g., "the test analyst shall be responsible for designing and implementing the test scripts required to test the application under test ...") . Issues of reporting, management, and liaison should also be specified.

▶ *Inputs and outputs* – specifying those artifacts (the items created and/or used within phases) required as inputs to this phase to ensure successful testing of the application under test (such as the test plan, the software itself, and the requirements documentation), artifacts created during this phase (such as test designs, test scripts, and test result record forms), and artifacts output from this phase (such as the tested software, completed test result record forms, and the test summary report).

▶ *Specific test techniques for this test phase* – describing any specific testing techniques (such as boundary analysis, equivalence partitioning, or state transition analysis; see [4]) or tools to be used within this testing phase such as test execution tools; see [15].

▶ *Reusable assets* – providing test practitioners with access to standard reusable assets (such as test plan, test script, and test summary report templates) that are shared across the project (or even across an organization). These assets can ensure that significant project time, effort, and cost are saved by preventing different practitioners on different projects from reinventing different versions of the same artifacts again and again. Standardization also makes it easier for staff to move between projects without having to relearn a new and different set of project documentation.

The preceding information is traditionally recorded in one or more testing documents (usually within the test plan document and the test specification document).

Although this approach to software testing has been widely adopted and used, as with the traditional development processes, this classic view of testing process has its critics:

▶ A key criticism leveled against the approach is that it is underpinned by the V-model, which is itself based on the frequently criticized waterfall model of software development. The relevance of the classic view of test process is often questioned when applied to more contemporary, agile views of software development.

▶ Where the approach is used on small, simple projects with low complexity, practitioners often complain that there is "too much process," and that the reality is that "experienced testers don't need so much detailed guidance." In effect, the process itself is criticized for taking too much time and effort to follow.

▶ Paradoxically, the use of a formal and prescriptive testing process may also be criticized for preventing testers from finding defects; many a well-hidden defect has been unearthed by the intuition of a skilled and experienced tester. Testing places high reliance on practitioners who are able to track down defects using their creative and lateral thinking skills, but a highly prescriptive testing solution is often thought to constrain and inhibit such skills.

2.7 Summary

Since the earliest days of programming, when engineers manually set noughts and ones on huge electromechanical devices, pioneering practitioners have looked for ways of making the process of developing programs easier, quicker, and more reliable.

Once, software was used in just one or two places around the world by a handful of people to implement the complex algorithms needed to decode secret military messages. Now, the world runs on software; it is everywhere – in your home, in your car, in your mobile phone, sometimes even inside you (think about the complex calculations made by heart pacemaker devices or the new generation of intelligent digital hearing aids). Today, a world without software is absolutely unthinkable.

As the technologies for developing software have evolved and increasing numbers of software practitioners have found employment[4] in more and more companies, producing ever larger and more complex software systems, the need to find easier, quicker, and more reliable practices for delivering that software has become absolutely critical.

In the early days, practitioners began to share the successful practices that they had found, often through trial and error, with their colleagues. As the IT industry matured, such best practices began to be documented and distributed, resulting in the appearance of papers and books on waterfall and spiral software development methods, for example.

While of initial value in managing relatively simple software projects where customer requirements were unlikely to change across the duration of the project, many workers became increasingly dissatisfied with these early methods as continuous improvements in the capability of programming technologies encouraged developers to produce systems of ever-increasing size and complexity, and as the number of software disaster stories began to accumulate.

---

[4] It is an incredibly sobering thought that in the 1940s there were just a few people in the entire world who could implement a computer program, but that today each year some 85,000 software engineers leave U.S. universities, with an additional 400,000 Indian graduates joining them, while China's education system produces some 600,000 developers annually! Inevitably, these numbers can only increase year after year.

Increasingly, the need to be responsive to changing customer needs, to be able to quickly develop, test, and deliver useful functionality to the customer in a planned and managed incremental manner, the need to reduce the cost and effort of development, and the need to deliver high-quality software led practitioners to challenge the role of traditional approaches to software development and testing.

In the twenty-first century, software development needs to be agile; to deliver quality software that meets the customer requirements and that is delivered on time and within budget.

Because, bottom line, if you can't – your competitors will.

3 Agile Development and Testing

Nanos gigantum humeris insidentes –
We are but dwarfs standing upon the shoulders of giants.

Bernard of Chartres

3.1 Introduction

The long history of software development is too frequently characterized by failure rather than by success. When you consider that the practice of software development and testing has spanned two centuries (and arguably three or more centuries[1]), it seems incredible that such a high proportion of projects are unsuccessful. One highly respected industry report, for example, suggested that as many as 76% of all software projects fail to come in on time, to budget, or to customer satisfaction [2].

Growing dissatisfaction with the failure of traditional heavyweight approaches caused a number of workers in the field of software development to begin to question the role of ponderous, inflexible, and frequently ineffective development processes.

From the 1980s onward, new lightweight or agile approaches to developing and testing software in an effective and efficient manner began to appear, which challenged the need for cumbersome and ineffectual process. Such approaches frequently focused on the need for good communication in projects, the need to adopt smaller, more easily managed iterations, and the need to be responsive to changing customer requirements.

This chapter provides a review of the most prominent agile methods that have been used to develop and test software. Specifically, the agile approaches covered in this chapter include the following:

▶ Rapid Application Development (RAD),
▶ Extreme Programming (XP),
▶ the Dynamic Systems Development Method (DSDM), and
▶ Scrum.

Each of these agile approaches is discussed at a relatively high level in this chapter; greater detail is presented in Appendices A through D, respectively.

---

[1] If we include the patterns developed for guiding the actions of weaving machines, for example, or even the astronomical software druids ran on their early silicon and granite hardware systems.

The chapter concludes with a brief overview of the key features of a number of other agile methods and approaches, including

▶ the Enterprise Agile Process (previously XBreed),
▶ Ruby on Rails (RoR),
▶ Evolutionary Project Management (Evo),
▶ the Rational Unified Process (RUP),
▶ the Essential Unified Process (EssUP), and
▶ the Software Process Engineering Metamodel (SPEM).

Inevitably, this is a snapshot of the agile methods because it is by necessity a very fast-moving subject.

3.2 Rapid Application Development

The RAD first appeared in the 1980s, when James Martin developed the approach in response to increasing dissatisfaction with the failure of earlier methods such as the waterfall model of software development [5].

These earlier approaches were characterized by being highly prescriptive, with developers following an inflexible series of development phases in which requirements were gathered early in the process and then set in stone throughout the rest of the project. Typically, customer involvement was limited to the initial requirements capture and final acceptance testing, resulting in an unacceptably high number of delivered systems that did not match the actual customer needs (which had almost certainly changed since they had been first documented anyway). Cost and time overruns were the norm for such projects and, since much of the testing was left to the later phases, the systems were frequently delivered with major quality issues.

Initially inspired by the work of other prominent workers in the field of development and testing, such as Barry Boehm, Brian Gallagher, and Scott Schults, and following a gestation period of several years, Martin's thoughts on rapid software development were finally formalized as RAD in his 1990 book, *Rapid Application Development* [16].

The key goals of RAD are

▶ high-quality systems,
▶ fast development and delivery, and
▶ low costs.

RAD seeks to break down the approach taken in monolithic waterfall projects into smaller iterative steps, increasing the opportunities for the customer to be involved in the development and to be exposed to earlier prototypes and working increments of the developing system. In fact, the development of software prototypes is a key aspect of RAD, providing a means of exploring the customer needs for the system through informal testing and managing customer expectations of how the final delivered system should look and perform.

RAD proved to be of benefit over traditional development approaches in a number of areas:

▶ *RAD's iterative approach* to developing software meant that testing could begin earlier in the development process and could continue more frequently through-out the project. This approach significantly reduced the risk of late identification of serious defects and the associated cost overruns and late delivery frequently seen in waterfall projects.

▶ *Closer customer involvement* in the development process, with early opportuni-ties to test how well the software met customer needs using the prototypes, meant there were less show-stopping surprises when the system was finally delivered.

▶ *Accepting that requirements would no longer be set in stone* at the very begin-ning of the project and that changes could be managed effectively through-out the development using requirements planning workshops and joint applica-tion design workshops, helped ensure the delivered software would more closely match customer expectations.

▶ *Tighter project management* of development priorities, costs, and timescales through the use of techniques such as time boxing [17] kept project progress on track and controlled the extent that the development could get out of control.

On the down side, for many practitioners who followed more traditional software development models, RAD gained the reputation of being an excuse for "hacking" or "opportunistic coding," as it has also been called [18]. It is possible that, as one of the earliest agile methods, RAD may have been perceived as having less rigor than the more established approaches. Also, RAD's focus on developing a series of rapid prototypes, many of which inevitably would not be carried forward into the final deliverable, was often blamed for wasting time and effort and jeopardizing progress. Finally, the process of prototyping was often poorly implemented due to a weak understanding of what prototyping actually involved [19], leading to a poor perception of the technique.

Despite some suspicion from the defenders of the more traditional development methods, RAD arguably set the scene for the development of a number of the later agile methods.

Appendix A contains further details of the rules and practices of RAD.

3.3 Extreme Programming

In the early 1990s, Kent Beck, a practitioner in the field of software development, had begun to consider how the process of developing software could be made simpler and more efficient. In March 1996 Kent embarked upon a project with a major automotive customer that would employ a number of the software development and testing concepts that he had been considering; the result was the genesis of Extreme Programming (XP [20]).

XP emphasizes customer satisfaction as one of its key drivers; the methodology aims to deliver the software the customer needs when they need it.

XP seeks to improve project success in four important areas:

1. *Communication* – XP encourages the team developing and testing the software to maintain effective and frequent communication both with the other members of the team and with the customer.
2. *Simplicity* – XP promotes the ideal of simple, clear, and understandable design, translated into similarly clear and understandable code. Even though the customer may not get to see the source code, XP encourages programmers to develop elegant and effective software solutions of which they can be proud.
3. *Feedback* – throughout the development project, the programmers obtain feedback on their work from other programmers and, crucially, the customer, who is exposed to early deliverables as soon in the project as possible.
4. *Courage* – programmers are empowered to respond positively and proactively to changing customer requirements and changes in the development environment (such as availability of new technologies).

By embracing these four principles, development projects are more agile and responsive; better communication across the team means that the developing system is integrated more easily and with fewer errors, plus the improved communication with the customer combined with good feedback ensures that the delivered software more closely matches the users' needs.

From a software quality perspective, XP emphasizes the importance of effective and efficient testing. An important goal of testing in XP is that test development should begin even before any code has been written, continuing throughout the coding process, and following code completion. As defects are found, new tests are developed and are added to the growing test suite to prevent the same bug from reappearing later and getting through to the delivered software.

Appendix B contains further details of the rules and practices of XP.

3.4 The Dynamic Systems Development Method

Developed in the United Kingdom in the 1990s by a consortium of organizations and agile practitioners, the Dynamic Systems Development Method (DSDM) is an agile framework that builds upon the principles of RAD. DSDM is based on an iterative development model, which seeks to be responsive to changing customer requirements, and which aims to implement the business requirements on time, to budget, and with acceptable levels of quality.

The DSDM is typically applied to information systems projects that are characterized by challenging timescales and budgets, and seeks to address many of the common reasons for information systems project failure, including exceeding budgets, missed delivery deadlines, poor quality, lack of user involvement, and lack of senior management commitment.

The DSDM is founded upon nine key principles:

1. Active user involvement is imperative.
2. DSDM teams must be empowered to make decisions.
3. The focus is on frequent delivery of products.
4. Fitness for business purpose is the essential criterion for acceptance of deliverables.
5. Iterative and incremental development is necessary to converge on an accurate business solution.
6. All changes during development are reversible.
7. Requirements are baselined at a high level.
8. Testing is integrated throughout the life cycle.
9. A collaborative and cooperative approach among all stakeholders is essential.

These principles were framed by combining the agile best practices and experiences of the DSDM consortium members. The first draft of the DSDM framework was delivered in January 1995, followed in February that year by formal publication of the framework [21].

Within its overall iterative approach, a DSDM project is structured into three distinct phases:

1. *Preproject phase* – this phase sets the context of the project and ensures it is set up correctly from the outset to give the project the best likelihood of success. Key products delivered from this phase include the initial definition of the business problem to be addressed, budget and resourcing, outline scope and plans for the feasibility study, and a decision whether or not to proceed with the project.
2. *Project life cycle phase* – this phase combines both sequential and iterative stages, which drive the incremental development of the system. Following the initial feasibility and business study stages, the project iterates through the functional model iteration, design and build iteration, and implementation stages.
3. *Postproject phase* – this phase covers postdelivery activities such as maintenance, enhancements, and software fixes, and is used to ensure the ongoing effective and efficient operation of the delivered system.

In terms of its continuing adoption and use, DSDM seems to have been more successful at being accepted by senior management than earlier agile approaches such as RAD due to the perception that it represents a more mature and formal agile method. This perception is further reinforced as a result of the frequent integration of DSDM and the PRINCE2 (PRojects IN Controlled Environments) project management method [22]. As a result, more conservative senior managers have been more receptive to the use of DSDM on larger/higher-profile projects with the result that a substantial and vigorous user population has been established around the globe.

The DSDM has also proven to be popular with development and testing practitioners, who have continued to refine and enhance the method; since its initial publication in 1995, DSDM has continued to evolve, incorporating new best practices and technologies wherever appropriate.

Appendix C contains further details of the principles and practices of DSDM.

3.5 Scrum

Scrum is a project management method for agile software development and testing that enables the creation of self-organizing teams by encouraging co-location of all team members (including customer representatives) combined with effective verbal communication among all team members and across all disciplines that are involved in the project.

A key principle of Scrum is the recognition that during a project, the customers are likely to change their minds frequently about what they want and need (often called requirements churn), and that such customer needs cannot be addressed successfully in a traditional predictive or planned manner. As such, Scrum adopts an empirical approach – accepting that the problem cannot be fully understood or defined, focusing instead on maximizing the team's ability to deliver quickly and respond to emerging requirements.

In terms of the genesis of Scrum, as early as 1986 Takeuchi and Nonaka [23] had observed that projects employing small, cross-functional teams were typically the most successful, and they coined the phrase "rugby approach" to describe the phenomenon. The first explicit reference to Scrum[2] in the context of software development came in 1990 in work by DeGrace and Stahl [24].

In the early 1990s, work on agile methods by Ken Schwaber and Jeff Sutherland, at their respective companies Advanced Development Methods and Easel Corporation, led Sutherland and Schwaber to jointly present a paper at the 1996 International Conference on Object-Oriented Programming, Systems, Languages, and Application describing Scrum [25]. Schwaber and Sutherland collaborated during the following years to further develop and document their experiences and industry best practices into what is now known as Scrum.

In 2001, Ken Schwaber teamed up with Mike Beedle to write up the method in *Agile Software Development with SCRUM* [26].

A major factor in the success of Scrum projects is the drive for efficient communications, with techniques such as daily short focused stand-up meetings combined with explicit team roles (e.g., Pig and Chicken; see Appendix D) to manage who may contribute to the meetings and in what manner.

Although Scrum was originally intended to be used for the management of software development projects, it can be employed in running software maintenance teams or as a program management approach: Scrum of Scrums.

Appendix D contains further details of the rules and practices of Scrum.

---

[2]   Scrum: a play in the ball game rugby in which two groups of players mass together around the ball and, with their heads down, struggle to gain possession of the ball. Typically held following an illegal forward pass.

3.6 Other Agile Methods

This section provides a high-level overview of the key features of a number of other agile methods and approaches to software development and testing. By necessity, this is only a snapshot of the current popular methods and does not seek to be a comprehensive catalog of all agile approaches. Because this subject evolves so quickly, it is recommended that the reader also refer to [26] as a useful source of updates on agile methods.

3.6.1 The Enterprise Agile Process (formerly XBreed)

Developed by Mike Beedle with the goal of developing "reusable software in record time," this twenty-first-century agile approach combines a number of best practices from other agile methods, such as XP and Scrum. Specifically, EAP [28] employs best practices from Scrum as the basis of its management framework and incorporates a subset of XP techniques for its development process.

A key feature of the method is the use of design patterns to create reusable objects; EAP creates a library of components that can be easily reused in new software projects to save time, effort, and cost of development and testing, while improving quality by the reuse of "tried and tested" components.

The EAP development process promotes the use of well-trained, skilled, and experienced practitioners to populate its teams, and encourages the use of effective knowledge transfer between team members, which, combined with a low communication overhead, helps keep the project running smoothly and efficiently.

3.6.2 Ruby on Rails

Created by David Heinemeier Hansson from his earlier work on the Basecamp web-based project management tool [29], Ruby on Rails (RoR [30]) is an open-source web framework that is optimized for "programmer happiness and sustainable productivity." Typically used by developers for relatively short client-driven web development, and often referred to as "Rails," RoR use is guided by two key principles:

▶ *Convention over configuration (CoC)* – In effect development by exception, the benefit of CoC is that only the unconventional aspects of the application need to be specified by the developer, resulting in reductions in coding effort. For example, if the developer creates a class "Part" in the model, the underlying database table is called "Parts" by default. It is only if one deviates from this convention, such as calling the table "parts_on_hand," that specific code needs to be written that utilizes these names.

▶ *Don't repeat yourself* – RoR promotes an approach where information is located in a single, unambiguous place. For example, using the ActiveRecord module of RoR, the developer does not need to explicitly specify database column names in class definitions. Instead, RoR can retrieve this information from the database.

Using the model-view-controller architecture [31] for organizing application programming, RoR incorporates a number of tools:

▶ *scaffolding*, for simplifying the generation of basic Web site models and views;
▶ *WEBrick*, a simple RoR web server; and
▶ *Rake*, a simple build system.

By providing these tools combined with an agile development philosophy, RoR can be seen as an example of a highly agile integrated development environment.

First released to the public in July 2004, RoR continues to find supporters in the web developer community with an impressive list of adopters (since 2007 RoR has been shipped by Apple with MacOS X v10.5 Leopard, for example).

3.6.3 Evolutionary Project Management

Developed by Tom and Kai Gilb, Evolutionary Project Management (Evo [32]) is a twenty-first-century agile project management method whose focus is on earlier delivery of critical results and on-time delivery of deadlined results. Evo is claimed to be able to provide more control over software quality, project performance, and project costs than more traditional project management methods.

Evo is particularly suited to developing large-scale software systems, involving complex technology and in rapidly moving environments. Evo aims to be highly responsive and adaptable to unforeseen circumstances while delivering rapid results.

Evo follows ten key process principles:[3]

1. Real results, of value to real stakeholders, will be delivered early and frequently.
2. The next Evo delivery step must be the one that delivers the most stakeholder value possible at that time.
3. Evo steps deliver the specified requirements, evolutionarily.
4. It is impossible to know all the right requirements in advance, but it is possible to discover them more quickly by attempts to deliver real value to real stakeholders.
5. Evo is holistic systems engineering; all necessary aspects of the system must be complete and correct, and delivered to a real stakeholder environment. It is not only about programming, it is about customer satisfaction.
6. Evo projects will require an open architecture, because project ideas will change as often as needed to really deliver value to the stakeholders.
7. The Evo project team focuses their energy, as a team, toward success in the current Evo step. They succeed or fail in the current step together. They do not waste energy on downstream steps until they have mastered current steps successfully.
8. Evo is about learning from hard experience, as fast as possible – what really works and what really delivers value. Evo is a discipline to make teams confront project problems early, but one that delivers progress quickly when provably, the team have got it right.

---

3   Sincere thanks to Tom and Kai Gilb for allowing me to reproduce this information.

9. Evo leads to early, and on-time, product delivery – both because of selected early priority delivery and because the team learns to get things right early.
10. Evo should allow teams to validate new work processes and get rid of bad ones early.

Benefits cited by Evo users include reducing the duration and cost of requirements capture by 75% over traditional methods, reducing the integration effort to upgrade from a previous code platform to a new code platform from hours to minutes, and improvements in the motivation, enthusiasm, and morale of developers and testers, leading to significantly higher staff retention.

The success of Evo can also be measured by the number of high-profile users (such as IBM, HP, and Microsoft) that have been involved in learning and using the method.

3.6.4 Rational Unified Process

Originally developed by Ivar Jacobson, Grady Booch, and Jim Rumbaugh at Rational Software Corporation, RUP is a use case–driven [7] iterative software engineering process that employs the Unified Modeling Language (UML) notation [33] to incrementally develop and deliver software. RUP provides industry best practice guidance on software development and testing to its users through a web browser interface, allowing the information to be accessed in a simple and easily distributed manner.

The RUP iterations are organized under a number of phases – inception, elaboration, construction, transition, and production – with development and testing activities grouped as a series of disciplines that run across the phases. These typically include business modeling, requirements, analysis and design, implementation, test, deployment, operations and support, configuration and change management, project management, environment, and infrastructure management.

RUP provides comprehensive information on all aspects of software development, including project roles and responsibilities, project planning and management, tasks and timescales, inputs and outputs, testing techniques and approaches, reusable project templates (such as test plan and test script templates), metrics, and guidance on process improvement.

RUP explicitly supports agile approaches by providing a customizable metamodel that allows users to select from the RUP best practices to create and maintain their own subset of agile best practices. RUP also provides access to predefined agile customizations, such as its XP process plug-in.

With its early origins in Ivar Jacobson's 1990s Objectory process [7], the development of RUP has been a highly inclusive process, and it has drawn from many sources including the experience of major industry experts, special interest groups, industry standards and guidelines, and the experiences of many thousands of ordinary practitioners.

Over the years, RUP has spawned a number of other agile methods and initiatives, such as the EssUP [34] and the Object Management Groups SPEM.

3.6.5 The Essential Unified Process

The EssUP [34] is a continued development of the work begun in RUP by process guru Ivar Jacobson, which identifies and promotes the use of a number of essential practices that include use cases, iterative development, architecture-driven design, team practices, and process practices, plus process improvement (through Capability Maturity Model Integration [35]) and agile development.

Adoption and use of EssUP are accelerated through the use of a set of "playing cards" – concise ready reference cards documenting the process best practices in a simple and highly accessible manner. Chapter 5 contains examples of these cards, and Figure 5.1 shows the Test Case and Test Results cards.

EssUP appears to be gaining in popularity and use, with both IBM and Microsoft incorporating its best practices into their respective process product offerings.

3.6.6 The Software Process Engineering Metamodel

SPEM [3] is, as its name suggests, a process metamodel that allows users to develop and maintain their own specific development and testing process.

SPEM is administered by the Object Management Group (OMG [36]) and based on the RUP metamodel, which the Rational Corporation donated to OMG for the purpose of supporting the development of a widely available open-source software process engineering metamodel.

Employing the UML notation [33], SPEM provides facilities for individual development and testing practitioners to create their own specific development method that incorporates those process elements appropriate to their own particular development needs and requirements.

3.7 Summary

Having worked in the software business for more than thirty years, I must admit to wondering if anyone will ever be completely satisfied with a particular means of developing and testing software.

It seems that, since the earliest days of process development, there have been practitioners who have either thought the resulting process was too lightweight or too heavyweight, that it guided them to do their job or constrained their creativity, that it gave them the freedom to use industry best practice or clipped their developer and/or tester wings.

I have often wondered if a major issue driving the development of new agile methods is a desire for IT practitioners to express their own individuality and their own creativity; even where perfectly usable and successful agile methods like Scrum and XP are available, there will be developers and testers who still find the need to pare these down to a subset of "essential" agile techniques, and to then add some bits of their own to form their own unique process.

On the other hand, it is an absolute fact that there are no two software projects that are exactly the same:

▶ There will be different-sized projects, with different-sized budgets and varying available resources (the case studies in Part 2 of this book illustrate this point well).

▶ The software being developed could be for internal use only, could represent a bespoke development for a customer, or could be a product offered for sale to numerous customers.

▶ The software might be being developed for a safety-, business-, or security-critical application.

▶ The speed of execution of the software may not be an issue, or the software might need to execute in real time or might need to be delivered as an embedded or pervasive solution.

Since there is no "one-sized" project, it is fair and reasonable to say that there can be no one-size-fits-all process. Viewed in this way, it seems entirely natural, even necessary, that diligent IT practitioners would find the need to define and document project-specific best practices for their own use and for that of their colleagues.

The case studies presented in the next section of this book provide an excellent illustration: real-world IT practitioners, working on unique projects, facing the need to deliver solutions in an agile manner, and needing to find their own interpretations of agile best practices.

In many of the cases studies, the authors have started from a point of adopting or using an established agile method, but have then had to modify or enhance the method to more closely meet the unique requirements of their particular project.

The third section of this book provides an analysis of the case studies, looking for common themes, identifying agile best practices that provided significant benefits to the project, highlighting agile methods whose use may need to be challenged in certain circumstances, and making a proposal for how you can quickly, easily, and successfully build and use your own effective and efficient agile process.

PART TWO

EVERYONE IS DIFFERENT: AGILE CASE STUDIES

People think computers will keep them from making mistakes.
They're wrong, with computers you just make mistakes faster.

Adam Osborne

This section of the book contains twenty real-world case studies from organizations or individuals who have adopted and used existing agile methods or who have developed their own agile approaches to software testing.

Each case study follows a standard format and concludes with advice on what aspects of the approach worked well and what aspects might be improved or removed in future testing projects. The headings include

▶ The case study title, author name(s), and a brief synopsis of the case study;
▶ Introduction – introducing both the author and the case study;
▶ Overview of the Testing Challenge – describing the particular testing challenges that needed to be addressed in this case study;
▶ Definition of the Agile Testing Process – providing details of the particular agile testing solution employed in this case study;
▶ Results of the Agile Approach – describing the outcome of the project and of the agile approach used in this case study; and
▶ Lessons Learned – documenting the lessons learned during the project, including what agile practices worked well, what could be improved in future projects, and what practices should be treated with caution.

The following quick reference table provides a summary of the characteristics of each case study to make it as easy as possible for you to identify case studies that most closely match your own testing needs.

Case Study Quick Reference Table

Case study	Market	Language	Platform	O/S	Proj Size	Test Automation	Author
1 (C4)	Survey & Reporting Solutions	Java	Web	Various	Medium	Yes	Gilb & Johansen
2 (C5)	Government	Various	Various	Various	Large	Yes	Nick Sewell
3 (C6)	Finance	C++	PC	WinXP	Small	No	Graham Thomas
4 (C7)	Telecoms	Citrix	PC Server	Win2K	Large	No	Michael G. Norman
5 (C8)	Finance	C	VAX	VMS	Medium	Yes	Nick Denning
6 (C9)	Life Assurance	Java	Web	Various	Medium	No	Geoff Thompson
7 (C10)	Finance	VB6–VB.net	PC	WinXP	Large	Yes	Howard Knowles
8 (C11)	Retail	Java	Websphere	Various	Medium	Yes	Colin Cassidy
9 (C12)	Various	Java	Various	Various	Medium	No	Martin Phillips
10 (C13)	Various	Various	Various	Various	Various	Yes	Stephen K. Allott
11 (C14)	Various	Java	PC	Various	Medium	Yes	James Wilson
12 (C15)	Finance	Eclipse Java	Windows	WinXP	Offshore	Yes	Peter Kingston
13 (C16)	Trading Systems	Various	Wndows & Unix	Small	Limited	Java	Richard Warden
14 (C17)	Professional Services	.NET	WebServer	WinXP	Medium	No	David Evans
15 (C18)	Various Fortune500	Java	Mainframe	Intel & Unix	Large	Yes	Jon Tilt
16 (C19)	Various	Various	Various	Various	Various	No	Isabel Evans
17 (C20)	Wiki	Lotus Notes	Web	Web	Small	No	Dass Chana
18 (C21)	SOA	Various	Various	Various	Various	Yes	Greg Hodgkinson
19 (C22)	Research	Java	PC	Windows	Research	No	Lucjan Stapp and Joanna Nowakowska
20 (C23)	Media	C#	.NET	Win Server 2003	Medium	No	Peter May

4 From Waterfall to Evolutionary Development and Test

Tom Gilb and Trond Johansen

SYNOPSIS

Evolutionary Development (Evo) focuses on early delivery of high value to stakeholders and on obtaining and utilizing stakeholder feedback. This case study describes, from a project manager's viewpoint, the results that one organization rapidly achieved after switching from using a waterfall approach to Evo. The major benefits of adopting an Evo approach come from reducing the duration of the requirements phase from four to five weeks down to just one week, and from paying greater attention to the quality requirements as opposed to the previous practice of concentrating solely on the required functionality, resulting in a happier workforce, happier clients, and more business.

4.1 Introduction

My name is Tom Gilb and I am an independent testing consultant and author of *Competitive Engineering: A Handbook for Systems & Software Engineering Management using Planguage* (2005), *Principles of Software Engineering Management* (1988), and *Software Inspection* (1993). My book *Software Metrics* (1976) coined the term and was used as the basis for the Software Engineering Institute Capability Maturity Model Level Four (SEI CMM Level 4 [37]). My most recent interests are development of true software engineering and systems engineering methods.

In 1997 Kai Gilb and I published a book entitled *Evo: The Evolutionary Project Management and Product Development Handbook*, describing an agile software development and testing project management method [32]. Evo is an iterative method in which a series of small delivery steps are taken until the project goals are reached and the software delivered. Key differences between Evo and other project management methods include an emphasis on achieving the requirements over slavishly following formal processes, and the focus on ensuring that testing starts early in the process, is conducted in each of the steps, and continues throughout the project.

This case study will focus on the adoption and use of the Evo method in the development of the Confirmit√ product from Oslo-based company Confirmit AS, which is where co-author Trond Johansen works as the head of project management.

Specifically, this case study focuses on the role and use of Evo in reducing the integration effort and timescales for developments and enhancements made to the Confirmit√ product, as compared with the previously used waterfall-based [5] development process.

4.2   Overview of the Testing Challenge

Confirmit√ is a powerful web-based software package that enables organizations to gather, analyze, and report on key business information across a broad range of commercial applications. Some twenty staff (including a quality assurance team of three people) work in the Confirmit AS research and development department and have responsibility for developing the core Confirmit√ functionality, as well as for developing custom bespoke modules for specific clients.

Early in the company's history, when Confirmit AS had just a few clients, the development process was fairly ad hoc and customer-driven. Changes to the software were made on an almost daily basis, driven by client feedback, and while this delivered stakeholder value quickly, the process also resulted in numerous defects, long working hours, and poor control of the software development and testing process.

As the Confirmit√ client base grew, Confirmit AS was faced with the need to become more effective and efficient in its development and testing of the product; it was clear that a more formal process was needed.

Initially, Confirmit AS looked to adopt a waterfall approach, incorporating process improvement via the Capability Maturity Model (CMM [37]). After following a waterfall approach for a number of years, a number of issues were identified:

▶ Risk discovery and mitigation was delayed until the later stages of the project.
▶ Document-based verification was postponed until the later stages of the project.
▶ There was dissatisfaction with the need to stipulate unstable requirements too early; requirements change is perceived as a bad thing in waterfall.
▶ Operational problems were discovered far too late in the process (typically at acceptance testing).
▶ There were lengthy modification cycles and too much rework and retesting.
▶ Most important, the requirements were nearly all focused on functionality, not on the quality attributes of the system.

With increasing dissatisfaction with their waterfall approach, Confirmit AS began to work closely with Tom and Kai Gilb to roll out and adopt an Evo approach in order to improve their development process for Confirmit√. In particular, three key goals were identified:

▶ *Reducing the integration effort* – that is, the amount of effort for each developer to get the latest build to work on his or her workstation so that they were able to code against the latest code platform;

▶ *Reducing the time in minutes to upgrade* – from a previous code platform to the most recent code platform from the past figure of three hours to a goal of two minutes; and

▶ *Improving the reliability of builds* – which historically had been an area where there had been significant quality issues.

Historically, the Confirmit AS development process for the Confirmit√ product had focused mostly on functional requirements, but with Evo the requirements process changed with the realization that *it is the product quality requirements that provide Confirmit AS with a competitive advantage over its rivals.*

4.3 Definition of an Agile Testing Process

While Section 3.6.3 provides a summary of the Evo process principles, the Confirmit AS interpretation of the Evo method was as follows:

▶ *Identify stakeholders* – end users, superusers, support, sales, IT operations, etc.
▶ *Define stakeholders' real needs and the related product qualities* – what was actually needed to support their business needs.
▶ *Identify past/status of product qualities and your goal* – that is, how much you want to improve.
▶ *Identify candidate solutions* for meeting your goals.
▶ *Develop a step-by-step plan* for
  ▷ delivering improvements to the process, and hence the product;
  ▷ providing deliveries every week (with respect to stakeholder needs and product quality goals); and
  ▷ measuring progress: are we moving towards our goals (again, with respect to stakeholder needs and product quality goals)?

Guided by Evo, Confirmit AS put in place a new requirements standard that meant that requirements had to

▶ be clear and unambiguous,
▶ be testable,
▶ be quantified,
▶ not involve solutions, and
▶ have a stakeholder focus.

The focus with requirements had to be on the day-to-day operations of the Confirmit√ users and not represent a list of what they might or might not like. Following this process, all of the requirements for a new release of Confirmit√ were defined and documented in just one week, as compared to the previous norm of four to five weeks.

In terms of Evo cycle time, a one-week-long Evo step was adopted in which the key activities were as follows:

- ▶ On the Friday:
  - ▷ The Project Manager (PM) delivers the detailed plan for the next week's version of the software (let's call it Version N) to the customer Chief Technical Officer (CTO) prior to attending a weekly project management meeting.
  - ▷ The CTO reviews and approves or rejects the design and records their comments.
  - ▷ The PM and CTO attend the weekly project management meeting to discuss the Version N detailed plan and review CTO comments.
  - ▷ The developers focus on general maintenance and documentation tasks.
  - ▷ The QA team runs final build and setup for that week's developed version (let's call it Version N-1), installs setup on test servers, and performs initial crash test[1] of Version N-1 prior to its release.
- ▶ On the Monday:
  - ▷ The developers first generate the tests required to validate Version N and then begin development of the code.
  - ▷ The QA team reviews the results of the continuous integration (CI) process and reviews test plans and tests for Version N.
  - ▷ The users begin to use Version N-1 and compile feedback for the developers.
- ▶ During Tuesday and Wednesday:
  - ▷ The developers continue to generate the tests required to validate Version N and develop the associated code.
  - ▷ The developers meet with the users to discuss the feedback from using Version N-1.
  - ▷ Incorporating the feedback from the users, the developers continue to generate the tests required to validate Version N and develop the associated code.
  - ▷ The QA team reviews the results of the CI process and reviews test plans and tests for Version N.
- ▶ On the Thursday:
  - ▷ The developers complete the final tests for Version N, code, and execute the tests. The developers also complete the graphical user interface tests for the previous week's version of the software (let's call this Version N-2).
  - ▷ The QA team reviews the results of the CI process and reviews test plans and tests for Version N.

---

[1]   A testing technique used to determine the fitness of a new build or release of the application under test to undergo further, more thorough testing [4].

4.4 Results of Using an Agile Approach

The adoption of the Evo approach has resulted in increased motivation and enthusiasm among the developers and testers. For example, developers reported that they are empowered and feel they have the scope for greater creativity.

The roll-out and adoption of Evo was relatively painless because the developers and testers saw the value of using the approach and embraced the method (even though some aspects of Evo were thought to be challenging to understand and execute). There may have been some scope for additional training pre-rollout to make the adoption even more successful.

There has been a paradigm shift with respect to the requirements process; previously Confirmit AS had focused on functional requirements, but following the Evo route, the focus was on product quality requirements. This was seen as a major value add over Confirmit AS's competitors.

Often, due to time constraints, testing was postponed so that the next development step could begin to plan. In the rush to complete the software, it was sometimes the case that it was not possible to compensate for these test delays, and less testing than was planned or wanted was actually completed.

LESSONS LEARNED

Overall, the move from an ad hoc waterfall style of software development to the iterative model promoted using Evo has been very successful; the adoption of smaller, more easily managed delivery steps, combined with a focus on customer quality requirements over slavishly following formal process, and with the emphasis on ensuring that testing begins as early as possible in the development and continues throughout the project, have all led to significant improvements in the speed and quality of delivered software and to more satisfied customers and happier developers and testers. Tangible benefits have included retention of existing customers, recruitment of new clients, and retention of more motivated and happier staff.

Specific lessons learned include:

▶ *The adoption of a weekly development, test, and delivery cycle has been very beneficial* – the developers, testers, customer representatives, and managers have fallen easily into the weekly rhythm and have a regular, well-defined, and predictable time period in which to achieve their tasks.

▶ As is so frequently the case in software development, *testing occasionally slipped* – in future improvements to the process, this needs to be addressed; time must be made during the Evo cycle to ensure adequate testing is completed.

▶ As with the introduction and use of any new, nontrivial technology, *it is key to ensure adequate training, mentoring, and consultancy* (process reviews or health checks) are planned into its roll-out. Tom and Kai were able to provide these, helping to ensure the successful introduction, roll out, and use of Confirmit AS's Evo approach.

▶ Although over time and under the influence of process improvement, *our approach to CI has been refined*, the CI process has proven to be successful and we intend to continue to use it for the foreseeable future.

▶ Finally, a very important lesson to be learned is that *there is always another lesson to be learned* – the goal of fine-tuning our processes continues today, and will continue into the future.

5 How to Test a System That Is Never Finished

Nick Sewell, European Managing Director of Ivar Jacobson
Consulting Ltd.

SYNOPSIS

In a fast-moving environment where requirements are changing all the time, in order to support the customer's needs, the testing strategy has to be superagile. How do you keep the relevant documentation up to date? How do you communicate the changes to your team? How do you ensure your testing covers the changes? How can you guarantee that you deliver a system that works and meets the customer's needs?

This case study reviews the issues that are being faced by a large, multiyear project practicing incremental delivery, and shows how the team has used agile techniques to address these issues. In particular we will look at how using techniques such as daily builds, pairing testers and developers through an iteration, and the use of automated testing tools for regression testing have enabled the team to successfully test and deliver a new, high-quality release every six weeks!

5.1 Introduction

My name is Nick Sewell and I work for Ivar Jacobson Consulting Ltd. as the European Managing Director. I have over twenty years' commercial experience in the software industry – twelve of these ensuring that software teams deliver software successfully using a range of techniques.

In a fast-moving customer environment where requirements are changing all the time to support the user needs, the testing strategy has to be superagile.

For example, I have recently been working as a part of a team enhancing a large business critical information system that needs to be updated every six weeks to keep pace with an ever-changing variety of information sources and analytical needs. Traditional test approaches are not suitable in this kind of situation; the test strategy must be agile for the project to survive.

As we worked to develop and test the software, we needed to meet the challenges of:

▶ keeping the relevant documentation up to date,
▶ communicating the frequent changes to all members of the team,

▶ ensuring that the changes are thoroughly tested,

▶ ensuring that the changes don't compromise or break the existing system, and

▶ delivering a system that works and meets the customer needs every six weeks.

This case study identifies the issues faced by the project and discusses some of the solutions that were explored to address those issues, such as

▶ developing the test cases alongside the requirements,

▶ pairing testers and developers through an iteration,

▶ ensuring that all the documentation was updated as we went along,

▶ relaying information to the team by means of a daily Scrum, and

▶ employing automated testing tools to assist with the testing load.

It concludes with a review of what parts of our testing strategy actually worked and what clearly didn't.

5.2 Overview of the Testing Challenge

The project was first initiated in 1997 and involves the development of systems to provide key information to government departments on demand.

As information sources are enhanced or new sources identified, the systems need to be quickly updated. There is no apparent end date to this project, as it is inevitable that changes and new requirements will continue to be identified for the foreseeable future.

The systems are truly "business critical," requiring very high quality, reliability, and availability. Essential updates and enhancements must be implemented quickly, must be delivered on time, must be defect free, and must not degrade the quality or accuracy of the existing functionality.

The project runs on a rolling three-year cycle, with major reviews carried out at the end of each period. These typically result in changes to the personnel involved in the project and the underlying customer needs. They can also influence the overall development approach taken. I became involved at the last three-year review, one of whose recommendations was to adopt "a more agile approach."

This is a large agile project, with some thirty staff, including customer representatives. The project team changes regularly, with no one staying on the team for any great length of time, other than a core of five people. It is critical to project success that the productivity and quality are not harmed as a result of the high staff turnover. Continuously integrating new team members into the team is a major challenge; consequently, a great deal of attention has to be paid to keeping documentation up to date to ensure seamless handovers whenever people leave or join the project.

The project is run as a series of six-week iterations, with each iteration delivering production-quality code into the live environment. As a result of this rapid development cycle and the need to deliver high-quality reliable code into the live environment, testing is absolutely critical to the success of each iteration, as well as that of the overall project. The need to ensure that the code implemented in the current iterations meets the customer requirements and is reliable, while ensuring that the changes do not adversely impact the existing code base, means that testing must be continuous, comprehensive, effective, and efficient.

5.3   Definition of an Agile Testing Process

We decided that there were two aspects to the successful delivery of the system:

1. We needed to assemble the core of a great team that had the experience and talent to work using the new agile techniques. This core of five people needed to transfer knowledge to new team members as they moved in and out of the project.
2. We needed a lightweight and practical process to help us deliver on time, to budget, and to acceptable quality.

Rather than try to adopt a whole new process we decided to adopt a smaller number of agile practices taken from the Essential Unified Process [34]. The concepts within this process are delivered using cards – this means that minimal information is referenced when it is needed. The practices used were Iterative Essentials and Use Case Essentials.

The beauty of the Essential Unified Process is that it adopts a practice-based approach, where the practices underlying the process are defined separately in a way that allows you to select just the ones that will benefit your project. In this case we didn't have to adopt the other practices from the process (such as the component-based development or architecture practices) to be able to benefit from the use of use cases and iterations.

Figure 5.1 shows a couple of the cards that we used – these describe two of the deliverables the project needed. The diagram on each was ticked to show the level of detail required for that deliverable.

The practice approach provides a very agile way of using small parts of the process to add value where and when needed. Lightweight is the key adjective for this, and we took advantage of this to introduce the changes quickly and effectively.

We also followed the advice provided by the iterative practice for improving communications and introduced daily Scrums. The improved communication allowed us to minimize the amount of documentation we produced (although the minimum on this project actually turned out to be quite a lot!). Combining smart communication with fit-for-purpose levels of documentation turned out to be very important in supporting the testing effort needed to ensure high-quality and reliable delivery. Communication through simply talking has proven invaluable in ensuring that all stakeholders are headed in the same direction.

Due to the need for high quality, we placed the testing at the heart of the process. Our process encouraged the involvement of the test resources throughout the project

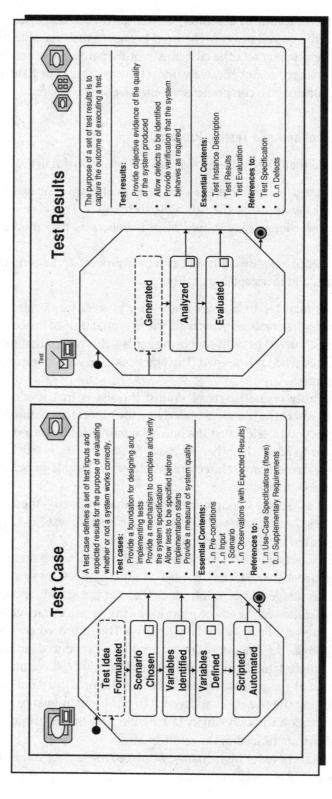

5.1 Some cards from the use case essentials practice.

in as many activities as possible (and in many more activities within this project than any other I have previously worked on).

For example, the testers were involved in working with the customers alongside the analysts, producing the test cases at the same time as the use cases (an integral part of the use case essentials practice [38]). This test-driven approach provided us with significant improvements in productivity and accuracy compared with traditional methods, and the software continues to be developed using this technique.

Similarly, we ensure that the requirements, both functional and nonfunctional, have a test built alongside them during their development. We have found that spending time on establishing traceability between the requirements, tests, and components provides the minimal level of documentation that is needed and adds value. This was especially true when the personnel changes within the team were so regular, new staff could understand the system by means of the documentation provided and quickly become productive with relatively little negative impact on the project.

The idea of having good people plus good process within the team was also extended to the customer; we took the approach that the customer representative was an essential part of the team and mandated that customer representatives be involved in the software development from day one. We followed the assumption that "the customer will only know what they want when they see it," and through having them on hand at all times we could make sure that we were building and testing the right thing. The agile principle of promoting good and regular communication works very well with the customer and cuts down the amount of time spent on clarifying or confirming issues.

5.4 Results of the Agile Process and Lessons Learned

The results speak for themselves: the project continues to deliver successfully, the reputation of the project has excelled, and other projects within the same organization are now looking to reuse the approach developed in order to improve their productivity and delivery records.

The key lessons learned from this project and which are continuing to be used in the later iterations of the project include:

▶ *User requirements and test cases* – you need them both up front. Following the use case essentials practice we have extended the role of use cases beyond being just an approach for gathering requirements. As the use cases are constructed, a test resource is on hand to identify the test cases that will be needed to cover functional and nonfunctional issues, quality, and integration. During the discussions with the customer representatives, where requirements were being identified, the tester would contribute by asking clarifying questions, such as, "How do you verify if that works?" Having these sorts of questions asked during analysis has proven to identify more details than we might otherwise have found at that time. This ultimately resulted in us producing a single document that covers what we would traditionally call a use case and a test case. This provided us with accurate requirements and the details of the testing needed to ensure that the requirements were met.

▶ *Pair developers and testers* – one effective technique we adopted was to pair a testing resource with a developer during the implementation of the code. We already knew about the benefits of pair programming, and we attempted to gain similar benefits by bringing developers and testers together. This solution was not perfect, as the perception of the developer was that the tester was acting as a policeman, sitting on their shoulder constantly directing her or him. We refined this approach so that the tester was involved in reviewing what had been delivered at the end of each day, so that this could be incorporated into the next day's testing.

▶ *Every day is test day* – I have heard it proposed many times during projects that "we can cut back on testing to meet the deadline!" Testing seems to be the first thing that is ditched when tight timescales start to make things difficult. The truth is that something can probably be delivered under these circumstances but the reliability and quality of such a system is often questionable.

Once a project has started delivering, it is vital that testing is continuous in order to keep to the levels of reliability required by the stakeholders. We have tried to promote the fact that testing is the central cog in our project, and that the testers need to be in communication with all members of the team in order to fully integrate the work completed by the requirements analysts, developers, and the customer community. If something is to be delivered, then it is the testers who make the final decision as to whether or not that something is delivered into the live environment.

In addition to daily builds and their associated tests, test cases are implemented during an iteration as the code is being developed. The testers work closely with the developers to help focus the effort on achieving deliverable code that can successfully pass the test cases. Because the testers are involved in the requirements-gathering effort, they are able to provide extra clarification points when a requirement is unclear. This means that we have analysts, testers, and customer representatives available to the developers to help clarify or confirm a particular requirement; this helps us cut down on the amount of documentation produced while improving the quality of the communications.

Each and every day in our iterations is a day that the testers will work with the team, with one common goal – successful delivery.

▶ *Automated testing of daily builds* – The use of automated testing tools for regression testing has saved the project significant amounts of time, effort, and cost, and has helped to ensure that the quality of the deliverable is maintained. The key to using these tools successfully is to have a testing resource who fully understands the tools and who has responsibility for keeping the scripts up to date every single day. The goal is to run automated tests every night, with any issues highlighted the following morning. Fixing these issues is a standard task all the way through the iterations – so there was an assumption that time would be spent on this activity and the iterations would be planned accordingly.

▶ *Role and use of Scrums* – One of the benefits of holding daily Scrums has been in promoting effective testing as the key to the delivery of higher-quality code. Scrums have also been instrumental in ensuring that testers, analysts, developers, and customer representatives are all working together as a team toward the same goal.

5.5 Conclusions

Overall, the importance of testing within a project that has to deliver high-quality code cannot be underestimated. Within this project, testing was given a great deal of emphasis and, specifically, testing *was*

▶ *introduced into the process as early as possible*, such as during requirements elicitation, with a tester working with the customer and the analyst;
▶ *present everywhere* within the practices that we used;
▶ *employed throughout each iteration*, with the testers initially working hand-in-hand with the developers, and later used just to review the code developed through the day;
▶ *the central cog of the development process*, with the testers providing close and effective communication between all the other stakeholders and helping the analysts during requirements elicitation, the developers during coding and delivery effort, and the customer community across the whole iteration; and
▶ *supported by the use of automated testing tools*, whose test scripts were used to ensure thorough and complete regression testing of the system under development, as well as maintained and used on a daily basis to highlight new issues and ensure they were corrected quickly, with minimum disruption to the project, and with as little cost impact as possible.

Finally, it seems like a no-brainer, but having well-trained, experienced, and enthusiastic people, combined with a practical, effective, and efficient process, helped us achieve noticeable success in a short period of time. Team agility can be achieved when the team buys into the agile principles and they are all given the opportunity to contribute to the successful end result. The practices of the Essential Unified Process provided us with a refreshing lightweight process that was usable, added value, and was palatable for the more agile-minded people in the team.

With agile practices and a good team, successful delivery becomes the norm.

5.6 Acknowledgment

I would like to express my gratitude to my agile mentor and company CEO Ivar Jacobson for his support in my writing of this case study and for his assistance in reviewing my material.

6 Implementing an Agile Testing Approach

Graham Thomas, Independent Software Testing Consultant

SYNOPSIS

This case study documents the introduction and use of an agile testing approach that is based on Extreme Programming (XP).[1] XP was introduced to a traditional development project where the classic view of the test process was proving to be an obstacle to keeping pace with a very demanding release schedule that involved a high volume of small changes to the system. The case study also explores the benefits of introducing test automation to assist with a faster release schedule and volume of changes, and discusses how automation can be successfully integrated into an agile approach.

6.1 Introduction

My name is Graham Thomas. I have a range of experience in software development and specifically testing, with formal qualifications in programming, systems analysis and design, and latterly in software testing. Most recently I have been involved as a program test manager looking after high-value testing portfolios of work.

I became involved with agile development and testing methods in the autumn of 2000, when I was working on a project with a small transatlantic software house producing systems for the treasury dealing markets.

This case study looks at my involvement in the project, starting at the point where I realized that traditional testing approaches were not working for an organization that was delivering customized releases combined with a high volume of small changes to an installed client base. The case study explores how we went about designing and running a change program to implement the adoption of an agile development and testing approach based around XP [20].

6.2 Overview of the Testing Challenge

City Street Traders is a midsized (220-person) software house producing solutions for the treasury dealing marketplace. At the time of the case study the company had

---

[1] See Appendix B for further details of the rules and practices of XP.

an installed base of systems with over thirty clients and was adding to that base at the rate of about three new clients per year. The company was also delivering upwards of 4,500 bespoke changes per annum to the installed client base. The company had sites in North America and London, with most, but not all, development being carried out in the United States. Testing, configuration management, and release management were performed in London.

The company had grown organically during the previous decade but was now beginning to experience problems with configuration management, organizational growth beyond process capability, and lengthening testing windows.

What was required was a development and testing approach that would

- ▶ shorten the lengthening testing windows,
- ▶ support the many client configurations, and
- ▶ allow the high volume of bespoke changes to installed systems.

The only answer that seemed to meet all of these requirements was an agile approach based around XP.

The anticipated benefits were that the organization could reduce the release windows from nine to twelve months down to less than six months, thus enabling an aggressive technology refresh program while still maintaining the lucrative bespoke enhancement business.

6.3 Definition of an Agile Testing Process

As described earlier, XP was selected as the base agile approach to be used on the project, with the following additional local agile process details:

- ▶ *definition of an organizational development methodology* – with variants for new product releases, bespoke enhancements, and emergency fixes;
- ▶ a *continuous integration development approach* – which included the adoption of development tools for
  - ▷ *static analysis and*
  - ▷ *automated unit testing*;
- ▶ *reduction of the release testing window* – from three to six months to four weeks,
  - ▷ based around smaller more frequent releases,
  - ▷ using test automation tools to give productivity benefits, and
  - ▷ development of a continuous integration release testing approach; and
- ▶ *implementation of automated configuration management*
  - ▷ to enable the management and control of customized releases and
  - ▷ to control a high volume of bespoke changes to the installed user base.

Some elements of the XP approach were not adopted, namely,

- ▶ *pair programming* – because of company management and developer resistance;

▶ *on-site customer* – primarily because of the nature of software houses developing products for a market rather than specific clients, and second for enhancement work because of the disparate geographic location of the clients. Expert business analysts were used as proxy on-site customers.

▶ *co-location* – was not possible because it would have meant splitting the release testing team across the two sites, London and New York, so in mitigation virtual co-location techniques were adopted, such as group working, videoconferencing, and the use of tools to share workstation control.

To support this radical change in the organization, a change program was initiated to manage and control the phased implementation, to ensure continuity of business, and to minimize any impact to productivity and ultimately revenue.

Care was taken to ensure that there was good communication with the stakeholders and sponsors. Workshops were held with developers, testers, and senior management to explain and sell the benefits of the changes. Frequent communication by e-mail, newsletter, and face to face ensured that all were kept updated with progress and developments.

Budget was secured for development, testing, and configuration management tools.

6.4 Results of the Agile Approach

The results of adopting an agile approach were mixed at best. The key benefits that City Street Traders gained from implementing the change program were as follows:

▶ *Definition of a development methodology* – the organization benefited greatly from the documented definition of an integrated development methodology, including analysis, design, build, test, and release activities. This development methodology comprised variants for new product releases, bespoke enhancements and emergency fixes. (City Street Traders was in a transitional stage from the size of company where everybody knew each other and what to do – less than 100 employees – to the point where there were too many people to know everybody – 200+ employees – and processes were starting to break down because there wasn't a common understanding across the organization.)

▶ *Release testing window shortened* – the release testing window was shortened from three to six months down to four weeks. This was partly achieved by having smaller, more frequent releases. The initial release test cycles took longer than four weeks, until the developers rigorously applied a continuous integration approach.

▶ *Identification of a core product set that would be tested every release cycle* – in order to enable a four-week release test, a core configuration of the product set was identified, the tests for which were then automated, giving a clear productivity and quality gain.

▶ *Closer working between development and testing teams* – the testers formed a closer working relationship with the developers because the release testers could focus on a smaller release, which was more current, and could therefore provide more timely feedback to the development teams, to the point where the developers would come to the release testers first with new ideas to get their feedback.

The results were mixed, primarily because, given the prevailing financial climate, City Street Traders only half-heartedly adopted an agile methodology, not wanting to endanger the current business model, productivity, and revenue streams.

A practical example of this was the developer's keenness to produce minimal documentation but without the balancing practice of pair programming. This led to reluctance by developers to refactor (see Appendix B) someone else's code because there was still strong individual rather than collective ownership.

6.5 Lessons Learned

The change program progressed more slowly than expected. This was in part due to a very flat organizational structure, which meant that it took longer than anticipated to get everybody onside with suitable tools for unit test and code analysis automation and configuration management.

The release testing team pressed ahead with automation of testing and reduction of the release testing window to four weeks but found it difficult to deliver in the four weeks because the development and configuration management changes had not been implemented. This led to lengthy integration delays caused in the most part by a lack of continuous integration by the developers.

What worked well included

▶ the drive for greater tool usage in development;
▶ the adoption of configuration management disciplines, which enabled greater control over the increasing complexity of the product configuration; and
▶ the closer working relationship between developers and testers, which produced a measurable increase in quality.

It could be argued that these disciplines could have been adopted anyway, regardless of whether an agile method, such as XP, was adopted.

There is always a danger with testing or quality-driven improvement programs that the rest of the organization does not take them seriously. There was a feeling that with this "testing-driven" change program, the changes were tolerated as long as they didn't cause any harm to the basic operating model of the company.

Additionally as the company grew and became established in the marketplace, it was observed during the sales process that potential customers were performing a more rigorous review of the development approach. There was a view that City Street

Traders' management was keen to wear the agile badge as a way of giving credibility to some of their established development practices.

What I would have done differently, with the benefit of hindsight, would have been to work harder to make the change self-propagating. Although the development team was already relatively small, I would have started with a smaller development team, let them establish the benefits, and then sell them onto their colleagues. Thus, a momentum for change would build up, mitigating against resistance and half-hearted adoption. The learning point from that experience is that just because the company is small, you do not have to change it all in one go.

7 Agile Testing in a Remote or Virtual Desktop Environment

Michael G. Norman, CEO of Scapa Technologies Ltd

SYNOPSIS

This case study deals with an agile approach specifically tailored toward the integration and deployment of packaged applications by or on behalf of enterprise customers.

The particular challenges of this case study were that no source code was available to the test team, timescales were very challenging, and the majority of quality issues were nonfunctional in nature.

7.1 Introduction

My name is Michael G. Norman. I have been involved with software test and performance for more than ten years, most recently having taken on the role as CEO of Scapa Technologies Ltd, a software tools vendor company. I was formerly involved in forming the Eclipse Test and Performance Tools Project (TPTP, formerly Hyades), which I ran in collaboration with colleagues from IBM and Intel and served on its Project Management Committee and the Board of Eclipse for around five years.

Scapa Technologies is involved with a range of testing engagements with its several hundred enterprise customers and tries to be methodologically neutral in the way it develops its tooling, making it applicable in both traditional and agile environments. In cases where it performs its own services, Scapa adopts a variation on the agile approach, which is tailored toward its predominant customer profile: integration and deployment of packaged applications by or on behalf of enterprise customers.

This case study describes a project where Scapa was engaged to test and produce very fast feedback on a set of applications that were being deployed by a telecommunications vendor via a remote desktop technology. The case study refers to Citrix technologies [39], but similar concerns and approaches apply to other remote and virtual desktop technologies from Microsoft, VMware [40], and a range of other vendors.

7.2 Overview of the Testing Challenge

In this particular project, the telecommunications vendor was neither the author nor the user of the applications under test; it was simply providing a secure hosted platform to allow others to have access to applications. Access was via secure token authentication [41] and the Citrix Secure Gateway into a Citrix server farm on Windows 2003 Server.

The whole platform was subject to a traditional long-term top-down testing project, which had been overtaken by political reality; the platform had gone into a phased live roll-out before the test process had delivered significant results, and issues were emerging in production. Specifically the platform was subject to instability (requiring frequent reboots) and the applications suffered from functional failure under load.

In this context Scapa was asked to test the applications to isolate problems and make recommendations about how they could be made more stable and less prone to failure under load.

7.3 Definition of an Agile Testing Process

In contrast to most approaches to agile testing, there was no source code available in this environment. Furthermore, a number of contractual frameworks that existed between the vendors involved, and the customer and Scapa, made it highly unlikely that source code would be made available within the timescales of the testing task.

In addition, the majority of issues raised were nonfunctional; that is, they related to performance and stability of servers either under multiuser load or after extended execution. The scope of the functional testing only required consideration of failures that could be detected by gross failure of the application and did not require detailed arbitration of results.

Another key element is timeline; there were twelve applications and the test timeline was twenty person-days (four weeks elapsed). The following conceptual framework was applied to provide a performance model within which tests were defined:

▶ *The Edge* – all systems "break" under sufficient load. System response time increases, the system becomes unstable, or both, beyond sustainable levels when the applied workload (in terms of transaction rates or number of users) is driven above a certain capacity. We refer to the set of acceptable workloads as the working Envelope of the system, and we are concerned with mapping out the characteristics of the Edge.

▶ *The Signature* – systems "break" for a particular reason, and there is a characteristic "signature" of associated system metrics, typically because one or another system resource saturates, serializes, or leaks up to a static limit.

▶ *Diagnostic transaction set* – there is usually a small set of transactions that show a set of differentiated "signatures"; that is, they cause the server to fail for a set of identifiably different reasons. Testing processes can be simplified if they are restricted to these transactions, and it is also possible to work with a test environment that differs from the production environment as long as the same signatures can be detected.

▶ *Calibration matrix* – a matrix of factors can be built that maps between the Edges of the Envelopes for the diagnostic transactions on various environments.

Simplifications:

▶ Since testing is on an exact replica of production, no calibration matrix is required.

▶ The edge of the Envelope (and corresponding signatures) is found for a set of "prototypical" transactions whose characteristics are constructed by reference to the architecture, not the business process. A judgment is then made as to how the production workload relates to the Envelope.

▶ Clear definition of pretesting dependencies and subsequent close involvement of the customer during testing to address remaining issues as they emerged.

▶ The reduction of testing documentation and complexity to a minimum:
  ▷ test plan – standardized across all twelve applications,
  ▷ test case design – standardized across all twelve applications with only detailed application-specific variations,
  ▷ systems performance metric collection – informed and very much constrained by the test case design and standardized across all twelve applications,
  ▷ stress testing and soak testing[1] using the same test cases,
  ▷ test summary report – maintained continuously with status updates to the customer on a regular basis, and
  ▷ template-based report for each application issued for review by the customer as the results emerge, followed by full signoff of report set with customer.

7.4 Results of the Agile Approach

Within twenty days the telecommunications vendor had an effective understanding of the performance and robustness characteristics of the twelve applications it had deployed onto the platform and had raised detailed concerns with a large number of its suppliers.

This in turn led to additional confidence within the telecommunications vendor that the phased roll-out was being managed effectively and that resolutions would

---

[1] *Stress testing* is a form of testing that is used to determine the stability of a given system or entity. It involves testing beyond normal operational capacity, often to a breaking point, to observe the results. *Soak testing* involves testing a system with a significant load extended over a significant period of time to discover how the system behaves under sustained use.

be found to the issues that were present in the initial roll-out, which allowed the planned roll-out schedule to continue.

The roll-out was ultimately successful, the applications were deployed successfully to the planned number of users, and the platform proved stable in use.

The agile methodology proved repeatable for subsequent versions of the applications deployed onto the platform.

7.5 Lessons Learned

Overall, the results of the use of an agile testing approach were good, and the agile approach was seen to have worked well.

In particular, the co-location of the customer integration team and testers worked very well, with the customer able to resolve environmental issues (availability of applications, logins, user profiles, security issues, etc.) that emerged during the testing. A useful side effect of this has been an increase in the awareness of the integration team of the role and need for effective and efficient testing of the applications they were deploying into their infrastructure (rather than assuming the vendors would resolve any issues) and a greater respect for the testing role.

The agile approach was applied tactically and coexisted with a much larger traditional approach and was able to provide effective results to specific concerns in a timely manner.

The approach of using architectural analysis rather than business analysis to define test cases was understood by all technical staff on the project and led quickly to detailed proposals for intervention in the system to increase capacity, to limit the impact of running over capacity, and to improve long-running stability.

Template-based test plans, test cases, reports, and so forth (see Appendices E, F, and G for examples of agile templates), and reuse of test cases worked well, both in simplifying the testing process and in articulating the approach to senior management. They also allow for significant reuse when new versions of the applications are to be deployed onto the platform.

8 Testing a Derivatives Trading System in an Uncooperative Environment

Nick Denning, Chief Executive Officer of Diegesis Limited

SYNOPSIS

This case study describes a project where our team was contracted to assist the resolution of quality issues in a commercially critical derivatives trading system and the challenges imposed by the demanding development environment in a financial institution.

After reviewing the testing requirements, the timescales and budget, and the difficult nature of the development environment, an agile testing approach was selected. This case study covers the selection process for the use of and the results obtained from using an agile approach.

8.1 Introduction

My name is Nick Denning and at the time of this case study I was the managing director of Strategic Thought Limited, a company I founded in 1987, which we subsequently floated on AIM[1] in 2005 and which now specializes in the development and sale of financial risk management products. At the time the events in this case study took place, we were an IT consultancy with a strong reputation for work in the Ingres Relational Database Management System arena. A particular strength of ours was to be able to analyze systems, identify performance issues, and make changes to the database configuration, the database structures, and the SQL code within the application.

Making changes to mission-critical applications, sometimes directly on the production environment, required a careful consideration of the implications for a change, and the ability to assess the risks and agree with a customer on the risk reward profile to justify implementing changes that bypassed the conventional release procedures.

Our successful approach to this problem resulted in a number of engagements to assist customers in building regression test environments so that they could continue to design, implement, and deploy changes to a solution quickly and confidently on

---

[1] AIM is the London Stock Exchange's international market for smaller growing companies.

completion of the engagement with us. A significant class of problems were not functional but rather performance related; solutions did not scale up under load. They might simply slow down and be unusable, and in the worst case they might run out of resources and crash. Our regression test approach began to incorporate a "performance pack" with which we ran tests on duplicate installations, using copies of production data and examples of transactions run a few days earlier in production, to identify the reasons for solutions failing. These projects then led to engagements associated with capacity planning to establish the upper limits for throughput on systems, such as prior to the deregulation of markets when a major increase in business was expected.

This case study describes a project where we were engaged to help our customer improve the reliability and availability of a mission-critical system. The case study describes an all-too-familiar problem in the software industry; the development of a business-critical software solution, initially built by an in-house team, with a focus on the delivery of key business functionality, to very tight timescales, but which after two years of development displayed serious quality problems during day-to-day use.

The quality issues were found in two main areas:

1. Functionally the solution was known to have a number of bugs within it when delivered, but generally it was possible for the back-office users to work around these issues. In practice, it was found that only experienced users could perform the work-around, and it took those users longer to use the system than had been expected. A dominating factor was a business desire for new capabilities to be delivered urgently, resulting in staff being rewarded by meeting delivery deadlines, resulting in an informal policy of deploying into production come-what-may and fixing bugs in production. As a consequence insufficient effort was put into testing prior to release.
2. Reliability and availability were also the issues; under circumstances of heavy load, or indeed unexpectedly and without warning, the solution could crash, after which it could take a number of hours to recover.

Given the business-critical nature of the solution, combined with the time-critical nature of the derivatives market, these quality issues were unacceptable; unless options (a particular financial instrument) could be exercised at precisely the right time, it would not be possible to realize the profits earned through those options.

This was not a theoretical risk – in fact this worst-case scenario had already manifested itself; the customer had lost substantial amounts of revenue because the system had crashed on these critical "end-of-period" dates, and it had not been possible to recover the system and exercise these options. Although difficult to quantify precisely, events of this nature could, in the worst case, cost the company in excess of hundreds of thousands of pounds (which does not include the intangible but important effect of loss of reputation). This event, and the likelihood that it would occur again in the future, provided the customer with a compelling reason to investigate how the problem could be solved.

Strategic Thought was approached by the customer to assist them in the development and testing of the next phase of this project. The next section reviews the testing challenge facing our team.

8.2 Overview of the Testing Challenge

The development and testing of the replacement software solution presented a number of challenges:

▶ The nature of the business need meant that the software solution would be a substantial and complex system, automating a wide range of innovative functionality which had previously generated substantial revenues for the business.

▶ As valuable and knowledgeable resources, who were very busy managing the day-to-day business of the customer, there was relatively limited time available from the users to participate in a major testing program (even though there was commitment from the users to assist, provided the amount of time could be maintained within acceptable bounds).

▶ There was a substantial development pipeline planned, and the testing approach needed to integrate closely with development in order to avoid interfering with the development plans as far as was practical.

▶ The specification was incomplete and poorly documented, making test planning and design very difficult. Historically, the test approach had been to make the solution available to the users for testing once it was complete and for the users to sign it off once they were satisfied with the solution.

▶ Historically, there had been very limited defect tracking documentation available, and no defect tracking system against which bugs could be formally logged, tracked, and fixed.

8.3 Definition of an Agile Testing Process

In determining the testing approach to be used, there were a number of issues to be considered:

▶ The characteristics of the development and testing process (as described earlier), plus the historical situation we inherited, meant that this was a "special needs" testing project.[2] The common manifestation of this problem in the IT industry is to exclaim that the system is too poor to salvage and should be rewritten from scratch because the issue of understanding the problem is so large.

▶ We had to find an approach that would accommodate the magnitude of the challenge, work with it, and deliver progressive improvement by identifying and

---

2 Indeed the classic joke came to mind of the person who, when asking for directions, was told, "if that was where I was going, I wouldn't be starting from here!"

isolating the most significant defects as quickly as possible. These would then be fixed on a case by case basis. At the same time, we also had to provide confidence that the ultimate goal of a high-quality robust system was achievable.

▶ Although initially we had the commitment of all of the key stakeholders, we knew we would have to work hard to ensure that we retained this support throughout the process.

The details of our agile testing approach are as follows:

▶ *The software solution is correct* – Despite the problems that we knew existed, we put forward the hypothesis that the software solution was correct (even with the work-arounds and reliability issues). This provided us with a working baseline from which to proceed.

▶ *User test run-through* – Using a copy of the current version of the software, we asked the users to run through the standard tests that they would normally undertake to validate the system and to show us the results that they would expect.

▶ *Employ test automation* – We captured these tests (including the navigation through the software and the specific verifications required) using functional testing tools (classic capture–replay tools) and printed out the results, both screen shots and reports, provided these to the users, and asked them to check and sign off these tests.

▶ *Minimum test harness* – We developed a process to reliably prepare a release package, installation instructions, and a set of minimum tests to run all of the key functions of the system to prove that all major functions would run without crashing. It is disappointing how many releases were deployed into production and crashed, often because of configuration and release errors rather than software bugs.

▶ *Regression testing baseline* – The signed-off automated tests provided us with a suite of regression tests, which gave reasonable test coverage over all components of the system. It was then possible to run the tests from a common baseline and get identical results on successive runs.

▶ *Incremental new test development* – Working closely with the developers and users, we then built a set of specific tests for the new functions being developed and worked with the users to define precisely what the new behavior of the system should be and where any other changes to the system might be anticipated.

▶ *Test new build* – The automated regression tests and the new tests were then run against the new version of the system. The assumption was that if the system was correct following the new development, then there should be no changes to any part of the system except those containing new functionality.

▶ *Review and analyze defects* – However, of course, in practice the system was not correct; differences started to appear in a number of areas. Each unexpected result was reviewed with the users to investigate the problem further, working through each example to identify the bug.

▶ *Log, fix, and retest defects cycle* – Once a bug was identified, it was logged and passed back to the developers for correction. Once fixed, the software was retested using the regression testing tools, iterating round this loop as many times as was necessary until all the bugs were resolved.

▶ *Changes to facilitate testing* – In the options market, option pricing depends on the time to expiry, that is, the difference between current date and the expiry of the options contract. The solution took the current date from the computer system clock. We needed to change the software to take the current date from a database field so that if we ran the same test on different days we would get identical results.

Finally we got to a point where we had resolved all the material bugs and the system was successfully released. Following release, only one bug was discovered, which we were then able to track back to an item that had been signed off incorrectly. This result confirmed the suitability and success of the agile approach that we had adopted.

8.4 Refining the Agile Testing Process

Having achieved this significant initial success, we then subsequently repeated the process for the second release. A number of improvements were introduced in the testing process leading up to this release:

▶ *Refine test automation* – A number of additional regression test tools were deployed. Of particular help was a tool that compared databases, so that we could inspect every record in pairs of tables and identify any differences in those tables and report them. This proved to be very useful in identifying a range of unexpected differences in the system's data that were not immediately apparent to the user (since they related to trades that the user might not be inspecting for some months until they were closer to the expiry dates of those trades).

▶ *Address system performance* – A performance pack was developed that was able to capture system load information while regression tests were executed. We could then compare the performance data of runs and identify any increases in run times or system load. These could then be inspected (in conjunction with profiling tools) to identify any specific areas of code that were generating problems.

The testing team continued to work with the software for a further year, before finally handing over the regression test environment to the developers to be integrated into their normal development and test approach.

In the longer term, the results of this approach were impressive. There was only one major crash of the system following the second release, and the system was never unavailable on key end-of-period dates.

A tremendous success, one would think. Well it was, in many respects, and it provided a model that has been reused many times in similar circumstances for other customers. However, as you will see in the next section of the case study, this was not the universal perspective of all parties involved!

8.5 Lessons Learned

This section describes lessons learned on the agile testing project in the following areas:

▶ developer relations,
▶ a project is a project,
▶ how to decide when to release,
▶ definitive evidence, and
▶ the epilogue.

Developer Relations

We had enthusiastic buy-in from all parties when we started the project; in principle the approach was well received, though there was some initial skepticism about whether it would work in practice, and some surprise when the results promised were delivered. However, in one particular area we experienced significant push-back; our relationship with the developers started to break down when the bugs began to be found!

As is the case in many parts of the finance sector, staff are paid bonuses based on their ability to deliver high-quality solutions into production. There was an expectation that we would not find much wrong with the system and that our efforts were going to be a bit of a sideshow. However, we found so many bugs that the first release was two months late going into production.

In some organizations there is a significant "blame culture." The testing process shone a spotlight on individuals when they were developing their code. So from the developers' perspective, the test team became "the enemy."

The situation became worse; as the developers gained an understanding of how the testing process worked, and by introducing subtle changes to the code each time the system changed, they were able to make the test scripts fail. We did not realise at the time but subsequently learned that there was a deliberate initiative to make changes to the solution user interfaces in order to disrupt the testing process so that the testers would be perceived as the obstruction in the development process.

In order to address the issue of poor developer relations, in all future projects of this nature we followed the following approach:

▶ *Identify facts and do not speculate on the causes* – having identified the facts, let the developers do the investigation so that they can become heroes for having found the cause of the problem and, as a minimum, have time to build a story for their managers.
▶ *Ensure that the design approach takes into account all aspects of the deliverable* – such as changes to the code, changes to the regression test harnesses, preparation

of test data. In this way, we estimate and optimize the time taken to perform all these activities to complete a change. Too often we found design decisions were taken to minimize the development process at the expense of the testing activity and to the detriment of the overall delivery. If a developer has the choice of a three-day work package that incurs ten days of testing effort as opposed to a five-day work package that incurs two days of testing effort, too many times the developers chose the former. The approach needs to motivate best behavior for the overall team.

▶ *Ensure that test specifications are included in the work package* – in order to define the completion criteria and to ensure the work package is complete when the test criteria are satisfied. Any subsequent bugs are not the developer's responsibility but rather that of the person who wrote the test specification. Thus, the developer has a structured approach to completion and does not waste time in random testing "in the hope" of finding a bug. Problems will arise later inevitably, but they will be integration problems arising from issues that had not been predicted.

▶ *Developing the previous points, regression testing cannot remain separated from the development process* or it is doomed to failure in the medium term. Use of the tools and maintenance of the test harnesses have to be undertaken by the developer and changes in the code and in the regression tests associated with that code made as part of the same work package or else the regression tests will not be maintained.

▶ *Management responsibility for development and testing must be delegated to as low a level as possible* – the test manager should be responsible for the definition of best practice, for quality standards, and for owning the regression test environment in order to ensure that it is being run every night so that new bugs are isolated as quickly as possible and passed back to the developers. However, the developers must maintain both the code and the associated test harness.

▶ *As a consequence of the best practices set by the test manager, we can develop an integrated set of test components* that linked together support system testing but can be decomposed into elements that can support both integration testing and module testing. This enabled us to shorten development cycles considerably by reducing the time for development of individual modules, the time taken for testing, and the number of bugs detected at a late stage.

A Project Is a Project

A fundamental aspect of our approach in managing the testing was to view testing activities as "just another project," and as such, to ensure we followed good project management best practice, such as that presented in PRINCE2 [22]. This approach included

▶ *identifying the project sponsor, agreeing terms of references, and confining yourself to those terms of reference.* You cannot expect to solve all the problems the organization is experiencing, so focus on solving those you are asked to address and ensure that you retain the confidence of the project sponsor by reporting on progress against plan for the agreed objectives;

▶ *identifying all the people affected by the project and ensuring that there is a mechanism for keeping them apprised of developments and progress*;

▶ *creating and following a project plan*, identifying the tasks to be undertaken by all participants, and ensuring that they are tasked through the project steering committee to deliver against the plan;

▶ *identifying early when there is risk that an objective may not be delivered by the client's staff* and giving the project sponsor sufficient warning so that there is a reasonable chance of the situation being resolved;

▶ *budget for testing a "rate of run project" and accept that there will be a regular monthly cost regardless of the level of work*. Once the initial test tools are available, running through the regression test process is highly dependent on the delivery by the developers; so one is a hostage to fortune if a testing organization undertakes work on a fixed-price basis. However, if you have testers who are also developers, you can consume time to benefit by getting testers to undertake some development-related tasks; and

▶ *ensuring that when your role as a consultant is completed, then you exit*. Define the exit criteria, meet them, and go! We are all passionate about testing, and it needs to be a permanent function, so help the customer to recruit a member of staff to continue the good work using the framework you have put in place.

How to Decide When to Release

It was expected that our approach would find problems; the challenge we faced was how to report them and how to prepare senior management to deal with them.

In our case, many problems once discovered were considered to be so serious that they had to be fixed immediately, and the new release they were associated with could not be delivered until they were resolved.

This was the single most significant factor in delaying the releases. In retrospect, we should have worked harder to create a regime where if the release was at a state where it was an improvement and there were no new known problems being introduced, then we should have proceeded with the release anyway on the basis that we were at least improving the quality of the code.

An alternate approach, and one that would have managed the expectations of the stakeholders more effectively, would have involved us making it clear that there was a significant probability that we would find so many issues, that the overall testing effort was likely to take at least three months, and perhaps up to six months. This would also have allowed the stakeholders to change their overall approach to the project – perhaps taking a different view on how to proceed.

As a result, even though the agile test approach was finding defects, getting them fixed, and improving the quality of the software, we were seen as the cause of the late release, rather than as the agents of improvement.

Definitive Evidence

It was found that using software tools allowed the creation of highly valuable reports. Experience showed that when the situation is extremely serious you can nevertheless create hope by performing analysis using heat-maps[3] and other categorization reports to identify where the trouble areas are and what the trend lines are.

These types of reports provide definitive evidence to enable senior managers to get involved in solving the problem by allowing them to determine where the problem is, and to take action based on hard evidence created from metrics. Producing trend graphs shows that, even in a dire situation, once the trend line starts to improve, the management action taken can be demonstrated to be having a positive effect.

Epilogue

Using the lessons learned from this project, we undertook a number of similar projects for other major financial institutions. The benefits of implementing this successful agile approach for these other customers include

- ▶ improving the functional quality of the delivered software;
- ▶ improving system robustness and availability;
- ▶ verifying that the performance of the software was capable of satisfying specific throughput levels (through rigorous performance testing);
- ▶ establishing the upper limits of scalability to support business planning, so that system hardware upgrades could be planned; and
- ▶ identifying, isolating, and rewriting performance bottlenecks to improve performance and scalability.

The agile testing approach described in this case study continues to be a useful and effective solution that will continue to be used and refined in future projects.

8.6 Results of the Agile Approach

Despite the issues described earlier, the approach described in this case study was a great success. Furthermore, it has worked extremely well on a number of subsequent projects too.

An important finding of this and the subsequent projects is that, as is usually the case, improving quality turns out not to be a technology problem, but a people issue and a leadership challenge.

---

[3] Also known as tree-maps, heat-maps provide an effective data visualization technique for concise display of project data.

9 A Mixed Approach to System Development and Testing: Parallel Agile and Waterfall Approach Streams within a Single Project

Geoff Thompson, Services Director for Experimentus Ltd

SYNOPSIS

This case study describes a project for which I was the test program manager for an FTSE 100 life assurance company that was delivered using both waterfall/V-model and agile approaches alongside each other in separate but dependent projects.

9.1 Introduction

My name is Geoff Thompson. I have been involved in software testing for nearly twenty years. In addition to automation, I have in my time been a test analyst right through to a test program manager. In that time I have experienced or directly used many life-cycle delivery approaches, such as waterfall [5], Timeboxes [21], V-model [4], Rational Unified Process [7], Interactive [27], Agile and Scrum [26].

I am currently the Services Director for Experimentus Ltd, a U.K.-based software quality consultancy, specializing in process improvement, project management, test, configuration management, and requirements management.

I am a founding member of the Information Systems Examination Board Software Testing Board and also a founding member of the International Software Testing Qualifications Board [42], and am currently the U.K. representative to the Board. I am also the founder and chairman of the U.K. Testing Board (www.uktb.org.uk).

The following case study describes a project for which I was the test program manager for an FTSE 100 life assurance company (the BigLifeAssurance Insurance Co. Ltd [BLA Ltd]) that was delivered using waterfall/V-model and agile approaches alongside each other in separate but dependent projects.

9.2 Overview of the Testing Challenge

The two main drivers that caused the BLA Ltd Mortgage Service project to be the critical project that it was, were as follows:

▶ Legislation had changed, meaning that BLA Ltd needed to change its mortgage sales system or it would have to stop selling mortgages (at the time mortgages provided 28% of its yearly revenue).

▶ BLA Ltd also saw an opportunity, through this change, to convince a larger group of independent salesmen to include BLA Ltd on their roster of insurance providers, and hence increase market share.

The initial architectural and design work started in January 2004, with a release date set to 31 August (the legislative change date).

The release was put under further pressure in March when the business decided that their IT department could not deliver the nice web front end they wanted, and it went out to a supplier (Webfrontendsrus) who had built a simple front end for a very small insurance company previously.

As a bit more background, BLA Ltd currently had 5% of the market and was almost the market leader (there is a lot of competition in this market); the insurance company that Webfrontendsrus had already worked for held just 0.01% of the market. The solution Webfrontendsrus proposed was therefore very simple and certainly not stable enough for a company the size of BLA Ltd; but, with excessive pressure from the business, the IT department at BLA Ltd agreed to include it within the overall delivery project (confirming that it would need significant customization).

So, what was a complex internal project had just multiplied in complexity and 50% of the development had been outsourced.

To make matters worse, BLA Ltd insisted on a waterfall approach, whereas Webfrontendsrus proposed the use of an agile approach; we were clearly in for an interesting time.

9.3 Definition of an Agile Testing Process

The specific details of the agile process adopted by Webfrontendsrus included:

▶ Co-location of designers, developers, and system testers in their offices.

▶ As will be seen later, it was not altogether clear what the involvement of test was within Webfrontendsrus's agile method. What was clear, however, is that they believed they didn't need the customer's input and they had the contract written that way.

As far as we could ascertain, this was it.

9.4 Results of the Agile Process

For clarity I have broken the results into two streams, the waterfall (BLA Ltd) and the agile (Webfrontendsrus).

▶ Results of the waterfall approach (BLA Ltd):
  ▷ With careful use of the V-model approach, the ability to plan and implement testing early in the life cycle was achieved.
  ▷ Even though the test analysts and developers were co-located and productivity should have been higher, the code wasn't ready on its scheduled delivery date. Development wanted to deliver something that worked and so asked for, and got, a week-long extension.
  ▷ On delivery to system test, the code installed first time – this had never been seen before!
  ▷ A system test pack of 200 test cases was run within two days of delivery, without a single defect of any consequence being found. In fact we found only ten cosmetic issues. This had never happened before at BLA Ltd. So we reran the tests again, still finding no serious defects.
  ▷ I then asked my test analysts to recheck their tests to ensure they were accurate; they were.
  ▷ We therefore completed system test six weeks earlier than planned, saving BLA Ltd £428,000 (in planned, but unused development time for fixes, and testing costs) and reducing the delivery to live by six weeks (six weeks before the legislation came into force).
▶ Results of the agile approach (Webfrontendsrus):
  ▷ No data are available as to what documentation was written or what tests were run.
  ▷ Code was delivered to BLA Ltd to run acceptance tests against it with just four weeks left before launch.
  ▷ There was a security flaw identified initially that meant that if you logged in then pressed the back button on your browser, your original login details remained in cache and allowed you to press the forward button and get straight back into the system! It was sent back for fixing.
  ▷ On receipt of the next version, most of the management information functions didn't deliver the right reports and the way in which the data were collected and stored meant that retrieval could take up to three minutes (completely unacceptable).
  ▷ Eventually the delivery was descoped to 25% of the original scope to ensure something was ready to go live, on time, and to stay legal.
  ▷ The now infamous quote by Webfrontendsrus's managing director to the IT director of BLA Ltd at this time was, "If you could stop finding errors we could put the time in to make sure that you get the full scope delivered!"

▷ Six months after the initial delivery date, Webfrontendsrus delivered software that provided 90% of the required functionality; three years later the balance of the initial functionality is yet to be seen.

▷ BLA Ltd did go live with a solution on time and so stayed legal but, due to the issues with Webfrontendsrus, never managed to grab the additional market share they were looking for.

9.5 Lessons Learned

The biggest lesson learned through the BLA Ltd project was that the in-house team had actually worked in a pseudo-agile way (we just didn't realize it at the time):

▶ We co-located development and test resources.

▶ The system testers tested code as it was built (hence the request for an additional week in development).

▶ Unit tests were automated using JRun.

▶ Daily short progress meetings were held throughout the delivery to ensure everything was on target.

▶ The V-model principles of early test design significantly enhanced our approach to delivery.

▶ All documentation was delivered with the initial drop of code.

Webfrontendsrus, however, appeared to have used agile as an excuse to adopt ad hoc and unstructured methods:

▶ None of their team had identified roles; developers did their own unit testing and the system testing (no trained system testers were used).

▶ No documentation was delivered.

▶ Code was rewritten on the fly, with no knowledge of the risk or impact of the change.

▶ Resources were employed without the requisite development skills (in effect to make up the numbers required).

BLA Ltd has now adopted a far stronger supplier management position regarding the quality of third-party software, defining the required development approach (and building in audits to ensure they are followed), demanding access to review system tests, and trying (as much as contracts will allow) to work in partnership with third parties.

While they still use the waterfall approach on the older maintenance releases, BLA Ltd has successfully implemented projects using Scrum as their prescribed delivery method for all new developments.

10 Agile Migration and Testing of a Large-Scale Financial System

Howard Knowles, MD of Improvix Ltd.

SYNOPSIS

This project describes the migration and testing of a large-scale complex business-critical financial software system from MS VB6 to VB.NET.

Since the project involved the direct conversion of the existing functionality of the system into VB.NET with no other enhancements planned, all the cost and effort involved were seen as overhead by the users.

Because of the need to reduce cost and timescales, an agile approach was selected for the project.

10.1 Introduction

My name is Howard Knowles and I am the MD of IT consultancy Improvix Ltd. With thirty-one years' experience in the IT arena covering the full software development life cycle, I have been involved in process adoption and improvement for the past fifteen years.

This case study describes a project in which I was engaged as the test manager by a leading international financial company to migrate their business-critical system from Microsoft VB6 to VB.NET. The project arose due to Microsoft's ending of support for VB6 and the difficulty in hiring (and keeping) VB6 developers to continue maintenance and enhancement of the system.

10.2 Overview of the Testing Challenge

Two factors defined the testing challenge facing the conversion project:

1. A regression test suite did not exist for the system to verify the migrated software. As part of gaining user buy-in to the conversion project, development of an automated regression test suite had been promised as a deliverable.
2. Development of the software would continue during the conversion because a change freeze was unacceptable to the users.

The system in question has been continually maintained and enhanced for over eight years in small increments, relying on informal developer and user acceptance testing. Whereas this approach has been successful in delivering a quality system, there has been no use of automated testing, and no formal regression test suite has been produced.

This presents a challenge when considering conversion from VB6 to VB.NET. It was clear that this would involve wholesale change to a high percentage of the code base. The existing testing approach was not designed to cope with this type of change. The business need is to ensure that the converted system functions properly and can be cut over with no business interruption. However, because no direct business benefit exists in terms of new features, all costs involved in the conversion are seen as an overhead.

The application is organized as a fat client/fat server system. The server accounts for around 80,000 lines of code. It abstracts the underlying database and includes business logic. The client code, around 120,000 lines, includes around 200 forms and also includes business logic. The behavior of the system is highly data-dependent.

10.3   Initial Approach

The server code was converted to VB.NET as a separate task from converting the GUI. The changes required to convert the server were relatively small. Following conversion using Microsoft's conversion tool, the manual correction of remaining errors could be accomplished in a few hours.

Most of the conversion effort was required in converting the client code. The initial approach to the conversion of the GUI code was functionality-driven:

- A survey of the user community identified the most-used functions in the system.
- The plan was built around converting the code to support these functions, most-used first.
- The actual conversion was done using Microsoft's conversion tool, followed by manual correction of remaining errors.

The initial plan for testing the conversion was to prove the functional equivalence of the converted system by producing automated functional tests for the identified functions and executing these against the VB6 code and VB.NET code and comparing results.

10.4   Identified Problems

An initial iteration showed many problems in both the conversion approach and the testing approach for the client code:

- The scale of the conversion problem was huge – 4,500+ fixes were required after the use of the Microsoft conversion tool.

▶ Manual correction was proving extremely time consuming, repetitive, and prone to error.
▶ Acquiring the right staff, with both VB6 and VB.NET skills, was difficult.
▶ Estimation of the effort required proved almost impossible.
▶ The testing task was also enormous – over 100 test cases were identified to test the first few functions, each requiring implementation in two environments.

The first iteration overran by more than 100% and did not deliver the planned functionality. Integration problems prevented a successful build that could be deployed automatically, meaning developers had to manually install the system on testers' workstations. Testing was performed manually because the system did not implement sufficient functionality to support the planned automated tests.

10.5 Analysis of Iteration 1

A postmortem of the first iteration identified a number of problems with the conversion approach and the testing approach:

▶ The testing was not focused on proving that what was changed worked (i.e., the GUI code). It was looking more abstractly for general functional equivalence. Business logic was not being changed and so did not require testing. Planned iterations to implement user functions were too long, which created integration problems and delayed demonstration to users, resulting in user unrest.
▶ Too much functionality planned in each iteration presented test implementation and execution problems.
▶ A lack of developer unit testing allowed many bugs to be passed through to the build that were caught in functional testing, increasing costs.
▶ Manually fixing conversion problems would require too much effort to allow the conversion project to keep pace with the development of the VB6 code base without imposing a lengthy code freeze, which the user community would not accept.

10.6 Definition of an Agile Testing Process

A complete change to the conversion approach and testing approach resulted from the analysis of the first iteration. Fundamental to this approach were the following:

▶ *Very short iterations* – conversion of one form per iteration. This allowed very early feedback on the approach and allowed early demonstration to users that something was happening.
▶ *Continuous integration* – With such a large code base, it was essential to keep all converted code building all the time. Each build also invoked unit tests and automated functional tests.

▶ *Complete build per iteration* – Each iteration produced a build, creating confidence that the build process would deliver the final system and allowing any correction of the build process to happen in very small increments.

▶ *Test first design and coding* – Unit tests using NUnit [43] were built into all code changes and incorporated into the continuous integration build process.

▶ *Testing what has changed* – Functional tests focused on testing the changes made to correct conversion problems rather than testing the user functions. These focused on testing the user interface behavior of controls/forms that required changes.

▶ *Identifying generic solutions* – This involved the identification of solutions to common classes of problems. An enhanced version of the Microsoft conversion tool from ArtinSoft [44] was used to reduce the number of conversion problems, including automated conversion of a number of popular third-party controls. Also, the adapter pattern was used to wrap .NET controls and provide COM-compatible interfaces to avoid code changes [45].

▶ *Automated application of generic solutions* – The generic solutions were coded as batch edit commands and applied automatically using scripts. As each occurrence of a problem was addressed, either an existing solution was applied or a new solution was created.

▶ *Automated conversion from VB6 label* – When performing a build, a subset of a label of the VB6 code base was converted to VB.NET by running the ArtinSoft conversion tool and then running the SED batch editor conversion scripts [46]. This allowed development of the VB6 code base to continue in parallel with the VB.NET conversion, as the application of all conversion fixes was automated.

▶ *Optimization of forms to convert* – Through an analysis of the occurrences of conversion problems, an optimal set of forms was chosen that covered all known problems. A milestone in the project was completing the conversion of these forms, because this represented finding a solution to all the known conversion problems. Through the use of generic solutions, once this set of forms was converted, the solutions could be applied to all remaining occurrences of the conversion problems.

▶ *Sample testing* – This involved the sample testing of occurrences of generic solutions; once the initial optimal set of forms was converted and tested, the remaining occurrences of conversion problems would not all be tested. A sample of the occurrences would be tested to ensure the generic solutions worked when applied to different occurrences.

10.7 Results of the Agile Approach

The results of adopting and following the agile approach were:

▶ *Analysis of conversion errors* – An analysis of the conversion errors remaining after running the ArtinSoft conversion tool was performed to identify the smallest number of modules that needed to have postconversion fixes applied and tested. This identified thirty-four modules that between them contained at least one instance of all the postconversion problems that existed in the VB.NET code. Once a generic solution was found to the problems in these modules, they were applied to the remaining modules.

▶ *Build process* – The build process automated the conversion (using nAnt [47]) by starting with a copy of a labeled version of the VB6 code, running the ArtinSoft converter, applying the batch edits to correct postconversion problems, compiling the VB.NET code, running unit tests, and packaging for distribution. This gave a repeatable process for the conversion, and the automation of the build allowed continuous integration, ensuring that the target could always be produced and any problems in building were detected early.

▶ *Iterations* – The iterations rapidly progressed from converting a handful of modules to adding in sufficient modules without any conversion problems to produce a running build suitable for testing. This allowed functional testing to commence early in the project. The approach of creating generic solutions using batch edits proved successful and allowed additional modules with postconversion problems to be rapidly added to the build.

▶ *Unit test* – Unit testing proved successful in detecting coding errors and resulted in fewer bugs finding their way into the functional testing.

▶ *Manual test* – Manual testing of the GUI functionality proved satisfactory and efficient. Developers were familiar with the features of GUI controls and forms and could easily exercise them to prove the functionality was correct without a large investment in test design and planning.

▶ *Automated test* – Automated testing fell by the wayside due to problems with tools and resources, but this did not adversely affect the outcome. The combination of unit testing and manual testing proved sufficient.

10.8 Lessons Learned

As a result of completing the project, the following lessons were learned:

▶ *Identifying targets of test is vital to testing success* because there will never be enough time or resources to test everything, so prioritization is essential. Identify what is being changed and test that and that alone.

▶ *Test early and often*; find defects as early as possible, correct them in a timely manner, and continue testing frequently throughout the project.

▶ *Ensure unit testing of all code changes*, testing first and often. This might be a target for test automation in future projects.

▶ *For a conversion to a new environment, building and deploying are very important*; so develop these approaches first and ensure that all subsequent development uses and tests them. This also enables testing to progress smoothly by ensuring the availability of a deployed build.

▶ *Save time, effort, and cost by using generic solutions* (patterns) and trusting that a generic solution can be tested in a subset of where it is used.

▶ *It is worthwhile investing time to create automated solutions for common problems* and applying these generic solutions (patterns) automatically with scripts, which is repeatable and efficient. Generic solutions can then be tested in a subset of their implementations, thus reducing the targets of test.

▶ *Automated testing is not a panacea* – Manual testing can deliver excellent results when suitably targeted, particularly for GUI code changes where there is little dependency between the changes and therefore the tests. Good test management with manual test packs and exploitation of reuse opportunities can achieve good test coverage rapidly, avoiding the overheads of automated test script development.

▶ *The effort required to develop an automated regression test suite for a mature system may well be greater than the effort required for major enhancements, conversions, and upgrades.*

Agile Testing with Mock Objects: A CAST-Based Approach

Colin Cassidy, Software Architect, Prolifics

SYNOPSIS

This case study examines the practical application of Java mock object frameworks to a system integration project that used test-first development and continuous computer-aided software testing (CAST).

Mock object frameworks allow developers to verify the way in which units of software interact – by replacing any dependencies with software that simulates them in a controlled manner. The case study explores the problems encountered with this approach and describes the subsequent development of SevenMock – a simple new framework that overcomes many of these issues.

11.1 Introduction

My name is Colin Cassidy. I'm a software architect for Prolifics – a systems integration company that specializes in IBM technologies. Coming from a software development background, I have ten years' experience in the IT industry. I have performed a number of roles, including software architect, systems analyst, developer, and development process engineer. This has been mainly in the retail, telecom, and finance sectors.

My interest in software testing stems from a desire to build better software and to find better ways of building that software. Having practiced development and testing on a number of project types ranging from the very agile to the very structured, I have experienced the problems caused by too much automated testing as well as those caused by too little.

This case study describes a Java system integration project that used test-first development and continuous automated regression testing. It explores the benefits and challenges of creating effective automated unit tests and describes mechanisms deployed by the project team to overcome the issues they encountered.

11.2 Overview of the Testing Challenge

This case study describes a project that was undertaken for a major U.K. retail chain to update their existing bespoke order management system.

The system was originally designed to operate on a version of IBM's Websphere application server platform that had over time been superseded. The customer had also purchased a commercial off-the-shelf (COTS) application to replace and enhance an important part of the existing bespoke system.

The objectives of the project were twofold:

1. to migrate the existing system to operate on the latest version of the IBM platform, and
2. to integrate the existing system with the COTS application.

Although all previous testing of the existing system had been manual, we decided that test automation should play a significant role in regression testing. The key factors in making this decision were:

▶ the large size of the project,
▶ the high number of changes being made, and
▶ the large number of parties involved.

After carefully considering the project requirements and resources, the following types of testing were decided upon:

▶ automated unit testing,
▶ automated integration testing,
▶ automated performance testing, and
▶ manual (UI-based) system testing.

This case study is concerned primarily with the development of automated functional tests at the unit and integration levels.

11.3 The Software Migration Testing Challenge

The software migration challenge was slightly unusual in the sense that we were not changing the behavior of the existing system in any way. The only thing that was really important from a functional testing perspective, therefore, was for the system to behave in exactly the same way before and after the completion of the software migration.

Since there were no existing tests and the internal design of the system was not well understood, we judged that the most effective way to regression test the software migration would be to use an automated record/playback (or capture–replay) style of testing tool at the system interface level. The system had a small user interface that could be tested manually, but the rest of the system was operated via XML (Extensible Markup Language [48]) message interfaces to other systems. It was therefore relatively straightforward to create a message recorder that extracted system messages from the input and output message logs. Starting with a fresh system database, a test harness then took the messages, replaying the input messages and verifying the outputs.

The system users were engaged to help develop and run through a set of test cases, which were duly recorded. The resulting scripts were then run before migration and against each incremental release of the migrated system.

Within the scope of the migration activity, this mechanism worked very well. The system needed to be built and deployed to the application server before any testing could commence, but this was appropriate given the lack of any functional change.

One minor problem encountered was that sometimes parts of the output messages could be difficult to predict – for example, if they were time-dependent. Our solution to this problem was to arrange for the system time to be artificially fixed by the test. It would also have been possible, although involving slightly more work, to write a more intelligent message verifier.

11.4 The COTS Integration Testing Challenge

The COTS system purchased by our client was a sophisticated and special-purpose piece of software that was designed to be installed on a server and to be controlled by a separate bespoke application. In our case, the bespoke application was the existing order management system. The objective of the project was to adapt this application to make it work with the COTS system in a way that met the stated business requirements. The task involved extending its user interface, writing control logic, and integrating with various legacy systems.

System requirements for the project were defined by performing a combination of top-down (business-driven) and bottom-up (technology-driven) analysis. In many cases, the business processes had to be changed to fit in with the way that the COTS system operated, which resulted in a significant amount of functional change to the existing bespoke system.

In order to reduce project risk, we followed an agile approach to software engineering that we have developed and refined through its use on many projects. Our approach is based on the Rational Unified Process (RUP) framework [7]. It adopts many agile practices, including early development and short (two- to three-week) iterations, with each iteration combining analysis, development, and testing activities. It also recognizes the importance of software architecture in attaining consistency and resilience to change, but at the same time developers are allowed to work unconstrained within their allocated unit of work. Agile development techniques such as pair programming and test-driven development were also adopted.

The implication of this way of working, however, is that there will always be a certain amount of change all the way through the project. Good change management was therefore critically important, as was the ability to understand the state of development at any point in time. The project manager needed to be confident about which requirements were implemented and working, irrespective of any other requirements that may have changed.

One practical way of achieving this was through automated regression testing. Such tests can be written at the unit or integration level (or preferably a combination of the two). However, due to project constraints, it became apparent to us that we would be limited in the number of automated integration tests that could be written and maintained.

Specifically, this limitation was caused by the difficulty of writing integration tests that were sufficiently focused on individual software requirements. In terms of code coverage, a single integration test would typically exercise a very large part of the system and, consequently, test many requirements. This was initially seen as a good thing but, as the test base expanded, we found that some parts of the system were being tested many times by many different tests. This made those parts of the system very difficult to change without also modifying every related test. In addition, integration tests (even automated ones) can become quite slow to execute, which made it disruptive for our developers to run these tests on a regular basis (for example, before committing changes to the source control repository).

A partial solution to this problem was to focus developer testing on the writing of automated unit tests. Execution of these tests by the developers before committing code was made a mandatory part of the development process. Once code had been committed, it was then automatically built and tested a second time by a continuous build server that would send out email notifications in the event of a failure. As such, a test failure could never remain undetected for more than a few minutes – a factor that vastly reduced the amount of time required for detecting and fixing any related bugs.

A small number of automated integration tests were retained as a sanity check, but the bulk of the integration testing was performed manually by developers at the point where each build was prepared for release to system testing.

11.5 The Unit Testing Challenge

When writing unit tests for a piece of software, the first decision that needs to be made is the granularity of the test units – if the units are too coarse, there will be a large number of tests for any given unit of code and the result will be hard to manage. If the units are too small, it will be difficult to relate the tests back to the software requirements in any meaningful way.

In order to support both unit testing and general maintenance, any well-designed system should be composed from a set of readily identifiable, cohesive units that individually perform well-defined functions and interact with each other via simple interfaces that hide implementation complexity.

In our case, the existing system was constructed from a set of components that were implemented using the Enterprise JavaBean (EJB) component standard [49]. These components were a logical choice for our unit testing and, consequently, the vast majority of our unit tests were written at the component level. They could easily be verified against system requirements through our software architecture model – a piece of high-level (and lightweight) design that charted the structure and interaction of the components against system requirements.

Despite being an obvious target for unit testing, there were no existing tests in place that we could use, and we encountered a number of challenges when creating new ones. These included:

▶ finding a way to run tests against their target components without the complexity and speed implication of automatically deploying them to the Websphere application server each time they were executed;

▶ introducing a mechanism that allowed a component's dependencies to be selectively replaced for testing, enabling it to be tested in isolation of other components;

▶ creating tests that were precisely targeted at particular features without unnecessarily constraining the way that the rest of the system worked;

▶ testing of poorly factored existing interfaces, whose behavior was heavily dependent on (although not immediately apparent from) the parameters passed to them; and

▶ trying to understand the purpose of existing code that, due to being outside the scope of our project, had no available requirements documentation.

11.6   Unit Testing with Mock Objects

Our unit tests were written by developers in Java code and executed with the JUnit framework [50]. In most cases, the code under test had dependencies on other system components and so, by default, this would have led to the execution (and therefore validation) of a large part of the system with each test. In order to avoid this situation, the developers forcibly stopped the code under test from calling other parts of the system. Instead, it was made to interact with test code that mimicked the original system by using mock objects – Java objects created by the test that are directly interchangeable with the real thing.

In their most basic form, mock objects can be pieces of code written by developers that use programming language mechanisms such as inheritance or interface implementation to make them interchangeable with existing system code. However, mock objects written in this way tend to be unwieldy and hard to maintain. Instead, developers commonly use one of the freely available dynamic mock object frameworks such as EasyMock or Rhino Mocks (for Java and .Net, respectively [50]). Such frameworks aid the test developer by controlling the creation of mock objects and monitoring how the system code attempts to interact with them. Figure 11.1 illustrates the typical use of a dynamic mock object framework by a unit test. When the test is run, the sequence of events is as follows:

▶ The unit test initiates the mock objects framework and requests a dynamic mock for each dependency of the code under test.

▶ The mock objects framework creates the dynamic mock(s).

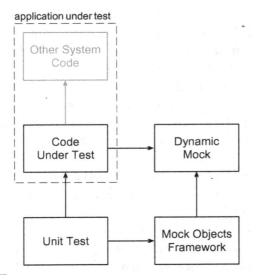

11.1   Replacing dependencies with mock objects.

▶   The unit test creates a set of "expectations" that tells the mocks how it expects the code under test to interact with them and what responses they should provide.
▶   The unit test invokes the code under test, ensuring that it will use the dynamic mocks in place of any other system code (i.e., code that is outside the test scope).
▶   The code under test executes, calling the dynamic mock instead of the real thing.
▶   The dynamic mock verifies whether it has been called correctly. If so, it returns the canned result it was given. If not, it throws an error that will let the unit test know that the test has failed.

After evaluating some of the existing dynamic mock objects implementations, we chose to use EasyMock. EasyMock allows a developer to create expectations by effectively "recording" a set of calls made to the mock object by test code. The EasyMock framework stores details of these calls but does not act further on them until it is put into "replay" mode. At this point, the framework knows that setup is complete and so it will verify that the calls are repeated by the system under test.

This mechanism is simple to use and has the advantage that the tests will not be broken by refactoring (i.e., making changes that do not affect behavior) of the system under test. For example, if a developer were to use an integrated development environment (IDE) to change the name of a particular operation, the tool would automatically update all references to that operation, including those in the test. Mock objects frameworks that do not use a mechanism like this tend not to be supported so well by common development tools, making their use a little harder.

11.7   The Mock Objects Challenge

The first challenge we encountered with the mock objects approach to testing was finding a way to replace existing component dependencies with mock objects. For new code, this is relatively straightforward since it is good practice to separate units of code, allowing them to be assembled flexibly in different ways without necessitating internal changes. Such an approach supports unit testing quite naturally.

There are two popular patterns that enable this way of working: the *service locator* and *dependency injection* patterns [51]. With a service locator, the code to identify and create new components is defined in a single place – within the service locator. When one unit of code needs to call another, the service locator is asked to provide a service or component that supports the required interface. Unit tests are then able to reconfigure the service locator as required to substitute mock objects.

With dependency injection, the dependencies of a given unit of code are determined at the point of initialization or invocation and are passed directly to the unit for it to use. A unit test is therefore able to call this code directly, supplying mock objects for any dependencies that do not fall within the test scope.

We have used both approaches but tend to favor dependency injection for its simplicity and recent popularity. For existing code, some level of refactoring is often necessary and desirable, although it is sometimes possible to avoid change by employing a technology-dependent solution such as the Java/EJB-specific XJB test platform [49].

When starting to examine the legacy code, we were lucky to find that there was a clean separation of technology-related (application server) code and core business logic. This helped enormously with the migration challenge but also made it possible to run unit tests against the system code without first deploying it to an application server, which is a slow and involved process to automate.

The second major challenge we encountered was that, even with a focus on unit testing, our automated regression tests eventually started to affect the ease with which system code could be modified. A number of contributing causes were identified:

▶ In normal use, EasyMock performs a deep equality comparison on supplied parameters. If any part of the parameter graph differs from the expectation, the test fails. Although it is possible to write custom "matching" logic for EasyMock, it is cumbersome to do and makes tests harder to maintain if widely used.

▶ Many of the existing system interfaces were (XML) message-based or were poorly factored, containing operations that could behave in many different ways depending on the parameters supplied. This resulted in a large number of tests exercising the same operations, which compounded the problem of EasyMock parameter matching.

▶ When some of the tests became quite long and repetitive, it occasionally became difficult to tell which expectation was causing a test failure. The reason for this is that EasyMock, in common with other mock objects frameworks, evaluates the expectations itself. If an expectation fails then the only reference back to the code that created it is the resulting error message.

In order to improve the situation, we refactored system interfaces and tests where it was practical to do so, treating the tests as production-quality artifacts and putting a corresponding emphasis on their design. We also took care to ensure that tests were linked back to documented requirements using comment tags so that they could be easily reviewed. This made it easier for developers to tell whether or not a test was failing for a genuine reason and for them to fix the test without compromising its original purpose.

11.8   Results of the Agile Approach

The agile approach to automated unit and integration testing brought a number of clear benefits to the project:

▶ The focus on thorough and continuous automated regression testing certainly reduced the overall number of bugs at any point during the project's life cycle, but it also helped developers to work side-by-side without inadvertently interfering with each other's efforts. Unit testing with mock objects allowed the development of code units in virtual isolation of each other.

▶ Since each unit test was focused on a particular part of the system, it could therefore be quite thorough. In some cases, for example, it was used to simulate failure conditions or housekeeping functions that would be hard to arrange or observe through the user interface.

▶ Writing tests before code forced developers to reason about what the code needed to do before deciding how it was going to work. This separate definition of function and design tended to produce cleaner code and tests that were well aligned with stated requirements rather than the developed solution. In turn, this made the tests and code easier to verify.

The things that worked less well were generally related to the pain of improving the quality and test coverage of legacy code. Poor code encourages poor tests and poor tests can slow the pace of change. The choice and use of tools is also vitally important. Arguably, however, most of these problems were uncovered by the adopted approach rather than fundamentally caused by it.

11.9   Lessons Learned

In summary, we learned a great deal from the project. Some specific lessons that we will be taking to future projects include:

▶ Use mock objects to enable unit tests to focus on the unit of code under test and nothing else.

▶ Pay as much attention to the design and quality of tests as you would to production code.

▶ In each test, check as much as necessary but no more. Carefully consider the scope and purpose of each test and think carefully about the most effective way to implement it without constraining system code.

▶ Adopt test-first or test-driven development to ensure that developers are disciplined about test writing and that they mentally separate function from design.

▶ Ensure that tests can be traced back to system requirements or that the requirement being tested is immediately clear from the test. This makes code easier to audit and maintain.

▶ Adopt and follow an effective change management process and consider the use of a change management tool [52].

Finally, following the conclusion of the project, I put some effort into evaluating how our development approach could be improved for the future and in particular how we could make more effective use of mock objects. I drew up a shopping list of features that my ideal mock objects framework would have. A summary is as follows:

▶ a simple mechanism to support flexible parameter matching – the testing of some parameters or attributes of parameters, but not others;

▶ the production of messages when mock expectations fail that allow the developer to determine exactly what has failed and why – ideally pinpointing both the test and the expectation;

▶ allowing for creation of mocks against existing classes or interfaces;

▶ supporting the ability to test calls to class constructors;

▶ being simple to use and maintain; and

▶ allowing the relaxation of call sequencing checks, if required.

I evaluated a number of mock frameworks against these and other criteria. Most (including EasyMock) did quite well, but they fell short on one or two important points. I also had the idea that a mock objects framework could be simpler and more effective if it shifted the responsibility of evaluating expectations back to the test by using call-backs. This would allow the test developer to implement the most appropriate set of assertions for any given test. If an expectation was to fail, then the error report would point directly to that line of code.

This prompted me to write my own Java-based mock objects framework called SevenMock [51], which is now an active project on the SourceForge open-source software development Web site.

As desired, SevenMock is a very simple piece of software but evaluates well against my stated criteria compared with the other frameworks that I investigated. It has a few restrictions of its own – it can only test against classes (not directly against interfaces) and it doesn't support relaxed call sequencing at the time of writing. In practice, users have found that its restrictions are easy to live with and feedback has been generally positive. Additional feedback and code contributions via the SourceForge Web site are very welcome.

12 Agile Testing – Learning from Your Own Mistakes

Martin Phillips, IBM Software Group, Hursley

SYNOPSIS

No one in our newly formed team had done this "agile" thing before, and while more and more colleagues in other parts of our company are doing "agile," it seems that everyone does things slightly differently. There are no mandated processes that we must follow, only guidelines, experiences from other teams, and best practices – but what everyone else does doesn't necessarily work for you. Learn from yourselves as you go along, change your process to match your working environment and your team, and don't be afraid to try something for an iteration or two to see if it works.

12.1 Introduction

My name is Martin Phillips and I work for IBM. I've been in software development for almost nine years, working mostly on functional testing of "off-the-shelf" middleware. This software was developed primarily using the waterfall model [5] (with twelve- to eighteen-month cycles), though more recently projects have been more iterative (with two- to three-month iterations).

For the past six months I've been the test lead for a newly formed agile development team, and am responsible for delivering a new middleware product for an emerging market.

This case study describes the challenges we have faced testing the product and what lessons we have learned.

12.2 Overview of the Testing Challenge

IBM is very aware of the commercial value of emerging markets; like many companies, it wants to get a foothold in these new areas quickly, but with products that meet the high expectations that customers have of IBM.

Developing with an agile approach enables our team to develop a functional product with early and frequent beta releases. This allows us to get feedback from a variety of potential customers and to incorporate that feedback into the product before it is released for sale.

The team is eighteen-strong and all were new to the agile process. About 50% of them were able to attend education on agile development before the project started, though none of the test team happened to be part of this group. The group consists of:

- one architect,
- seven developers,
- five testers,
- one documentation writer,
- one project manager,
- one people manager,
- one User-Centered Design expert (part time), and
- one sales manager (part time).

The goal of the project is to deliver the product within ten months. We are doing two-week iterations and have just finished iteration 12, with six iterations to go before our target release date.

The product is an enterprise-quality, distributed Java application that integrates with an existing off-the-shelf product. It must support a variety of distributed platforms (Linux, Solaris, HP, AIX, and Windows) in addition to supporting the zOS mainframe. The product includes a command line interface, an Eclipse plug-in graphical interface, a graphical installer, and all the associated documentation.

In addition to the functional requirements of the product, we also need to test the installer, graphical interface, and documentation, and additionally conform to corporate requirements. These requirements include accessibility and globalization, including translation into ten different languages and running on operating systems running in any locale worldwide.

All in all, quite a challenge.

12.3   Definition of an Agile Testing Process

The details of the agile testing process we are currently following are shown as follows, but this process has grown and developed over time and I'm certain it will continue to change and evolve:

- *Co-location of test and development* – This allows test input during the design and development phase, and development input in the test phase.
- *Unit tests, developed along with the code, are run in every build* – Any unit test failures result in a "bad build," which must be fixed immediately.
- *Static analysis is run against the code in every build* – Any static analysis problems result in a "bad build," which must be fixed immediately.
- *Automated build verification test (BVT) of every good build* – tests basic core function on a single distributed platform.

▶ *Automated functional verification test (FVT) of every good build* – test more functions, including across every operating system that we need to support.

▶ *Development uses "stories" as the unit of function* – Each story has "success criteria" that must be demonstrated at the end of the iteration. These success criteria clarify any ambiguity when trying to determine if a story was complete.

▶ *Reduced test planning* – Only do actual test plans for the more complex stories. Simple stories are tested using exploratory testing [53].

▶ *Automate what we can* – Rather than automating everything, we automate only key tests because automating everything would take too long. Try to automate the tests that will give best coverage and the most complex areas of code.

▶ *Pseudo-translation and accessibility testing every iteration* – We used tools to test that all visible text is translated/translatable and that GUIs are accessible in every iteration. This prevents a backlog of problems building up in these areas and reminds development to write their code appropriately.

▶ *Define "test stories" as part of the planning process/burndown* – This allows us to track large test work items such as setting up the automation infrastructure, adding major new test automation function, and "test-only" work-items such as globalization verification testing and translation verification testing.

▶ *Introduction of system verification tests (SVTs) as test/development stories* – System tests such as long runs, stress, load, large topologies, and so forth, take a lot of time and effort to do properly, so these are entered as stories in the planning for the iteration. If the SVT stories do not get prioritized into the iteration, the testing does not get done.

▶ *Everyone is a software engineer* – There is no hard line between testers and developers. People specialize in certain areas, but developers do some testing when they are free, and testers do development and fix defects when they are free.

▶ *Low defect backlog* – We carefully track the number of open defects toward the end of each iteration with a requirement of no high-severity defects and a target of less than fifteen low-severity defects open at the end of every iteration. This prevents a defect backlog from growing over time.

▶ *Lessons learned and reflections for test in every iteration* – Along with the development side of things, the test team have a "lessons learned" session at the end of every iteration. We have actions for what we can change in our testing process to make things better. This keeps our testing processes as up-to-date and meaningful as possible.

12.4   Results of the Agile Approach

Even though, as of the date of the submission of this case study, we are still working toward the final release of our product, already we are able to report the following benefits of the agile process that have been apparent to us:

▶ *Early demonstration of product to stakeholders* – Having functional drivers at the end of every iteration allows us to give early demonstrations of the product to interested parties. These stakeholders include the sales team, beta customers, upper management, and, in some ways most important, the development and test team itself.

▶ *Inspiring confidence in the customers* – Allowing beta customers to try out the software gets them interested early, shows them how the software is developing, and starts to give them a feeling of confidence in the quality of the product, assuming the beta releases are of sufficient quality. I know that agile process says that every iteration exit driver should be of high quality, but we heartily believe that a bit of extra testing on beta drivers is not wasted effort.

▶ *Managing the managers' expectations* – Demonstrating to your management chain that you have something that works keeps them feeling good about continuing to spend the money to support your team.

▶ *Inspiring the sales team* – Demonstrating your product to the sales teams gives them a good idea of what will be possible with the product, familiarizes them with its capabilities, and lets them start thinking about which customers may benefit from the product.

▶ *Keep it clean* – Having builds that work all of the time makes it very easy to spot defects as soon as they are integrated into the code base. It makes it much easier to track down the cause of problems and get them fixed, fast!

▶ *Don't underestimate the value of the feel-good factor* – Finally, working on a product that "works" almost all of the time certainly gives me a really good feeling. In the past I've worked on waterfall projects where the code sometimes failed to compile for weeks at a time, and, even if it did compile, it didn't work for months! The frustration that causes is terrible. Working on this agile project, where I can install almost any build and expect it to be functioning fully, is a real joy, and happy people work much better than depressed ones!

12.5 Lessons Learned

The lessons learned from this project so far include the following:

▶ *Deliver testable function as early as you can* – With very short iterations (two weeks for us), it is imperative that development deliver testable function as early as they can to reduce last-minute integration and testing. A hard cutoff for integrating new function, leaving at least two days of testing (and defect fixing) time is crucial to getting a functional and tested driver for the end of the iteration.

▶ *Do not underestimate the time and effort required to develop and maintain an automation infrastructure* – We had a complex, distributed, asynchronous system to test, which made choosing an automation framework very difficult as we found there were few existing frameworks available that could help us. We ended up using STAF and STAX (available from sourceforge.net), which have been flexible enough to do what we wanted. Even using these tools it took us five iterations before we got the infrastructure in place to be able to run an automated

BVT and a further five iterations before we managed an automated multisystem FVT.

▶ *Communication is absolutely key to the success of iterations and the product* – Make sure that you communicate with the developers to ensure that you understand what the product is supposed to do, reviewing the designs as soon as they are produced and before implementation starts. Challenge them if you have differing thoughts. Also ensure that you validate the requirements with what the stakeholders actually want by talking with them.

▶ *Test early and test often* – Testing as soon as you can is good: testing the developed code directly after the development team has coded it finds bugs early and, while the developers still have the code they wrote fresh in their minds, makes finding the problems easier. Additionally, testing the small units of function that are developed makes the scope of what needs to be tested clearer. Getting early drops of testable function in an iteration is good in that it allows us to test earlier and eases off some of the pressure from the last few days of the iteration, but it can sometimes allow regressions to slip past if no automated regression tests are written.

▶ *Ensure the GUI is stable before using automated GUI test tools* – It was decided not to attempt to perform automated GUI testing. Our understanding of the automated GUI testing tools was that they are useful only if the GUI is fairly stable. With a brand new product being developed from prototypes and adding new functions frequently, we decide not to spend time trying to automate the testing of the GUI. This has turned out to be a good thing in that it forces us to get real people looking at the GUI, trying out different things and finding usability and accessibility issues that would not have been discovered by automated tests.

▶ *Select tools in haste, repent at leisure* – Take time to choose your tools. We changed some of our tools several times, and the cost of changing whatever tool you are using is wasted effort. Automation frameworks, change management system, defect tracking systems, design document repository, and so forth – get it right at the start because it is difficult to change halfway through and has a high cost in time and effort. This may seem anti-agile to spend lots of time deciding things up front, but I believe that the cost of spending additional time up front to get things right is worth it.

Agile: The Emperor's New Test Plan?

Stephen K. Allott, Managing Director of ElectroMind

SYNOPSIS

"Steve, about every five years," Ross Collard once told me, "you'll hear about the NGT in software testing." "The NGT?" I questioned. "Yes, NGT – the next great thing." Ross was one of my first ever teachers of software testing and in those early days in 1995 I learned a remarkable amount from him about how to test and what it means to deliver quality software.

Toward the end of the 1990s the NGT was RAD (Rapid Application Development) and five years later, in 2005, the NGT for me was agile testing. This was to be the savior of testing projects throughout the Western world. Nothing could stop it or stand in its path. Nonbelievers were cast aside as the NGT drove a coach and horses (or tried to) through the established numbers and acronyms of my beloved software testing world (IEEE 829, DDP, ISO 9126, TickIT, ISO 9000, RBT, Test Strategy, MTP, IEEE 1012, IEEE 1044, Test Cases).

Books and papers were written, seminars delivered, and agile manifestos created for all to worship and wonder at. It was time to cast aside the restrictive clothing of software test documentation and formal methods and enjoy the freedom of exploratory testing in a context-driven world. The Emperor's new test plan was born!

13.1 Introduction

My name is Steve K. Allott and I am a chartered information technology professional (CITP), who has worked in the IT industry for over twenty-five years, after graduating with a computer science degree. My background includes software development and project management at telecommunications and financial organizations, and since 1995 I have specialized in software testing and quality assurance, founding my own company, ElectroMind, in 2002, which is currently focused on providing test process improvement "health checks" for companies in the financial, telecommunications, retail services, and e-commerce sectors.

I also serve as the program secretary for the British Computer Society Specialist Group in Software Testing (BCS SIGiST) and am the Executive Director for IT Integrity International, a not-for-profit organization involved in researching areas such as IT security, workforce education, and IT governance.

Illustrated with real examples from my consulting and training experiences over the last few years, this case study contains my perceptions on the Next Great Thing – agile testing.

The question mark in the title for this chapter is deliberate!

13.2 The Emperor's View[1]

I am not trying to say that those promoting agile are simply twenty-first-century snake oil salespeople, but neither shall I conclude that it's a bandwagon of requirements nirvana on which businesses should jump wholeheartedly without a second thought. In my experience of over thirty years in IT, agile could be the bees' knees (you see how old I am), the best thing since sliced bread, or the software testing equivalent of the Betamax or Sinclair C5.

Will agile be the answer to all our software testing and quality assurance issues? As a consultant I can honesty say, "It depends."

My agile story is based on a collection of anecdotes and observations from the testing departments of corporate U.K., with the company's real names and identities disguised, mainly because by the time the ink is dry on this book, they will all have learned from the process and moved on.

I started my own consulting company in 2002 and initially delivered training courses and strategic consultancy based on traditional methods and standards such as ISEB (the Information Systems Examination Board) ISTQB (International Software Testing Qualifications Board) and IEEE 829. After a few years we'd realized the world was changing – getting more complex and faster in every sense of the word. Our articles and seminars on rate of change over time were developed and we published our FAST (Funded, Autonomous, Supported, Technical) methodology and started to follow the agile developments.

In my recent experience as an independent consultant in software testing and quality assurance I have found agile to be both a blessing and a curse: a blessing when it has delivered real business value, a curse if it is used simply as an excuse to ignore commonsense testing approaches. The agile approach has transformed some development shops and significantly enhanced their relationship with the business. Have they been lucky not to have a major systems failure or pragmatic about the way they integrate the iterative testing with the traditional end-to-end approaches? Me thinks the jury is still out and we have a long way to go to understand, let alone solve, all of the problems.

13.3 Common Themes and Patterns

This section provides a snapshot of testing problems found during a variety of consulting assignments throughout the United Kingdom and Northern Europe.

---

[1] Mature testers and conference aficionados may recognize my nickname as the Emperor of Testing following an amateur production of a play in Scandinavia many of your Earth years ago (once upon a time in the West).

Scale	0	1	2	3	4	5	6	7	8	9	10	11	12	13
Key Area		Controlled					Efficient				Optimizing			
Test strategy	A						B				C		D	
Life-cycle model	A				B									
Moment of involvement			A				B				C		D	
Estimating and planning				A							B			
Test specification techniques	A			B										
Static test techniques					A		B							
Metrics						A			B			C		D
Test automation				A				B			C			
Test environment				A				B						C
Office environment				A										
Commitment and motivation	A					B						C		
Test functions and training				A			B			C				
Scope of methodology					A						B			C
Communication			A		B							C		
Reporting	A				B		C					D		
Defect management	A				B		C							
Testware management			A		B						C			D
Test process management	A			B								C		
Evaluation							A			B				
Low-level testing					A		B		C					

13.1   Composite TPI chart from a number of clients, 2005–2008.

Over an eighteen-month period I've been fortunate to have worked closely with the senior IT management of leading companies in a variety of sectors including investment banking, travel, mobile telecommunications, on-line retail, and utilities (gas, electricity). This work includes assignments done in association with a well-known London test house and one in Ireland.

The methodologies employed were a mix of agile, fragile, and traditional. Typically the technologies in use were mainly Microsoft-based, including Visual Studio Team System (VSTS), Team Foundation Server (TFS), SQL Server, Windows XP, and .NET with some use of UNIX/Linux, Oracle databases, and Citrix Metaframe. Most engagements involved the ubiquitous test management tool – HP Quality Centre.

As I worked with these many companies, a pattern of behavior emerged as depicted in the composite test process improvement (TPI) chart (Figure 13.1). Essentially, where organizational and process maturity is relatively low, significantly more effort is needed to make agile methods work in practice. My observations over the past few years will probably not be a surprise to anyone working in the software testing field:

▶ The first observation is that of constantly changing business priorities, which leads to frustration and demoralization within the test teams. Often a project is started as high-priority to get it moving and then as time goes by it gets forgotten a little and moved down the list. Test teams find it difficult to plan in this situation, whether using agile techniques or not.

▶ Second, the often frantic demand for new functionality by the business managers seems to forget about the complexity of what's already out there.

▶ Third, with weekly and sometimes daily release cycles, the intellectual exercise required to think about likely modes of failure is compressed into a timeframe which I believe is bound to lead to problems later on in the release cycle. People just do not have the time to think and come up with that "eureka" moment anymore.

▶ Finally, the test teams I have worked with were small, enthusiastic, and had an important role to play as gatekeepers and firefighters, yet many seemed to have little influence over the business demands or the investment in new tools and technologies to help them improve their own career opportunities. Many groups were asked for metrics to prove their case and explain their added value, yet struggled to record even the simplest numbers due to lack of time.

In summary, many of the agile projects I have been exposed to have suffered from

▶ no documented test process;
▶ no formal test policy, strategy, or plan;
▶ many tests, but with no formal design;
▶ no test (or other) metrics;
▶ no proper test environment (some tested in "live" environment);
▶ no documented test basis; and
▶ testing/testers not involved early enough.

13.4 Lessons Learned

These are the lessons I have learned through my exposure to the NGT:

▶ *Agile verses fragile* – As mentioned earlier, I have seen both agile and fragile projects. Fragile is apparently the buzzword for a "fake agile" project: this is where some, but not all of the buzzwords are used, yet the test teams lack the expertise and disciplines to actually follow through and carry them out to a successful conclusion. I've seen some development groups totally embrace the concept and redesign, build, and unit test their flagship Web site in a few weeks with no recognized testing function other than some user acceptance test (UAT) done by the project's business analysts on behalf of the user community. They used Extreme Programming techniques. It was agile. It worked. It may not work for you but in this context it was amazingly successful and cost-effective.

▶ *Islands of enterprise* – Many times I find that developers, business analysts, project managers, operations people, infrastructure, and architecture experts are all working in isolation with no overall knowledge of the "big picture" of what the systems are supposed to do. Only in the test group does all of this expertise supposedly comes together; to perform an end-to-end test of a business process at either a systems or UAT level requires knowledge of the back-end systems and databases, interfaces, protocols, and much, much more than just the small changes developed at the front end in the Scrum. This increases the knowledge and skill levels needed in the test team. I do not believe that the software testing industry has yet found the right balance, and part of the problem is the awareness (or lack of it) of what testing is all about.

▶ *No one-size-fits-all solution* – There are no simple answers or one size fits all. The problems are essentially the same; however, the solution within each organization is unique – it depends on the organization's culture, level of investment, likely resistance, and buy-in from all senior stakeholders to give people time to "sharpen the axe."

▶ *The value of embracing agile* – In one large organization we worked with, agile has consistently delivered new and valuable (revenue-enhancing) business functionality month in, month out; it has fundamentally changed the relationship between the business and the IT group and, although we normally expect UAT to be done by the users, in this case the IT group has taken on that responsibility on the users' behalf. They will look to try and solve the problems of doing an agile development as well as coping with end-to-end testing and especially nonfunctional testing such as performance, usability, accessibility, and security.

▶ *Tool support for agile* – The tools, methods, and techniques within the industry are all starting to adapt to agile methods. We are starting to find that using commercial-strength test management and test automation tools is not as essential as it once was if you adopt the true agile principles. There are many open-source test tools available that can help. Maintaining traditional automated test scripts within a two-week sprint is a nightmare and often impossible to do well. And what value do the automated regression tests provide? Perhaps some comfort level, but do they find any new bugs or give you good information about the quality of the new code drop? Maybe the time would be better spent using exploratory techniques. (With a control mechanism like session-based test management these can be very effective in some situations.)

▶ *Process improvement* – Paradoxically the process improvement community does not yet appear to have models that will be of use in an agile environment (e.g., TPI, TMM) and yet technical capability and organizational maturity are required, in my experience, for agile to work well. Testers in the organizations I have worked with almost exclusively relied on their experience and domain knowledge to design tests, whereas I would expect agile testers to also be highly skilled test professionals; with a crazy workload they will need to use techniques to get better coverage with fewer tests, use softer skills to negotiate a better position, and have the technical skills to set up their own test data and test environments.

▶ *Breathtaking pace* – One retail web company released software three times a week at a breathtaking pace. Attempts to try and consider testing outside of the Scrum functionality for a particular sprint always seemed to get delayed until the next release, by which time all the code and impact had changed anyway.

▶ *Experience counts* – At a U.S. software company, a small, well-funded and managed, more technically able team delivered better testing in half the time with fewer resources than a conventional test team.

13.5   Conclusions

These then are my personal opinions based on recent experience, and since I am still learning about "agile testing," they are subject to change:

▶ *Agile methods are seen as the NGT* – Everyone wants to get on board; they are good (or bad) depending on the context; they may scale depending on the organization and its maturity in the test department. In my opinion, agile does not sit on its own as the NGT. It's just another tool in the toolbox which may help, it may not. It is worth a look. You decide.

▶ *Don't forget the skills and people challenges* – As long ago as 1976, in my first programming job at a telecommunications company, I had to write Program Acceptance Tests (PAT) (yes I know it is tautologous but that's life) and show them to my manager BEFORE I wrote the code. Sounds a bit like test-driven development to me. Are we not going "Back to the Future"? I believe that some of the disciplines we had back in the old days, without being too nostalgic, have been lost and need to be rediscovered in our test groups; testers need to own their own career, learn agile methods, learn the test techniques, and vastly improve their own technical knowledge and abilities if they are to succeed in the brave new world.

▶ *Apply common sense* – Traditional also works if you do it properly; you cannot build a hospital in a day! We must not forget the end-to-end and non-functional aspects of testing and quality. We don't know how to communicate to management and the businesses, and the businesses don't seem to like or care about IT anymore.

▶ *Not quite mainstream, yet* – Agile testing techniques are not yet in the mainstream or fully understood; they are not methods or techniques as such that stand up to a lot of scrutiny. However, there are some good ideas and principles that can and should be adopted by anyone wishing to make testing better, cheaper, and faster.

▶ *Size (and complexity) matters* – Using an "agile" method for testing (or development) should always be explained "in context" of the size or complexity of the system under test and not just as a theoretical exercise. How many developers, how many testers, how many screens, interfaces, how many servers, and so on – these questions must be answered – how can I write down on small A5 cards my "requirements" for an air traffic control system or a new missile defense system. Being used to weekly and sometimes daily releases at some web clients, I asked one project manager (attending a training course I was running) when the next release of their radar software was due (expecting "next month") and she said four years hence, just in time for the next Olympics!

▶ *Don't neglect the documentation* – The way in which tests and test plans are documented should be examined. In very complex object-oriented systems there are often thousands of tables and hundreds of "screens," so keeping track of it all is a nightmare and I can understand why there is so little documentation either for design or for test.

▶ *The pace of change* – The pace of change is often so fast that the ink is not dry on the code or the test (whether test-driven development is used or not!) before the next change comes charging along; this seems to create a strange effect where people ignore several changes and don't worry about the related impacts (i.e., they are so swamped with work that they do their best and fix and test what they can without doing a full impact analysis). This leads to integration, regression, and performance faults much later in the project.

▶ *Don't throw the baby out with the bathwater* – The skill levels required to adopt "agile testing" should be examined in more detail. I have met some very clever people who can and do test in an agile way. But they know the traditional test design techniques as well and I think they apply these perhaps without really knowing it. Can we teach good testing techniques to large numbers of testers?

▶ *Avoid NGT for NGT's sake* – We must get a more joined up and collaborative software testing industry where we share ideas and resources rather than compete for the NGT. The poor customers have been confused by promises from certificated experts and new methods that are amazing; in truth, it's a complex world and we need skilled analysts to help solve the problems where business people stop ignoring the complexities of what they have built.

14 The Power of Continuous Integration Builds and Agile Development

James Wilson, CEO of Trinem

SYNOPSIS

This case study will examine how organizations can benefit from applying continuous integration build (CIB) solutions; it will also look at how adopting agile best practices can increase development productivity while introducing performance management techniques, as well as examining the role and use of testing throughout CIB.

14.1 Introduction

My name is James Wilson and I am the CEO of Trinem, based in Edinburgh, United Kingdom. I cofounded Trinem with Philip Gibbs in 2001 after working for a number of years as an IT consultant, primarily delivering software configuration management (SCM) services and solutions. Since 2001, Trinem has implemented SCM projects that have inherited various forms of technologies, methods, and scale.

Trinem has implemented processes, and had their technology implemented, for a wide spectrum of organizations, including NASA (United States), Bank of New York (United Kingdom), HBOS (United Kingdom), Belastingdienst (Holland), Syscom (Taiwan), SDC (Denmark), and GE (United Kingdom and Holland).

This case study illustrates the challenges, approaches, and benefits that I have encountered while developing agile application development processes.

This case study will also explore some of the key technologies that were used, both commercial and open source, to augment the implementations delivered by Trinem and myself.

14.2 Agile, Extreme Programming, Scrum, and/or Iterative?

Invariably when customers ask for consulting services to assist with the implementation of SCM and application development best practices, they already have an idea of what is happening in the industry. Typically the customer would talk at length about the latest development methods, the newest techniques, and the most popular processes that will increase productivity, reduce costs, and convert their currently unremarkable development teams into superdevelopers who would be the envy of their competitors.

In addition to managing the varied interpretations of the latest "fads," the endless meetings would involve representatives from all walks of the enterprise IT/business management world, including developers, testers, release managers, configuration managers, project managers, production control, business analysts, change control board, architects, etc.

These meetings would attempt to address the ideal "standard" that should be adopted across the enterprise. It very quickly became apparent that there was no one "standard" that could meet even one customer's enterprise requirements; the ideal was understood and seemed logical, but the implementation and management of any one method didn't appear comprehensive enough or scalable.

After years of getting involved in such exercises – understanding, implementing, and reworking the various development methods available – I embarked on a cherry-picking exercise of selecting the strongest elements of multiple techniques, in order to create a concoction that I embraced as our "best of breed." In addition to adopting the strongest facets from each method, it was also designed to be scalable and manageable from an enterprise SCM point of view. Some purists may argue that technology can't/shouldn't be used to manage agile development; I believe it's essential.

14.3   Definition of an Agile Testing Process – The Application Development Life Cycle

The majority of my experience has involved the generation of software development life cycles – how they are managed, by whom, and for what purpose. I used this experience to create a template from which I could include the best practices encouraged from the numerous best-of-breed development methods at my disposal; my main sources of references being Extreme Programming (XP [20]), Scrum [23], iterative development [7], and agile development [18].

From these methods, I focused on developing a life cycle that could encompass the following best-of-breed practices from these best-of-breed agile methods:

▶ From Extreme Programming, I selected refactoring, spike development, user stories, and minor releases.
▶ From Scrum, I selected Heartbeat Retrospective [54], dynamic information, and sprints.
▶ From iterative development, I selected spiral process.
▶ From agile development, I selected working software, response to change, and collaboration.

The keystone for my life cycle was user stories: the ability to articulate requirements in sufficient detail to allow a reasonable development estimate to be made. In terms of managing user stories with technology, Harvest packages and their related electronic forms were designed to capture the necessary information for a standard user story.

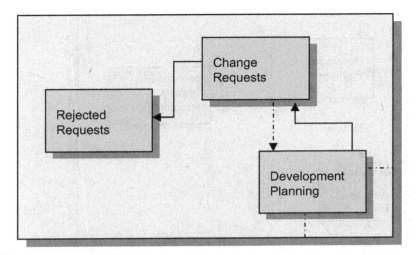

14.1 Life-cycle workflow 1.

Once the user stories were created, it was necessary to undergo formal validation and iteration planning (development planning) – the process of assigning user stories to particular iterations, or sprints, based on resources, effort, and priority. Modeled in Harvest,[1] this process looked as shown in Figure 14.1.

You will notice that the terms are not literally extracted from the methods in which they originally belong; this was to reduce the "cultural shock" and make the transition more seamless for the end users.

From iteration planning (development planning) the user story could be sent to the development team, either as a planned piece of work or as a support and maintenance development.

Depending on the customer requirements, support and maintenance could also take on the role of "spike development," as per the XP method [20]. For this particular customer, the principle of working on the latest version of the code, in an isolated environment on the branch, lent itself to support and maintenance development but could have easily been labeled "spike development" with no functional changes to the SCM product.

The resulting life cycle process was further developed as shown in Figure 14.2.

It is in development that the continuous integration builds were implemented; this will be covered in more detail later in this section.

Assuming a successful build was produced, the user stories would then be promoted through the SCM product to a staging area where the business acceptance could take place. Once the business had accepted the changes, they would be promoted for a minor release.

In the event that the business required rework, the user story was demoted back to development where the necessary changes could be made and the user story reused

---

[1] The majority of SCM products on the market today allow users to define the life cycle and, subsequently, the processes in which they want to work. In this case study I will be referring to the functionality and terminology of CA's SCM product, which I will refer to as Harvest for clarity and to avoid confusion with the term "software configuration management."

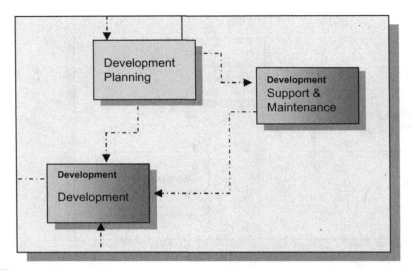

14.2 Life-cycle workflow 2.

to repeat the process. The advantage of using a tool for managing the process means that workflow information can be continually tracked – identifying the proportion of "new development" versus "rework," for example, may be an extremely useful metric of the productivity of the team, how accurate the requirements are being specified, or the capability of the assigned developers (see Figure 14.3).

This completes the end-to end application life cycle, as shown in Figure 14.4.

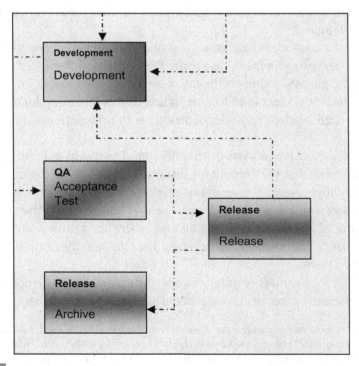

14.3 Life-cycle workflow 3.

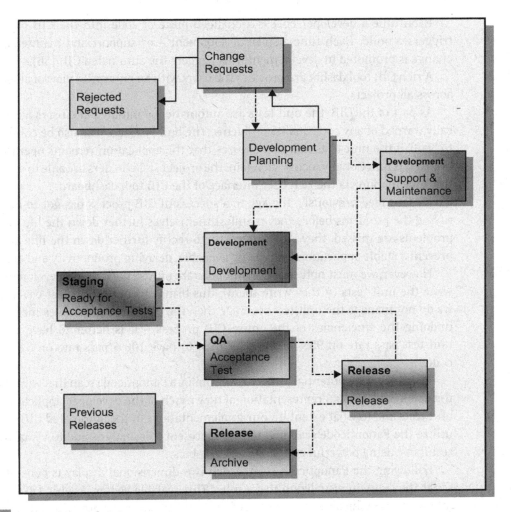

14.4   Life-cycle workflow 4.

From Figure 14.4 the process should become clear with respect to what has been implemented and how it has been influenced by various development methods.

14.4   Continuous Integration Builds and Automated Unit Testing

The key benefits of implementing the best-of-breed life cycle is that it integrates seamlessly, both from the process side and the technology side, with the desired CIB and testing.

In my opinion, the key advantages of CIB are

▶ consistently working software,
▶ automated unit testing, and
▶ panopticode scanning.[2]

---

2 Panopticode is a project dedicated to making code metrics widely understood, valuable, and simple so that their use becomes the norm, thus raising software quality (see [55]).

Each time a developer checks a changed piece of code into the CIB tool, this triggers a build. Each time a spike development – or support and maintenance – change is promoted to development, this triggers the automated CIB [56].

A rich CIB tool dashboard provides the users with an enterprise view of all builds, across all projects.

As part of the CIB, the unit tests are automatically initiated and users automatically warned of any code quality problems. The build process can also be configured to "fail" if the unit tests fail; this ensures that the application remains operational, even if it is functionally incorrect. Again, the project stakeholders are able to visualize this information via the rich user interface of the CIB tool dashboard.

As described previously, the key to a successful CIB process has got to be identifying the problems before they manifest themselves further down the life cycle. If problems are missed, they are more costly to rectify further down the line and can prevent a stable application from being available, delaying productivity and delivery.

However, we must note that the unit tests are only as good as the developers who write the unit tests (*if* they write them); this brings us on to unit test coverage. If we do not manage the unit test coverage then the unit testing becomes ineffectual, undoing the efficiencies of the entire CIB process – it is better to have an 80% unit test pass rate on 95% of the code than to have 100% pass rate on 5% of the code.

To manage this potential problem, we employ a Panopticode scan that will provide the users with a visual representation of how much of the developed application has unit tests and to what extent. In our implementations of the automated CIB tool we utilize the Panopticode scanning tool to represent this analysis and to visualize the results by using powerful code coverage graphics.

Following the Panopticode scan, a rich two-dimensional display is generated to assist the users in visualizing the results. This scalable vector graphic (SVG) is an interactive, graphical representation of the unit test coverage; green, yellow, and red represent coverage greater than 75, 50, and 0%, respectively. Black represents the areas of the application where no unit test coverage exists (blue is "not applicable"). Two-dimensional boxes represent methods, and these are grouped by the classes in which they belong.

Again, by using the Panopticode scanning tool it is possible to manage the code complexity of the applications. By identifying the complex areas of an application it is useful to assign developers to refactoring activities – the rework of complex areas to make them less complex and more useable.

As with the code coverage, we can generate an SVG graph that will assess the complexity and provide a code complexity number (CCN) rating. The code complexity display uses a style of graphic display similar to that used for code coverage: green, yellow, red, and black represent CCN ratings from 1–5, 6–9, 10–24, and 25+, respectively (1 being the least complex and 25+ being the most complex).

With the Panopticode scans, we now have a comprehensive system for identifying the most complex code and the areas in which unit testing is not sufficient. In addition to the Panopticode scanning, the CIB tool also has various options to include code analysis tools, including CheckStyle and PMD. These can be very useful for checking the quality of the code at build time.

14.5 Management Information and Metrics

Since the implementations are managed through a suitable SCM tool, it is possible to make use of the metadata that are generated and stored in the underlying database.

The process includes the following high-level activities:

▶ user story definition and validation,
▶ iteration planning,
▶ spike development,
▶ development estimates,
▶ iteration durations,
▶ rework/new development,
▶ acceptance, and
▶ minor release.

We can make use of the data generated (manually input data or system data) to produce useful management information and metrics. For example, we know the number of developers in a team, the number of user stories, and the development estimates for each user story. Therefore, we can produce metrics to assist the iteration planning process by assessing the capacity versus utilization metrics.

Since we know the iteration start dates, iteration duration, and number of development days (actual/estimated), we can calculate the burn rates (Heartbeat retrospective), iteration velocity, and project velocity [26].

All of this information can again be displayed to the appropriate stakeholders using the rich graphical user interface (Figure 14.5).

Figure 14.6 illustrates the new development versus rework; note how iteration 4 has a predominantly high level of rework. Development managers (Scrum masters) can use this information to assess the reasons why there is a rework peak: poor requirements, complex code, or a change in business requirements, for example.

Again, there are sufficient data within the SCM tool to assess the velocity (progress) of each iteration and the overall project. With the correct management of user story metadata, combined with SCM workflow, it is possible to determine these statistics.

Taking this a step further, we can use these data to visualize trends and make predictions; consider the graph in Figure 14.7.

The dashed line in the graph plots the velocity of each iteration, whereas the gray solid line provides the velocity of the overall project. By overlaying trend lines we can also make reasonable assumptions for the delivery of the current user stories – fluctuations in the iteration velocities may be attributable to changing, or additional, requirements.

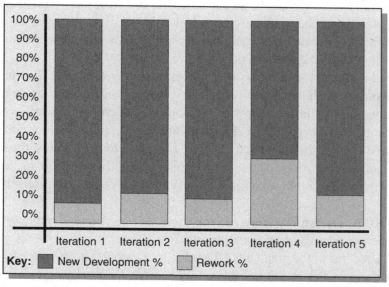

| Development Planning | Development | Defect Management | Release Management | Peer Review |

Iteration State Date: 06-02-2008 ▼

Iteration End Date: 06-06-2008

Assigned Developer: thornbow

Iterative Development Cycle: 1

System Release:

⊙ 5   ○ One Day
○ 1l   ⊙ Two Days
○ 1:   ○ Three Days

Iteration State Date: 05-05-2008 ▼

Iteration End Date: 05-09-2008

Total Number of User Stories: 3

Total Number of Days: 7

Iteration Velocity: 33.33 %

Project Velocity: 4.44 %

Create New Iteration

14.5 Graphical display of user story attributes.

14.6 Graphical display of rework ratio.

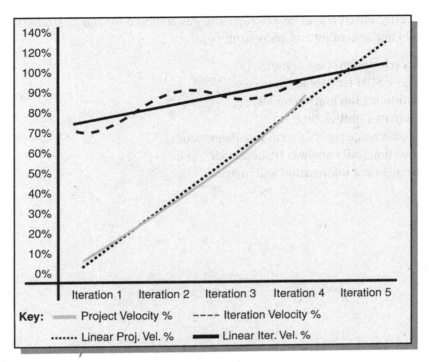

Graph of iteration and project velocity.

14.6 Lessons Learned

In my experience, there is not one method that can solve all development problems within any organization; however, there are compelling reasons to utilize various techniques to achieve better quality of code more quickly.

The main objectives of the "best-of-breed" agile development process were to

▶ gain control of application development,
▶ prove compliance and governance,
▶ provide flexibility for the developers and other SCM users,
▶ deliver increased productivity,
▶ ensure increased quality of code (leading to a decrease in defect costs),
▶ be responsive to business needs, and
▶ reduce time to market.

A significant achievement for our customers was the ability to leverage their technology to support the "best-of-breed" agile development. Certain methods almost dictate the absence of any SCM tool to support the agile processes; this is just not an option with large-scale, N-tier applications.

Effective enterprise agile development was achieved for our customers by successfully implementing and addressing

- ▶ life cycle and process design,
- ▶ flexible SCM technology,
- ▶ continuous integration builds,
- ▶ automated unit testing,
- ▶ code coverage analysis (unit test Panopticode),
- ▶ code complexity analysis (Panopticode), and
- ▶ management information and metrics.

15 The Payoffs and Perils of Offshored Agile Projects

Peter Kingston, Contract Test Manager

SYNOPSIS

This case study describes my experiences of working on a project where we combined two potentially highly beneficial, but apparently incompatible, approaches to developing software: offshoring and agile methods.

Although ultimately successful, with the delivery and use of the system developed using this combined approach, there were a number challenges to overcome (such as the issues of not having a co-located team, of culture, of language and its interpretation, and of reliable reporting and estimation).

In addition to describing the solutions to the challenges of agile offshore projects, I also review the positive aspects of the project (such as reductions in effort, cost, and timescales; extended development and testing time; and establishing a process for future agile offshore projects).

15.1 Introduction

My name is Peter Kingston and at the time of this case study I was working on a contract as a test manager for a financial products company, The Remortgage Corporation (TRC).

My career in IT spans more than twenty-five years, beginning as a software developer before moving into systems analysis and then management. For most of the last decade, I have been a professional software test consultant and have a wide variety of experience of the software testing industry. I have gained much expertise from working as a test analyst, test manager, and test consultant in a variety of industries including finance, retail, government, and petro-chemical. In addition, I am an accredited provider of the ISTQB Foundation Course in Software Testing [42].

TRC operates in a highly competitive market place; there are many companies producing similar financial products for a relatively small number of potential customers. As a result, organizations like our own have to ensure our development process is as lean and mean as possible. Our customers demand products with ever-increasing functionality and usability, developed in shorter timescales and with lower cost, and with higher quality!

As a result, we need to constantly review our development approaches and to look for opportunities for driving down costs and increasing the quality of our products. During our review of development approaches, we identified two particular approaches that seemed to offer the sort of benefits we were looking for:

▶ *Agile development* – With its focus on effective and efficient development and testing, agile appeared to provide a means of reducing development costs, ensuring that we met our delivery commitments and (done properly) improved quality (both meeting requirements and reducing defects) through early and frequent testing.

▶ *Offshoring* – With its focus on distributed development using lower-cost resources, offshoring also provided the opportunity to "extend the length of the development day" by, for example, having practitioners in different time zones picking up the development effort at different times.

The purpose of this case study is to share a number of interesting experiences gained in setting up and running an agile offshore project involving a U.K. and Indian development and testing team, but with an added complication of the product marketing team being located in the United States.

The system developed through our agile offshore project has been successfully delivered and is being used by a number of our customers.

15.2   Overview of the Development and Testing Challenge

In 2007, TRC began a project to migrate and enhance a large existing product (TRC-Legacy) to a new platform (and new name – TRC-Heritage). In its existing form, TRC-Legacy had the following characteristics:

▶ The product focused on the remortgaging market and had been purchased by ten U.K. customers, who were still using the tool to support their everyday business.

▶ Legacy had originally been implemented using Power Builder and employed an underlying Oracle back end.

▶ The product had been under development and enhancement for some ten years and during its initial development had been implemented by a team of some sixteen analysts and programmers, plus two dedicated quality assurance representatives.

▶ In its final incarnation (Legacy v6.0), the product consisted of some 450 distinct screens.

In terms of the replacement TRC-Heritage product:

▶ The new system was to be *developed using Java on the Eclipse platform* [57, 58], plus some third-party GUI control products.

▶ The migration project had *very challenging timescales* (i.e., our marketing team had obtained market intelligence that indicated that a competitor product would be launched within three months) and *very challenging budgetary constraints*. We were told we had ten weeks to migrate, enhance, and deliver the replacement system.

▶ As a result *it was decided to employ an agile approach* to ensure that the timescales would be met and to reduce the cost of development and testing. An agile approach was also anticipated to help us be flexible in terms of likely changes to requirements and to ensure product quality was maintained by allowing testing to begin as early as possible in the project and to continue throughout the development.

▶ To reduce the cost of the migration further, it was also agreed that *much of the development work would be offshored* to a company in India, with marketing responsibilities given to a team in the United States.

15.3 Definition of an Agile Offshore Approach

The details of our agile offshore approach were as follows:

▶ *Staff*
 ▷ The U.K. team included one project manager, two developers, one test manager, and one test analyst/tester.
 ▷ The Indian team included one team leader and five developers.
 ▷ The U.S. team included one marketing manager.
▶ *Agile requirements*
 ▷ *Use cases* – Where new requirements were needed (this was, after all, mostly a migration-style project), they were elicited using a use case–based approach. The majority of new requirements were obtained from our U.S. marketing manager and involved some intensive transatlantic teleconferences (where, oddly, we still suffered from language issues – more on this later).
 ▷ *Requirements documentation* – Requirements were documented using a commercial product [59]. This product included a web-based interface that allowed our Indian and U.S. colleagues to be able to review, comment on, and make use of the requirements. In practice, this was a very successful aspect of the project, and as long as we phrased the requirements in a concise, clear, and unambiguous manner,[1] the results (i.e., the code implemented against the requirements) were good.
▶ *Iterative approach*
 ▷ *Two-week iteration period* – We employed a two-week iteration period. We had previously seen projects where iterations based around a week-long period

---

[1] You might justifiably argue that all requirements should be phrased in a concise, clear, and unambiguous manner in any project; however, the differences in culture, language, and idiom on this project meant we needed to be ultracareful in terms of how requirements were documented.

had been successful (more on this later) but the work items were too large on this project; hence, our use of a two-week period. (Interestingly, we believe a week-long iteration might have been possible had we not had the additional communication overhead of offshoring the project.)

▷ *Time boxing* – The two-week iterations were time-boxed [17]. Where rapidly approaching time-box deadlines meant that not all the requirements for that iteration could be implemented, the decisions on what requirements would be left out were based on priority values assigned to the requirements in the requirements management tool. (Risk and priority were in effect attributes associated with any particular requirement.) It was also possible to include information describing relationships between requirements in the tool, such as dependencies; this allowed the U.K. project manager to assess the impact of proposals from the developers about omitting specific requirements.

▶ *Agile meetings*

▷ *General* – Wherever possible, all meetings would include the whole team (typically Indian and U.K. staff, with occasional attendance by the U.S.-based marketing manager). Because of the communications challenges of offshoring, meetings were considered to be an essential aspect of making the project successful, and great importance was placed on holding and attending them. To avoid too many meetings and not enough work, all meetings were as brief and focused as possible (following the principles of the agile project management method Scrum [23]).

▷ *Initial project startup and planning meeting* – This meeting was convened on the Friday before the project was to begin to kick off the project, to introduce the staff to each other, confirm roles and responsibilities, review and agree on tasks and timescales, agree on our offshore working protocol (such as the when and how of communications), and to plan and prepare for the first iteration (to begin on the following Monday).

▷ *Two-weekly Friday iteration startup meetings* – These meetings were used to review the results of the previous iteration, to document any lessons learned, and to plan and prepare for the next iteration (which would begin on the following Monday morning). The meeting would involve a review of the requirements for the next iteration, their priority and any risks and/or dependencies, and agreement on the tasks and timescales. The test plan for the iteration would also be discussed and agreed.

▷ *Weekly conference call progress meetings* – Held midweek on the Wednesday, these brief meetings were really just to confirm that all members of the team were on track and that there were no problems, risks, or dependencies that might cause the team to fail to meet its deadlines.

▷ *Local daily stand-up meetings* – We also ran daily fifteen-minute stand-up meetings[2] first thing each day with the U.K. team for the purposes of reviewing

---

[2]   In effect, Scrums [23].

what the team had achieved the previous day, what it planned to do today, and what issues, risks, or dependencies might disrupt its plans. We asked the Indian team to follow this approach as well.

▷ *Project closedown meeting* – At the end of the project we scheduled a large videoconference meeting that included all the stakeholders from the project (which was planned to coincide with the U.K. presence of our marketing manager) to formally close the project, review the deliverables, ensure all artifacts were filed, and to review and document all of the lessons learned during the project (many of which were rolled up from lessons documented in previous meetings). This was a very valuable event both from a process improvement and project administration perspective, but also from a human perspective. By then, our resident offshored resource had returned to India, and it gave all the team members on both continents the chance to thank each other and to say goodbye – quite an emotional moment, as it turned out.

▶ *Agile development approach*

▷ *General* – Since we were developing using Java and Eclipse, we largely followed the agile Eclipse Way development process [60].

▷ *Pair programming* – We employed an agile development approach using pair programming (as per Extreme Programming [20]).

▷ *Continuous integration* – The developers used a continuous integration (and test) approach. This would continue daily at a local level, with a weekly (on Thursday close of business) email consolidated build and test in the United Kingdom. In practice, this did cause some quality issues (see Lessons Learned).

▷ *Test-driven development* – Developers were expected to review the requirements and design their tests before coding began.

▷ *Automated unit testing* – Developer testing was automated using the popular JUnit tool [50].

▶ *Agile software quality management*

▷ *Test management and planning* were based around the iteration plan, with functional tests planned at the end of each iteration (plus rerun regression tests from previous iterations – see later bullet point). Unit testing (and evidence of unit testing) was provided by the developers as they coded. A key goal was for testing to begin as early as possible and continue frequently throughout the project.

▷ *Test coverage* was achieved by ensuring that each requirement had one or more test cases associated with it and that each test case had one or more test scripts associated with it. This was a very straightforward process using the requirements management tool selected for the project [61], and it was possible to produce extremely useful test design, implementation, and coverage reports as and when needed.

▷ *Unit testing* was very successfully achieved using the JUnit tool.

▷ *Acceptance testing* – Use cases were also employed by the test analyst to generate acceptance testing scenarios, which was found to be a very natural and straightforward solution to producing realistic and effective acceptance tests.

▷ *Regression testing* was achieved using a Java-based capture–replay tool [62], allowing us to automate the acceptance tests in the form of Java scripts, which we were then able to replay against new builds and releases of the product.

▷ *Pair testing* was a technique we developed to be a software quality equivalent of the pair programming techniques the developers were using. Our test manager and test analyst worked together to design and implement the tests needed to verify functionality, which were subsequently recorded by the capture–replay tool (to be reused against later builds and releases).

▷ *Test automation* – As described earlier, JUnit and a capture–replay tool were used to automate the testing process wherever appropriate. In the case of the capture–replay tool, we also used it to set up, initialize, and manage the complete regression testing activity.

15.4 Results of an Agile Approach

The replacement TRC-Heritage product has been successfully implemented and is now in use with a number of our existing customers; it has also been sold to several new customers.

Bottom line, the migration has resulted in a replacement product that has been updated to match current market needs, is in service with existing and new customers, and has earned (and continues to earn) significant revenue for our company.

In terms of the overall project results:

▶ *The product matches the customer requirements well*. The new product requirements were largely obtained through our U.S. marketing manager and have enabled TRC to make sales of the product to new customers, as well as providing an upgrade to our existing customer base. The team (including the nontechnical U.S. marketing manager) felt that the use case approach had been a success, allowing requirements to be captured, reviewed, and easily understood by all the stakeholders.

▶ *Overall product quality has been good*. The early and frequent testing that our iterative approach supported has meant that a great many defects were detected and corrected way before release of the product. Since release, there have been no critical defects reported, and (at the time of writing this case study) two serious defects (both involving database access – which were quickly fixed) and just eight cosmetic issues (which have been fixed in the next release).

▶ *Overall project costs have been reduced*. A brief analysis of our project metrics shows that the overall cost of the project was 30% lower than running an equivalent co-located U.K.-based agile project. Although this information must be balanced by the fact that the project overran by 20% in terms of its duration, this has nevertheless been a very well-received result from the perspective of our senior management.

▶ *Reporting and estimating issues* – From a project management perspective, there were definite issues with reporting and estimating. Because of time zone differences, the difficulty with convening ad hoc offshored meetings, lack of formal cross-geo reporting tools, and the challenge of not having face-to-face communications when the weekly teleconferences were held, it was very difficult to have a clear picture of progress. Our agile approach highlighted these issues much more acutely than a traditional project approach would have done.

▶ *Two-week overrun* – Over the projected ten-week project duration, we overran by two weeks. This 20% slippage was largely attributed to the overhead associated with "round-trip communications" (i.e., where a request from the U.K. team, email or voicemail, was made outside of the Indian working day, picked up by the Indian team the next day, worked on, and then reported back to the U.K. team the next day). As the project proceeded, we did try to find solutions to this phenomenon, which I cover in the Lessons Learned section.

15.5 Lessons Learned

There were a number of lessons learned from our agile offshored project:

▶ *Fundamentally, offshoring is a trade-off between speed and cost of development.* This may not be such an obvious issue on a project employing traditional development and testing approaches, but the use of an agile approach did highlight the problems. For example, our feeling is that we could have run to shorter one-week iterations (with which we have had very positive experiences of in previous projects) if we had not had the overhead of long-distance communications to cope with. Instead, we had to adopt a two-week-iteration period, which meant that the team did not get into quite such a slick rhythm and were of necessity slightly less productive.

▶ *Reduction in productivity* – Now, the key issue is – was the reduction in productivity offset by the reduction in the unit cost of the offshored resources? In this project, our feeling (justified by metrics) was yes – in fact, overall we believe the project was some 30% cheaper than if we had based the work solely in the United Kingdom (and employed a co-located team).

▶ *Software quality lessons* – There were some very valuable software quality lessons to come out of this project:

  ▷ *Pair testing* – We definitely recommend the use of this approach. Metrics showed that when two testers worked together to design and implement tests, they
   • showed a greater understanding of the underlying requirements,
   • identified more and better data points (to test the correct operation of the code, as well as in terms of error and exception values),
   • were more productive (producing some 15% more tests per unit time than two testers working in isolation), and

- smiled more – this social activity made for happier and more motivated testers.

▷ *Test-driven development (TDD)* – The feedback from the developers is that TDD is a very valuable approach. The need to understand the requirements in sufficient detail to be able to design a test to show that the code meets the requirement before implementing the code means that the developers have gained a thorough understanding of the intention of the requirement before they come to code it. Some developers expressed the view that TDD would slow them down and reduce their productivity; in practice, there has been no appreciable reduction in developer productivity, but there has been a measurable improvement in the quality of the code (in terms of matching requirements more closely as well as in delivery of code with fewer defects in it).

▷ *Test automation* – The use of the JUnit testing tool has been an unqualified success and we would definitely use this again on similar projects. The results of the use of the capture–replay tool have been mixed:
  - There is a definite benefit in software quality from being able to rerun tests recorded in earlier iterations (we make sure that old defects don't reappear, for example).
  - Also, the more often you replay a given test script, the more return you gain on your investment. This is important, because these tools are a significant project investment (both in the cost of the tool plus staff training/learning time). We estimate that we needed to reuse a script four or more times to realize a gain in productivity versus an equivalent manual test. So for a short one-off project you need to challenge the use of these tools. Where you are likely to gain good reuse from the tools, there are economic gains to be made.
  - A good lesson to learn is that, to use these tools effectively, you must ensure you either have testers who have used the tools in the past or ensure that you budget time and money for training.
  - As a final thought, if your code base or application functionality changes too frequently between iterations, you may also incur additional cost from maintaining the test scripts. Although this sort of project chaos should clearly be discouraged by the project manager, script maintenance costs must be balanced against your return-on-investment metrics.

▶ *Requirements coverage* – If you do not know what the software you are developing is supposed to do, how can you possibly test it correctly? For any nontrivial project, the use of a requirements management tool is essential. The ability to elicit, document, and maintain the requirements for the system enables developers to know what they are developing, as well as allowing the testers to know what it is they are testing. In particular, the use of a requirements tool should allow the test manager to be able to make some informed estimates about testing timescales and resources and allow the test analyst to demonstrate complete test coverage of the requirements. A further bonus of using a requirements tool is the ability for remote stakeholders to use the product's web-based interface to inspect, comment on, and request changes to the requirements.

▷ *Testers beware of time boxing* – Time boxing is clearly a valuable tool in the project manager's arsenal to help keep development on track and to achieve delivery deadlines. However, during a couple of our iterations, the time allocated in the plan for testing was eaten into by overrunning development. If you plan to use a time-boxed approach, you must ensure that the time planned for testing is sacrosanct. We considered, but in the end didn't implement, making the functional testing activity a time box of its own that followed on immediately from the associated development time box. This is definitely something I would investigate in future projects.

▶ *Communications issues* – We learned some very valuable lessons about communications, and how good and bad communications can affect the choice of using an agile approach:

▷ *Lack of face-to-face communication matters.* It is difficult to build a rapport with someone on the other side of the world just using a telephone. As a result you lose some very valuable face-to-face cues, such as the confidence with which an estimate to complete is delivered during a telephone progress meeting. A true agile approach would of course have mandated the co-location of the stakeholders. One method that I have used that worked particularly well was to have one of the offshore team work onshore as a liaison (or even as translator). They are able to deal with people at both ends of the telephone and are often well placed to explain what the other team really means.

▷ *Find strategies to build a trusted relationship with offshored colleagues.* Find the time to engage in small talk, find out about their interests and hobbies, discuss family stuff, and even just talk about the weather. All parties need to find the means to understand and trust each other. Having an offshore team member working onshore is also a good way of building a trusting relationship with the remote group. However, it is important to make this person feel like a full member of the team and to include them in all activities, bearing in mind there are cultural differences. For example, one Indian colleague revealed, but only through general conversation, that three days earlier he had become a father for the first time but didn't think it polite to mention the fact. We were able to discuss cultural mores while "wetting the baby's head" before presenting him with some cuddly toys and packing him off home to meet his daughter.

▷ *Be polite, but firmly challenge all estimates.* It is all too easy for someone on the end of a telephone (and themselves under project pressures) to provide overly optimistic estimates of their progress. This is particularly true when the communications are infrequent – a team member may actually give an estimate that is too optimistic, believing that by the next time you were in communication, they could have brought a late task back on track. The best solution (and one we would look to use in similar future projects) would be to use an agile distributed development tool (such as in [63]) where individual worker's estimates and actuals are automatically collected as they perform the work and which are instantly available to the project manager to review.

▷ *Be aware of language/meaning issues.* For example, one of the Indian offshore practitioners, when asked how a particular delivery had gone, used to say "ship happens"; over the telephone and with the unfamiliar accent, this message was interpreted in a "negative manner" as something bad had happened, rather than in the positive manner it was meant to have been interpreted (i.e., that the software had in fact shipped).

▷ Funnily enough, we had similar problems with our U.S. colleague.[3] In one transatlantic teleconference, our project manager wanted to highlight what he thought was a key requirement and said something like, "let's place this issue on the table" (meaning "let's focus on it"). At the next weekly meeting, our project manager was surprised to find that no progress had been made on the requirement; it turns out that in the United States, to put something "on the table" means to put it aside and to focus on other issues!

▷ My final, and perhaps most interesting example, however, is of one offshore practitioner who was working onshore in the United Kingdom. He was perfectly polite when arranging meetings but would always ask to meet people "on" their convenience.

▷ *Find better means of more frequent communication.*
   • Make use of *instant messaging* technologies to keep in touch. Such technologies can be very useful to ask simple spontaneous questions or to seek clarification (but beware of time zone differences).
   • Consider the use of cheap *Internet telephony.* Although this may not be too useful for offshore sites where there is no working time-zone overlap, it can be a powerful adjunct to instant messaging, allowing workers to have cheap and easily available voice calls.

▷ Consider the role and use of *videoconferencing.* Although not so much in vogue as it was in the 1990s and early 2000s, the face-to-face aspects provided by a video link for holding offshore meetings might well provide a better means of obtaining subtle cues from body language and expressions that straightforward telephone calls can't.

▷ Consider the use of Web 2.0 social networking technologies. For example, consider having on-line virtual meetings in Second Life [64]. This may well be an approach that improves team cohesion and encourages effective communication.

▷ Ensure you only select tools that are *distributed.* For example, the requirements management tool we selected included a web-based interface that permitted our offshore colleagues (and, in particular, the U.S.-based marketing

---

[3] Winston Churchill was spot on when he said that the United Kingdom and the United States are two nations divided by a common language!

manager) to log on to the tool remotely, review the current requirements, and, where necessary, make comments or request changes to the requirements.

▶ *Make more use of tools that support 24/7 working* – Having tools that automatically replicate the code base and project data between geographically distributed sites would be a very valuable means of supporting the distributed working model we were looking to achieve. We discovered a very powerful approach that would have automatically replicated our project workspace between sites just after the project completed and we would definitely investigate its use in future projects of this nature [63].

▶ *Make use of process enactment tools.* In running an agile approach to developing the new software, it would be of value to have all of the practitioners follow the same process. Taken a step further, it would be nice if all the practitioners were constrained to follow the same process. There are products available that provide powerful facilities to implement and enact (enforce) a particular style of project management (such as agile) and which will also produce accurate real-time reports and dashboard displays of project progress [65]. Employing a distributed tool of this nature would be a powerful solution to drive an agile offshore project more effectively.

▶ *Try to harmonize working times across time zones.* As described earlier, over the ten-week project duration, we overran by two weeks. This slippage was largely caused by the problems of "round-trip communications" (i.e., where a request from the U.K. team – email or voicemail – was made outside of the Indian working day, picked up by the Indian team the next day, worked on, and then reported back to the U.K. team the next day). As the project proceeded, we did try to find solutions to this phenomenon – such as making sure we were in touch with the Indian team during their working period, and changing our respective start and stop times to improve overlap (i.e., asking one or more of the Indian team to start work an hour later than usual and finish work an hour later and doing the converse with the U.K. team). This certainly helped and meant that, toward the end of the project, round-trip communication became less and less of an issue.

15.6 Summary

The bottom line is that the project to migrate and update the TRC-Legacy product has been a success. Despite a two-week overrun, the agile offshored project used to deliver the new TRC-Heritage product was completed for an estimated 70% of the cost of running an equivalent traditional U.K.-based project.

When you add to this the fact that the product does what it is supposed to do (and sufficiently well for the existing TRC-Legacy customers to be very pleased to use the new TRC-Heritage product, as well as for TRC to be able to attract new customers to buy the product) and was delivered with surprisingly few defects, the exercise would seem to be an unqualified success.

In terms of specific quality management aspects of the project, we would give a big thumbs-up to our pair testing solution, as well as to TDD. The use of a requirements management tool, and in particular one that integrates with your test management and test design approach, was also of great value.

In terms of test automation, we have mixed results. While JUnit was unanimously agreed to have been a very valuable tool for the developer testing, we have some reservations about the capture–replay tools that can be used for functional and regression testing. If you are only going to use the tool once or twice, then you will almost certainly not recoup your investment. We found that reusing the test scripts four or more times saved time and cost compared with taking an equivalent manual testing approach. Each time you continue to reuse the test scripts after this point, it is all up-side.

Finally, if you are in a project that uses time-boxing techniques, insist on maintaining the time planned for testing in the time box – even if the developers are overrunning. If this is a frequent problem, consider breaking out the functional and regression tests as a separate and distinct time box of their own.

16 The Basic Rules of Quality and Management Still Apply to Agile

Richard Warden, Director, Software Futures Ltd.

SYNOPSIS
Agile is a label that covers a wide range of incremental development methods, languages (e.g., UML (the Unified Modelling Language – [33]), and management styles (e.g., Scrum [23]). However, whatever flavor of agile you choose, from Extreme Programming [20] to the use of ICONIX [66], certain rules still apply. This chapter reports some experiences from projects that reinforce the basics.

16.1 Introduction

My name is Richard Warden and I wrote and tested my first computer program on May 12, 1970. When I worked for the Swiss Exchange in Zurich as a test manager they called me an "Old Rabbit" – a complimentary term, I will add. That was eleven years ago and I have since spent much of my time immersed in UML and agile-related projects within financial services companies.

My career started in the Royal Air Force as an analyst, developer, and tester on large mainframe defence support systems. I then moved to Racal Electronics working first on business systems and then interactive computer-aided design (CAD) systems in positions of programming team leader, test manager, project manager, and head of quality assurance. Following this I worked for the K3 Group as a product and research manager. Since 1991 I have been an independent consultant.

The case histories relate mainly to trading systems and I will give a brief outline of their design rather than a complex architecture picture. There is a trading platform that is usually a client–server design where traders conduct business. The client is used by traders to create trades and is supported by server functions to provide a wide range of static data such as clients and contract types. Trades created from the platform have to be processed by a number of downstream systems such as clearinghouses, reporting and regulatory organizations, and risk management systems. Consequently, a routing or messaging system is employed to create the necessary transactions to distribute to these systems. This router has to work with very high reliability in real time and is a potentially difficult part of a system. The trading platform may vary in complexity according to the types of financial product being traded. Some may be specific to a particular instrument, such as the Swiss Exchange or electronic REPO market, and others may cover a range of financial instruments, such as Bloomberg's widely used system [67].

16.2   Project A: One Cannot Live by Scrum Alone

This project was to develop a replacement trading system, which is now common because many organizations are moving to second- and third-generation systems. Scrum was chosen to manage the development work.

A fortnightly Scrum cycle was chosen with daily Scrum meetings. Analysts, developers, and testers attended the Scrums and gave their reports based on the following three questions: What did I do yesterday? What am I doing today? Do I face any problems where I need help?

Analysts decomposed specifications into stories and all could monitor progress on the storyboard in the project office. Burndown charts were displayed so everyone could see the velocity and projected completion dates of the different development parts.

The first problem we found was that charts were unreliable – specifically projected completion dates. They would remain static for some time and then slip suddenly. Surely one purpose of Scrum is to identify slippage quickly? The problem appeared to be in calculating velocity with accuracy. As an analogy, the onboard computer in my car has to solve a similar problem to predict the range of the car. It knows how much petrol is left in the tank and past fuel consumption. The question is, how do you use past consumption in a predictor algorithm? Do you take the last 25 miles' driving as representative, or 50 or 75? Likewise, do you take the last Scrum cycle or use more? Furthermore, how do you normalize story counts so they are comparable across cycles, as stories ranged in size by a factor of 10?

Another effect we observed was that of sucking the pipeline dry at the end of a cycle. To maximize velocity, staff would be assigned to clearing as many stories as possible. For example, analysts would suspend work to focus on QA sign-off. Although the sprint velocity looked good, it meant delays had been created that were not visible in a plan and could delay later cycles.

However, the larger problems were as follows. Trading systems by their nature interface with many other systems. There was considerable work being done by these systems' owners to develop and test their interfaces with the routing system. They had to plan and execute their work and ensure that it was ready in time for final integration and user acceptance testing. Although analysts worked with external organizations to define and agree the interface specifications, there was no coherent development and delivery plan. It was left to testers to poll interfacing systems owners to determine availability. This was problematic as there was no project plan and reporting mechanism that showed all these activities and their dependencies. In short, it meant that slippage in external work often came as a surprise.

One conclusion I draw from this experience is that Scrum, although easy to describe, is hard to implement without proper calibration to measure velocity accurately. More importantly, any project that has external dependencies requires a plan showing them and an associated reporting mechanism driven by the project office. In this respect Scrum appears limited and the danger is that people do not understand the limitations.

16.3 Project B: Risk does not Go Away if You Are Agile

In this project the aim was to replace the routing mechanism for a trading system. The trading platform had already been developed and was not the main subject of testing.

A risk-based approach to testing had been considered, but management decided this was not necessary. The main grounds were that all parts of the system were critical and therefore of equal risk. Also, there was considerable confidence in the trading platform because it had been fully tested. There was a feeling that, because agile inherently mitigates against risks, no further risk analysis was required. How true is that?

I see agile mitigating risks in two areas. The first is in the business risk category, namely that of minimizing the risk of developing the wrong system, a system that does not support business operations. This is achieved by involving users directly in the agile process to incrementally specify and sign off stories. The second is in the project risk category. An agile approach is meant to reduce the risks of delivering late by decomposing the project into stories that Scrum, or similar management approaches, can manage well.

What agile does not appear to cover is product, or system, risk. I make this as an observation and not as a criticism. Product risks are risks associated with failure of an internal component of a system. They can be related very much to architecture and design; for example, in a network system you avoid building single points of failure. A product risk register usually drives two elements in a project. By identifying high-risk components, developers can reduce the impact of their failure by redesign (e.g., by building multiple routes through a network). The Internet is perhaps the ultimate network design, having been proposed to keep operating in a situation of global conflict. The second element is to reduce the probability of failure in the first place. High reliability is achieved by focusing testing on high-risk components, and the risk register is used to identify test coverage required and the testing techniques, with metrics, that can provide them.

The lack of understanding of product risks regularly created problems that could have been forestalled. For example, transaction routers are tricky and complex and can have varying abilities to replay or rerun transactions in the case of failure. It was discovered that under several circumstances trades could be lost and not rerun. The impact on testing was severe. Financial products often require test cycles spanning days or weeks. That is, testing on day one has to be successful for day two onward to proceed. Now if some of the day one transactions are lost due to, say, a configuration error and in a router, and cannot be rerun, day two tests onward cannot be executed. If it is a router to a specific external system, then that system may have to be removed completely from the current cycle.

These risks could have been identified at the outset. However, without a risk workshop this information remained hidden until the risks turned into failures during test execution. Mitigating actions could have been put in place. Additional tests prior to major test cycles could have been run to show the router was configured correctly. Additional breakpoints could have been created. This meant additional cycles and test runs needed to be executed, consuming precious time and resources.

Another example of misunderstood risk was in the performance and capacity planning of some key servers. The Information Technology Infrastructure Library (ITIL) best practices [68] places much emphasis on capacity planning (i.e., can your systems cope with the expected workloads, both normal and peak). This, in turn, feeds into design, development, and testing. However, no capacity planning or related risk assessment was done. Consequently, integration and acceptance testing suffered because servers were unable to cope with even moderate test workloads, let alone volume and stress tests. The situation was only resolved with a moratorium on development and testing while new servers were procured, installed, and configured – more delays.

16.4 Project C: How to Be Agile and Operate at CMM Level 1

In the early days of this project the quality management system (QMS) included reviews of requirements, specifications, and other key documents with users and developers. Because this financial system integrated with many others, the analysis work was complex. General progress was slow and difficult and the project moved to an agile footing to create a more manageable project. During this transition, basic quality disciplines were no longer enforced; it was left to individuals to decide how they implemented the QMS. In project B, I described how agile should address business risks through close involvement of users. What happened was a slow degradation of quality in the analysis model as users were less involved. This happened in two areas.

First, existing specifications were amended without proper review. This made it difficult to examine a document and determine if it was current and trustworthy. Second, new documents were created with minimal desk-checking. In some instances there was no information on author and history, so they were particularly untrustworthy – we found they contained serious errors. As a consequence, testing was compromised, particularly test execution. Unreviewed documents had been turned into code that did not do what the user wanted. This gets you into the protracted cycle of errors created during early analysis not being found until late acceptance testing.

This relaxation of quality disciplines showed itself in some areas of development outside of the agile part of the project. Developers considered it reasonable to fix bugs in code but with minimal testing, leaving it to systems and integration tests to find them, even if it compromised those activities. Consequently, later stages of testing found errors that could have been removed much earlier had the QMS remained in operation.

Here are two examples. A router interface specification was written by an analyst, not reviewed with users, and not even placed under control of the project repository. It was given to developers who wrote the interface code and the analyst signed off their work. When the software reached integration/user acceptance testing, it failed immediately with a simple and obvious error that caused every transaction to fail. The users were unimpressed. A cursory inspection found more fatal errors in the specification.

The second example is where bugs were fixed in a router interface. The fix was tested and declared OK, which it was. However, when the developers declared the interface ready for acceptance testing they had not tested that the router was configured to the trading platform as opposed to their development environment. The router failed to pick up all transactions during an acceptance test run and took that external system out of testing for over a week. When asked about this, the developers did not consider it part of their quality responsibility to test whether the configuration was set correctly; this was for the testers to do.

In summary we had a project where individuals applied their own ideas of quality control. Some ideas were good, many were not. This created a lot of uncertainty and unpredictability. We were not in the repeatable environment of Capability Maturity Model (CMM) level 2, let alone the confident environment of knowing how to tailor our processes to new demands, CMM level 3. It felt like CMM level 1; many avoidable problems appeared through poor prevention and big gaps in the QMS, accompanied with the recriminations and closing of ranks that destroy team spirit.

16.5 What if D = A + B + C?

Now imagine one project, D, where all three issues combine, since this was the reality. We need to get the picture of how they interrelate.

The agile part felt like a project within a project. Despite the issues mentioned earlier there was good visibility of what was happening. The development work was generally successful within the sprints, as shown by low programming and design error rates found in later stages of testing. JUnit was used with considerable refactoring and code/unit testing. (As an aside, some of the development stories took significantly longer than expected and we suspect this was because the refactoring element was significantly underestimated.) Agile worked well from a verification viewpoint. Developers were "building the software correctly." This part felt under control.

In contrast the rest of the project felt less and less under control as time progressed. Errors and faults injected early into the project were surfacing during late stages of test execution. User acceptance testing and integration-in-the-large testing were combined. The idea was that as individual interfaces were released from a Sprint cycle they were put into user/integration test immediately. The lack of user involvement in the sprints led to simple yet high-impact defects getting through to test execution. Test runs had to be repeated many times but they only gave a slow increase in software reliability. In this respect the project did not work well from a validation viewpoint. It was not good at "building the correct software."

The critical issue was the lack of risk management. There was no risk register, let alone a process for populating it and identifying risk mitigation actions. Without a proper understanding of business, project, and product risks, how do you decide the appropriate techniques to manage, plan, develop, and test a system? How do you apply a QMS? How do you know if agile will work for you, and if so, which agile? Should it be an ultralight software factory run by Scrum or a heavy-duty project following ICONIX? Or should it be a combination of agile and traditional techniques?

What was not well understood was how Scrum would mitigate risks in this project, and areas where it would not. It reinforces the received wisdom that without a risk analysis your project will adopt a fatalistic approach. The North American saying is, "This project is like a log floating down a river with a thousand ants on it, and each of them thinks they're steering it."

What could have been the solution? In another institution the internal and external development parts of a new trading system were treated as two separate projects. Internal development was run as an incremental project. Instead of stories we had many use cases, but with increments measured in weeks and daily meetings it was not that different from Scrum. We developed burndown charts for testing, showing the velocity at which we could test and close bug fixes. An experienced bond trader was assigned to the team to act as a user, keeping the user view close to the developers and to act as an oracle for the testers. The external integration was managed separately with different business groups providing the testers to specify and run the tests once the trading platform had been delivered. The system went live on its planned deadline. But then, this project had a risk register, as did individual groups such as the testers.

16.6 Conclusions

Some conclusions were drawn in the individual sections but here I will cover the bigger picture. This case study provides an example of agile/Scrum misapplied. Agile is a solution to a problem; unless you understand the problem, *your* problem, you will make mistakes.

In this example the project needed revitalizing and agile was chosen to bring focus and momentum, which it did. However, in making the transition, no risk analysis was performed to understand what elements agile would *not* address. As we have seen, it did not address the larger integration issues, areas of product complexity, and the application of quality controls.

Agile/Scrum provided a good software production line but, without quality control on the specifications (reviews) feeding the "goods inwards" side, the quality of the "goods outwards" (software) would be in question from a validation perspective. One obvious problem was that end users did not perform the sprint QA/sign-off, this being done by the analysts who wrote the specifications. To my mind this was a fundamental error, because a major aim of agile is to involve users as soon as possible in the validation testing.

From an integration and user test perspective the project was highly reactive; there was little chance of following a test plan with any degree of confidence. Too many (unidentified) risks turned into reality, and too many principles had been broken.

Many problems in information and communication technology are wicked problems; that is, they cannot be solved by some linear problem-solving process. I would suggest that making a transition to agile from a traditional project background is one of them.

As food for further thought I leave you the four main characteristics of a wicked problem:

- ▶ First, a wicked problem contains many factors that all need to be considered. Overlook some and stakeholders will lose out, and you will end up with a solution that is not sustainable without much cost. In short, do not oversimplify the problem.
- ▶ Second, there is no standard solution to a wicked problem. Your situation is unique and you need to tailor the solution to it. Organizations often have their own culture of project and quality management that has grown over a period of time. If you are shifting to agile you need a solution that fits with your culture.
- ▶ Third, there is no perfect solution to a wicked problem; there will be trade-offs. The question is, how do you know how to compromise? Clearly you need to have addressed the first two points, understanding the factors and your take on the problems, to identify good compromises.
- ▶ Fourth, the problem changes as your understanding increases. The more you get into solving the problem the more you realize that what you thought were problems are only symptoms. This requires an iterative approach; that is, you must reassess the application of agile frequently and be prepared to amend your approach.

17 Test-Infecting a Development Team

David Evans, Director of Methodology at SQS

SYNOPSIS

A software quality services company had a good idea for a software product; they assembled a team of developers to build it and instructed them to run it as an agile project. Competent and experienced, but new to agile and skeptical of what seemed like radical new processes, the developers learned from first-hand experience that tests are highly valuable information sources, and that thinking about development from a test-first perspective leads to highly efficient, bug-free software design. They became "test-infected" – a condition where developers are so enthused about test-driven development that they refuse to return to their "bad old ways" of writing software without tests.

17.1 Introduction

My name is David Evans. I am the Director of Methodology at SQS, a pure-play testing and software quality consultancy. I am also the chief Agile Testing Evangelist in the company.

I have been in the software development and testing business for twenty years, first as a mainframe developer and tester, later moving to object-oriented C++ windows development and then .NET web development. In 2000 I joined Cresta, a testing consultancy, where I specialized in test automation, test methodology, and software quality practices. Cresta was later acquired by SQS.

In 2002 while carrying out a test strategy assignment for a global pharmaceutical company, I came across Extreme Programming (XP), which was being trialled by some of their development teams, and had to factor this into their enterprise-wide test strategy. I was fascinated by the agile process and impressed by the levels of quality and customer satisfaction these teams achieved.

When I was given responsibility for creating a software product based on testing metrics from Cresta's testing methodology, I knew the project needed to be agile. We were able to enlist a team of highly talented .NET developers, but none of them had worked in an agile project before.

17.2   Overview of the Testing Challenge

How to get developers to willingly spend roughly half their time testing, and get the customer to see the economic benefit of this!

The Project

Cresta was an innovative company of testers. Their core business was testing and test consulting, not software development, although many of Cresta's consultants were technical test automation specialists and some were ex-developers. The decision makers in the company were well aware of the need to develop tools to support the business and to improve the quality of project delivery. Rather than outsource this work, it made sense to do it internally, as it made use of the technical skills in the company and provided an excellent internal "laboratory" for research and innovation in software quality techniques. In 2004 they initiated a project to build a quality metrics dashboard, which would be called TestStrategist.

Developers and Customer

I was to be the lead software designer, but I was also doing programming, so it was important to have a *customer* (in the XP sense) from the business, someone who was ultimately going to be responsible for helping teams use the product and to sell it to clients. This was to be Edgar, a director and founding member of Cresta. "Pure" XP recommends a full-time customer in the team, but because the system we were building was based on an existing process that I had designed, a lot of the business knowledge was already in the team, and we relied on our customer mostly to take decisions regarding priority, so we could live with the fact that Edgar was not full-time on the team.

We also needed a good technical guy who could handle our hardware and network issues, as well as cut code – Scott was someone I knew and trusted and, although he was new to the agile way, I felt confident he would pick it up. As well as being a fine developer, he was a naturally organized team member who did the important job of setting up our team collaboration site and tooling to enable remote working.

For our main development resource we took on Monique, an external developer whose coding skill was known to us from previous dealings. When we interviewed Monique prior to joining the project we described the process we were intending to use and mentioned XP practices such as close customer collaboration, test-driven development, collective code ownership, and pair programming. She was clearly skeptical and showed classic developer defensiveness, especially at the idea of making "her" code so open to the scrutiny of others. She went home and told her husband of the extremely strange development practices that had been suggested to her, adding that we acted like we were asking her to join some sort of cult. Fortunately for us, she needed the work, and she agreed to join the team.

Testers?

Initially, it was just the three of us, all developers, as full-time members of the team. We did not assign any full-time testers since, as a testing company, we knew there would be an ample supply of those as we needed them. The strategy was to rotate test consultants through the team on a "tour of duty" to give them experience of testing in an agile environment and avoid losing a "billable" resource for the whole duration of the project. Before we could do that we needed to bed down our own process and that meant taking responsibility for all testing ourselves. This, after all, was not in any way inconsistent with accepted XP theory, which says that developers and customer are jointly responsible for testing. (The reality of most agile projects of nontrivial size is that dedicated testers add great value, since neither the developers nor the customer have sufficient bandwidth or experience to include all testing.)

Good testing intentions are not enough, and our challenge was to ensure we could "drink our own champagne" and show that we were a quality-oriented development team, as dedicated to testing as we were to development. We were well aware of the risk to the company's reputation of releasing a product that was not of the highest standard of quality. We also had to get to grips with the new concept of test-driven development (TDD). This is a challenge for developers who might not think that testing – especially at the levels required by TDD – is a productive use of their time. It is also a challenge for management, who may take the naive view that development time on all tasks is going to double.

We were all climbing a new hill and starting from the bottom. What we had on our side is that we worked well as a team: there was mutual respect from the outset and an eagerness to learn from each other's experience.

17.3 Definition of an Agile Testing Process plus Test Automation

Unit testing with NUnit, acceptance testing with FIT & Fitnesse, continuous integration, and exploratory manual testing.

Starting with Simplicity

As the team was new to XP (and to an extent still skeptical about it) we did not attempt to take on all aspects of the method at once. Certain things made sense from a business perspective and we concentrated on those first:

▶ We knew that, although we had a reasonably good idea of the fundamentals of what the dashboard application needed to do, the detailed requirements would evolve over time.

▶ We needed to demonstrate working software to our customer as quickly as possible.

▶ We needed to do the *simplest thing that could possibly work*. Two-week iterations, with a focus on running tested software at the end of every iteration, ensured we followed the principle of simple design.

The first lesson we learned as a team was that every requirement can be cut down to something simpler, until you have distilled the essential minimal "core" accompanied by "layers" that improve one or more aspects of that core functionality. This realization gives you a lot of confidence to meet deadlines, which is a critical success factor for iterative development.

Test-Driven Development: Unit Testing

Perhaps the most important practice that we embraced from the beginning was TDD. Unit testing is something that developers will avoid if they perceive it to slow them down, or if it forces them to switch context from their programming routine. Fortunately, the XP community has created xUnit, a remarkable family of open-source unit testing tools, each implemented in languages that developers use for programming. As we were coding in C#.NET, we used NUnit. It is a very elegant tool that makes unit test creation, management, and execution simple and highly effective.

Armed with the right unit testing tool, we adopted the test-driven approach from the outset. This proved to be an important success factor for us. Writing a unit test in order to "shape" the next small element of code can seem counterintuitive at first, but for us it quickly became a very natural and satisfying way to work. This was reinforced by the XP practices of *collective code ownership* and *pair programming*, so that, although the practice was new to us, all members of the team worked consistently and were able to support each other. The very high code coverage this gave us, combined with the very fast feedback regarding unexpected side effects and regression errors, became an addictive element of our process.

Enter the Build Captain

Once we had unit-level TDD ingrained in our development process, and a very large suite of tests, we began to observe and reflect upon our tests and the maturity of our technique. We read articles about good unit testing practices and patterns. We considered how we could get our slower tests to run faster. We learned about mock objects and specialist frameworks for testing ASP pages.

This period coincided with a new member joining our team. Owen was a test consultant who was looking for a change from what he was doing. We knew he was bright and capable, and certainly didn't want to risk losing him from the company, so we were glad to welcome him to the team. He was appointed originally as our first dedicated tester, although it was clear he had the technical ability to be doing development. I was interested in having Owen help us lift our testing process to a new level – not by being a manual tester to supplement our automated tests, but by implementing processes that helped us as a team to do more and better testing. He became our Build Captain.

Continuous Integration

Owen started by implementing continuous integration (CI). Our "development episode" process to date had been to get the latest code (including unit test code) from the source repository, build the application locally, run all unit tests, then do TDD for a task or feature, and run all unit tests again locally before checking in the code. This was fine up to a point, but didn't protect us against occasional integration errors caused when simultaneous developer changes were incompatible with each other.

Owen set up a build server and installed the continuous integration tool [56]. He configured it to monitor our source code repository, so that after a ten-minute "quiet period" after any check-in, an automatic task would get all the code, increment the build number (this was something we baked into the app), perform a clean build of the whole application, then run all the unit tests. If the software failed to build or any unit tests failed, the build was marked as broken.

This was visible on the CI tool dashboard, and an automatic email would be sent to the developer responsible for that check-in. A little icon in every developer's PC system tray turned from green to red. For added effect, the build server would announce its dissatisfaction to the whole open-plan office with a loud Homer Simpson "D'oh!!" As if that wasn't enough, Owen also rigged up a pair of green and red lava lamps to the server, which duly switched on the appropriate lamp according to the good or bad state of the latest build. (For the benefit of the remote workers in the team, and anyone else in the company, a regular grab from a web-cam pointing at the lamps was put on our team collaboration web page.) All this created a highly visible sense of quality and a team culture of putting quality as our top priority.

Green Bar Addiction

In agile development and testing, you are theoretically working through a list of tasks in priority order. Therefore, the new feature you are working on now is logically less important than fixing the defects in what has already been built. For our team, a "broken build" became a stop-what-you-are-doing-and-fix-it situation. We were happy to explain the lava lamps to any curious passerby. But we didn't want to do that when the big red one was bubbling away. Whatever else needed to be done, fixing the build came first, and even though the build server pointed the finger at the last check-in, it was in the whole team's interest to pitch in to get it fixed. Once the green lamp was glowing again, we could proceed with confidence in the knowledge that order had been restored.

This aspect of TDD is something of a revelation, even to a seasoned tester and developer: the only acceptable pass rate for unit tests is 100% – this is the only way to get the "green bar" in the unit testing framework. This criterion is absolutely necessary for getting a developer to accept responsibility for a broken build. Since all the tests were passing before you checked in your code, your code must be the cause of any failures – no matter how much you believe your change had "nothing to do with it," the tests are now failing. If a test suite already has failures in it, a developer would most likely dismiss any new failures as being unrelated to their code or caused by a flaky and unreliable test suite.

Getting FIT: Acceptance-Test-Driven Development

At this stage we were addicted to testing, proud of our healthily growing tree of tests and feeling satisfied to see the "green bar" at the end of every small development episode. However, we now had so many unit tests that we wondered if we were suffering from the syndrome of treating everything as a nail because we only had a hammer. With a smooth CI process in place, we knew we could afford to ramp up our testing further and introduce new tools for specific situations without it slowing us down.

I had been interested for some time in FIT, the open-source Framework for Integrated Testing, having heard it mentioned on various occasions and liking what I saw when I investigated it on the web. Owen, our dedicated tester, soon had us kitted up with a FIT server, and Fitnesse, the custom wiki wrapper for FIT.

The "arrival" of FIT allowed us to reassess the way we viewed TDD. FIT is essentially a collaborative test tool, designed to allow a customer to express acceptance tests in tabular format (alongside HTML documentation of the features to be tested), which the development team subsequently automates with simple code "fixtures" to connect the test data to the system under test.

We changed our process for writing stories so that, instead of documenting them as Word files stored on a server, we created new stories as wiki pages on Fitnesse. The beauty of this is that the story specifications can include the functional acceptance tests embedded in the descriptive documentation. It was easy for Edgar, our customer, to change details of stories and to select and prioritize our solution ideas. With the ability not only to write tests in the wiki but also to execute them and see the results, we were doing TDD at an acceptance test level. This is an important difference from unit-level TDD. For the first time, Edgar had true visibility and access into the details of the tests that prove the behavior of each feature. He did not have to just trust our unit testing, nor did he have to wait to try out features running through the GUI – he could open the relevant wiki page in his web browser, check the tests for completeness and accuracy, create new cases if necessary, and with a click of a button see the test data light up in green if everything was passing correctly. "I'm loving FIT" was the way he summed it up.

Exploratory Testing

As the project matured we rotated a number of testers from the consultancy through the project. One such tester, John, stood out as one who seemed to fit very naturally into an agile project. He was keen, he was confident, and he had no problem with telling developers what he felt they needed to know about the quality of the application. He also tuned in very quickly to where he could add value. He was surrounded by automated tests, but he saw developers being "too busy" to do the kind of exploratory testing that a professional tester is so good at. He put the application through its paces as a skeptical user would, creating interesting scenarios and unusual (but not unrealistic) usage sequences. He considered usability, noting how many mouse-clicks it took to perform common operations. He measured performance. He changed browsers and browser settings, and tried the application through a mobile phone. He checked how good our graphics looked at different screen resolutions.

Importantly, John brought lists of his observations, bugs, and anomalies to our planning meetings for triage. That way, the developers could comment on likely solutions and estimate how long it would take to address each issue. Edgar was then able to balance the cost and benefit of these against other features he wanted to add to the product functionality.

17.4 Results of the Agile Approach

Developers became great advocates of testing and helped to advance the state of test automation in a testing services company. We observed extremely low rates of field defects. The product was sold to many blue-chip companies and won an Innovation award.

Product Success

The first version of TestStrategist was brought to market after six months of development, and the first sale made soon afterwards to a large multinational company. We settled into a regular rhythm of bringing out a new release every three months. Only once did we have to delay a release, by one week. It was surprising how disappointed we were as a team over this "slip" – a sign of how proudly we regarded our record of delivering working software on time.

Edgar, as our internal customer, had the excellent idea of strengthening this concept by establishing a Client Advisory Board, where one key user representative from each of our clients could attend a quarterly planning meeting. This was partly a customer relationship exercise, but it was also a genuine opportunity for our clients to influence the ongoing design and development of the product, as well as get a preview of the features in each new release. This regular obligation to "face the buyers" lent a great sense of importance to each release and certainly heightened the team's commitment to quality and testing.

The product continued to enjoy success in the market and sold at a healthy price to big-name companies, including four in the U.K. FTSE top 10. It was also being used internally as a delivery dashboard on several of our company's test consultancy engagements. In 2005 the product won the *Information Age* award for "Most Effective Use of IT in Professional Services."

Test Infected

The proof of the success of the process was that we were delivering valuable software to paying customers and satisfying their new requirements regularly. Customer satisfaction was high and we had very low rates of field defects.

However, the most remarkable sign of agile success was how we worked as a team and how it changed our view of what was important in software development. As a development team, we had made a genuine transition where we no longer thought of testing as someone else's job. It was part of how *we* created good software.

We treated our growing test suites as genuine assets that returned real value on our investment. They served as both a guidance system during development and a reassuring safety net during refactoring. Quality was no longer optional, and the "cost" of writing tests was an essential element that was factored into the estimate to develop each feature.

We didn't think about writing code without writing unit tests first. We found TDD not only a natural way to develop, but also a safe way to develop. It was likened to the habit of putting on a seat-belt before driving: once you've formed that habit, it feels unsafe not to do it. We were test-infected, to borrow Erich Gamma's phrase [63].

Converting Unbelievers

Not only that, we were developers surrounded by a company of testers, and we wanted to be the advocates of this new age of collaboration-for-quality. We were convinced that the more developers learned about testing, and the more testers learned about development (especially the tools and processes that support developer testing), the better the software industry would become.

Monique, who had at first been the most vociferous skeptic, became a proud ambassador of agile and TDD. From joking to her husband that she was joining a cult, she would later be trying to teach him (and anyone else who would listen) the virtues of the agile way of working. Owen – who had cycled his roles through tester, Build Captain, UI designer, and developer – showed that his abilities and the opportunities offered by an agile project were not just a natural fit, but a virtuous cycle of reinforcement. It seemed that the more he learned, the more opportunities arose for us to improve, and the better and more agile we became as a team.

Parting

All true agile projects blur the line between development and maintenance – releasing live software early and following it with regular incremental feature releases. Rather than having a fixed project end date, the product owners can "call time" on the project when the expected returns to be gained from further development do not exceed the development team cost.

While it is one thing to draw the line on product development economics, it is more difficult to account for the value that accrues in a high-performing team. Over and above turning out software, our team was adding value to the company in the form of new skills, innovative ideas, advanced research, high morale, and leading-edge development and testing techniques.

When the time finally came for the management to take the decision to wind down the project and disband the team, the sense of loss ran deep. The team had been through a great deal and had bonded closely. What should have been a fond and celebratory farewell to the project instead felt like an unceremonious and rather sudden breakup, where cold economics had taken priority over human concerns, without any consideration for how the investment made in the team could be retained.

17.5 Lessons Learned

Be pragmatic and business focussed. Recognize and respect what is important.

The most surprising results of this experience were how we overcame the initial skepticism of new processes, converted the unbelievers, opened their minds to the benefits of testing, and made them hungry for other ways to get quality information that is timely, relevant, self-evident, and helpful.

For other teams embarking on this journey, these are the main lessons that we would share.

- ▶ *It's OK to be agile about your agile adoption.* You don't have to take on all the practices at once. Starting with the fundamentals (short iterations, simple design) will get your team into a steady rhythm, and supporting practices will follow naturally. Understand and prioritize other practices, then fold them into your process gradually. However, do keep the bigger picture in view: read books to learn how the method works holistically and how the individual practices support each other. Don't expect being "half-agile" to work in the long run.

- ▶ *Start from a position of trust.* If most of the team are new to agile development and testing, ensure that the team members who are experienced also have the people skills to understand the challenges and concerns the others will face, and the patience to help them come up to speed. If the whole team is new to agile, create an atmosphere of mutual respect and safety by getting some kind of team-bonding activity scheduled as soon as possible. Train the team together. Make it clear to all that having doubts and asking "stupid" questions is OK. In the long run this is much better than allowing people to carry on with misconceptions. In all cases, allow extra time for pairing and agile retrospectives to enable the team to "own" their process and feel comfortable with all aspects of it.

- ▶ *Respect the testers.* Ensure testers are treated as equal members of the team, and remove any barriers that hinder fast and easy communication between customer, testers, and developers.

- ▶ *Respect the tests.* Do not get into a mindset of "the code is the concern of the development team, the tests are the concern of the test team." There is only one team. That team creates tested code. Tests and code are of equal value and both are the concerns of the whole team.

- ▶ *Respect the build.* Use continuous integration and other automated testing processes to your advantage and have them provide fast feedback about code quality, either daily or on every check-in. But don't squander the value of that information by failing to respond as quickly as it comes. A "broken" build, including any failing test that previously passed, should always be the top priority for the team to fix.

▶ *Respect the team.* The people involved in any agile project are likely to work more closely than in nonagile projects. Remove impediments that prevent them from working well together. Encourage them to run their own retrospectives to improve their own practices. Be supportive of each other when occasionally life gets in the way. Don't mess with a team that is already working well together – the economics of headcount rarely stand up against the power of good teamwork.

Agile Success Through Test Automation:
An eXtreme Approach

Jon Tilt, Chief Test Architect, IBM

SYNOPSIS

"Automation, Automation, Automation" was the battle cry of our leaders as we embarked on our first "iterative" mission with a large team of twenty testers; within our agile iterative test approach, we have invested heavily in test automation, unit test, and continual integration.

After a number of years of operating this strategy, we had reached a point where the regression test took up to ten days to run through (35,000 tests), and we had to create an approach we called "laser-guided testing" to pinpoint the best set of tests to run each build. We can now run a complete targeted regression in less than a day!

We saw many benefits of our agile automated approach, but there are costs and pitfalls that are worth considering ahead of time.

18.1 Introduction

My name is Jon Tilt; I have been involved in software development for twenty-five years and specifically in software testing since 1996. I started testing in the functional test team of MQSeries, a large middleware product. Since then I have progressed through test management, test project lead, and test architect roles. I currently work for IBM's Software Group under the WebSphere brand and am the Chief Test Architect across a number of Enterprise Service Bus (ESB) products that generate in excess of one billion dollars of revenue each year. The products we deliver are primarily enterprise middleware offerings (application servers, messaging backbones, etc.) that many major Fortune 500 companies bet their businesses on.

This case study focuses on a project that I worked on that started about five years ago. It involved the delivery of a new ESB component using an iterative development approach; this was the first time our team had tried this method. Our team's focus was automation, automation, automation, from developer test through to system test, with strong leadership support and team buy-in to achieve this.

This case study focuses on the challenges of getting the project started and how we almost became victims of our own success. After several years of this strategy we had reached a point where the regression test took up to ten days to run through our 35,000 tests. In short, we had reached a point where we had too much testing!

Fortunately, our story ends happily, as we "innovated" our way out of automation overload. We created an approach we called "laser-guided testing" to pinpoint the best set of tests to run against each build. We can now run a complete targeted regression test in less than a day.

18.2 Overview of the Testing Challenge

We had been commissioned to develop a new component, written in Java, as part of a much larger middleware product. The component approached two million lines of code and had a delivery team of one hundred software engineers. The component is delivered as part of a Java Enterprise Edition Application server.

Our primary challenge was to fully integrate testing into the psyche of the whole delivery team. Our guiding principle was that "Everyone owns the quality of the product."

We needed to be able to continuously verify the product, finding defects as early in the process as we possibly could. By focusing on the quality of our drivers we strove to make later phases of testing more effective and efficient.

In order for this strategy to be effective we needed to front-load our testing as much as possible.

We also had to ensure the software performed correctly on a number of different platforms (Mainframe, Intel, UNIX, zOS, Windows, AIX, Solaris, HP-UX, Linux, IBM i series).

18.3 Definition of an Agile Testing Process

The development process introduced time-boxed iterations and full automation to our team for the first time. The key points include the following:

- *Time-boxed iterations*
  - ▷ Each iteration had to deliver "testable entities;" content was agreed jointly between developers and testers.
  - ▷ Continuous integration (at least twice-daily builds).
- *Test automation* included
  - ▷ clear direction from leadership team (good communications about what to test and when to test it);
  - ▷ dedicated automation infrastructure resource – people and hardware; and
  - ▷ developer testing, incorporating automated unit test, run as part of the build process; "stop the line culture" for unit test failures; rivalry between teams to have best code coverage of unit tests; charts to demonstrate results shown in department meetings; and function testing.
- Focus on end-to-end test automation (not just the execution phase).

▶ Over time, the number of tests increased to a point where a regression run took ten days!

  ▷ System test was largely manual for "consumability."

  ▷ Humans tend to understand variations better than machines.

  ▷ User-like tests (documentation, GUI).

  ▷ Laser-guided testing – invented to reduce the burden of our regression suite (laser guided testing is explained in detail in the next section).

The test automation was separated into two parts, which I will call *developer testing* and *functional testing*.

Developer Testing

Developer testing was a big cultural change for our team. We put a huge amount of emphasis on finding defects as early in the process as possible, when they are the cheapest to fix. Under the banner of developer testing, I include the build process itself (compiling and merging the whole product twice a day), automated unit tests, and, finally, a build verification test (BVT) that was run against each driver to verify basic functionality.

For the first time we actually measured the unit test code coverage using the open-source tool EMMA [69]. This was a real revelation, as we now had evidence of the rigour of each developer's testing. At first we exposed a number of groups who claimed they were thoroughly unit testing, but in reality had not added the tests to the automation. With leadership support this was quickly rectified. At each end-of-iteration department meeting, we displayed the coverage figures for each subcomponent team. At first this was used as a stick, but very quickly it became a carrot as teams openly competed with each other to achieve the highest figures.

Functional Testing

When we built the test team, we made sure that from the start we had an experienced automation specialist who was responsible for creating the infrastructure for running all our tests. We defined automation from the beginning to mean "end-to-end" automation. That meant that from a single button push, the infrastructure had to be capable of installing a new driver, configuring the environment as required, running the appropriate tests, evaluating the outcomes, and storing the results in a database. Too often I see teams interpreting automation to mean automate the execution step. While this has some benefit, the real costs of testing tend to come in the setup – especially in a multiplatform, multimachine environment such as our own.

Once we had the infrastructure in place it was up to the testers to write the material. We instigated a policy that a test was not deemed complete until it had run inside the infrastructure. This did lead to some heated debates with the project team, who of course wanted to see test progress. However, in the long run it proved to be the most effective way to ensure everything was correctly automated.

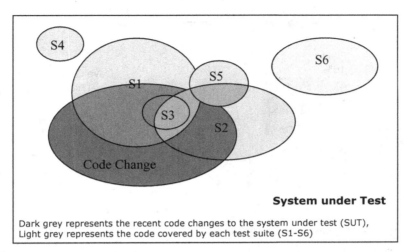

System under Test

Dark grey represents the recent code changes to the system under test (SUT),
Light grey represents the code covered by each test suite (S1-S6)

18.1   The principles of laser-guided testing.

With a team of up to twenty testers we managed to accumulate vast numbers of tests over the course of several releases. While this mass of collateral was a real benefit to the project, it was beginning to take on a life of its own as it got to the stage where a complete regression run was taking in excess of ten days to complete. The overhead of feeding the automation beast was now becoming a considerable burden to the team.

This is when test specialist Ian Holden and test manager Dave Dalton devised the concept of *cumulative test analysis* – a way of identifying the most effective tests to run, based on information about how they have run in the past, what system code they cover, and what has changed in the last product build (see Ian and Dave's paper describing the process [70]).

Since this was going to be a radical new approach to the way we did our testing, we needed to sell the concept to our leadership team. The first step was to rename "cumulative test analysis" to "laser-guided testing" or just "targeted testing," which I felt conveyed better the exciting approach to what we wanted to achieve.

At its core, targeted testing is very simple. You need two pieces of information: first, a map of what product code each test covers, and second, you need to know what code has changed in the product since you last tested it. If you have this information then it is possible to select the most effective tests to run against a particular product driver.

Figure 18.1 provides a simplified graphical overview of the principles of laser-guided testing.

In this example we can use targeting to select and prioritize the suites that need to run:

▶ S1 and S2 must run.
▶ S3 and S5 may add a small amount of value.
▶ S4 and S6 need not be run as they add no value to this change.

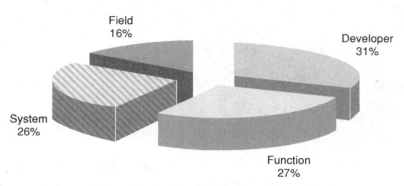

Where defects are found

18.2 Breakdown of defects found by testing phase.

I have deliberately simplified how targeting works, and when I do this everyone points out that there may be changes elsewhere in the product that have an impact on a piece of code that hasn't actually changed. This is of course true and has been taken into account in the targeting algorithms; however, those details would take another chapter at least and I won't go into them here.

18.4 Results of the Agile Approach

Overall our approach to agile testing has been very successful. Figure 18.2 shows the breakdown for who finds defects during the product life cycle. (When these figures were gathered, the component had been out in the field for over a year.)

Nearly a third of all defects discovered are found by developer testing (compile, unit test, and BVT), which is when they are cheapest to resolve. Adding in the defects found by our functional test automation brings the percentage of defects found by automation to well over 50%.

After our first product release, I wanted to work out how successful our automated unit test strategy had been, so I did an analysis of the defects found by the test team and compared them to the code coverage figures of each of our subcomponent unit tests. The results are summarized in Figure 18.3.

I believe this graph really shows the effectiveness of unit testing; the subcomponents that had the lowest automated unit test coverage had the highest number of defects found by the test team, and the subcomponents with the highest code coverage had the lowest number of defects.[1]

The total automation of our functional testing has also proved very successful as we now have an excellent regression capability, despite its initial high cost and the fear at one stage that it was going to devour all our resources.

---

[1] There are some anomalies in between the two extremes and these would need more detailed investigation. There may also be some correlation between the complexity of the subcomponent and the number of defects, but this is another area for future investigation.

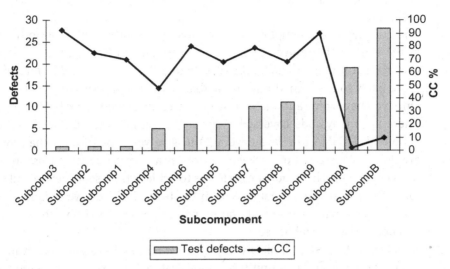

18.3 Analysis of defects found by test team versus code coverage.

The introduction of laser-guided testing meant we were able to reduce our team of regression testers (the team that was responsible for preparing the hardware, kicking off tests, and chasing test failures) by four people and move them into front-line testing. We were also able to reduce the cycle time of a complete regression run from ten days to only one day. The important thing to understand here is that, while we no longer run the entire regression suite, we believe what we do run is able to assess the quality of the build to the same extent but in a dramatically reduced timeframe.

18.5 Lessons Learned

Potential adopters of such approaches should not be overawed; this isn't rocket science. Here are some simple guiding principles that we identified:

- ► The earlier we find a problem, the less it costs to fix it.
- ► Successful agile quality is *not* a technology issue, but a cultural one:
  - ▷ Everyone in the team is responsible for the quality of our component.
  - ▷ Define the automation vision early and stick with it.
- ► Start your automation with something simple and build on it.
- ► Remember that over the course of time your automation will grow; plan for this and don't let it consume you.
- ► When starting out, be very clear on why you are embracing automation and early testing. The cost factor is the primary driver and helps get buy-in across the whole team.

▶ We spent a lot of time reiterating to the delivery team that everyone was responsible for the component quality and that we could achieve high quality through automation.

▶ There is always the temptation to architect yet another automation framework at the start of the project. Don't! Look around at the simple tools that already exist (like JUnit) and build on them as required. Developers and testers are much more likely to use something simple that is quick and easy to use.

▶ Once you have some automated tests in place, start measuring their effectiveness. There are many code coverage tools in the market, but start with something simple like EMMA (for Java coverage) to give you a picture of what your tests are doing. We started our measurements at a very crude level (just measuring class coverage). This made it easy for us to achieve high scores early and psychologically helped gain acceptance from the team. Later on we switched to more fine-grained analysis (method and branch coverage) but only after the process had become well established.

▶ All our figures were graphically displayed for all to see – a great motivator!

▶ We generated over 7,000 unit tests alone that ran as part of every build.

▶ Do remember – code coverage itself does not improve product quality, *actions based on its results can!*

▶ When your automation is running regularly and growing with each iteration, remember to keep an eye on its size and how long it takes to run. While the perception is always that lots of tests mean lots of good testing, beware of the automation beast and how it will end up consuming all the time and resource you have.

▶ We have had great success with our laser-guided targeting of tests, but it is also worth considering regular refactoring of your test suites. This way you can purge anything that is not adding value and help to keep your regression capability lean and agile.

19 Talking, Saying, and Listening: Communication in Agile Teams

Isabel Evans, Principal Consultant, Testing Solutions Group

SYNOPSIS

This chapter describes techniques to improve the interactions between people during agile projects.

The quality of communication is vital for agile projects; agile methods rely on close and collaborative working, so the relationships between team members strongly affect success. Agile methods emphasize people but they do include process; the reaction to and success of the processes depends on the people. We can use special techniques to enhance the communication between people, thus enabling our agile processes to be effective and efficient.

This case study provides examples of problems with communication that I have observed in a number of agile projects and some useful and practical techniques that can be used to address and overcome these communications issues.

19.1 Introduction

My name is Isabel Evans. I'm a principal consultant at Testing Solutions Group Ltd and I have more than twenty years' experience in the IT industry, mainly in quality management, testing, training, and documentation. During that time I have worked as a practitioner and a consultant with clients in many sectors, including financial, communications, transport, and software providers.

I've been a member of various working parties and groups to contribute to improvement in software quality and testing, and my book *Achieving Software Quality Through Teamwork* was published by Artech in June 2004. I'm interested in people and processes, how they interact, and how those interactions affect the success of projects and businesses. Agile methods emphasize people but they include process; the reaction to and success of the processes depend on the people.

In this chapter, I want to think about techniques we can use to enhance the communication between people to enable our agile processes to be effective and efficient. This is not a specific case study dealing with one customer or project but is distilled from a number of such engagements I have worked on and from which I have documented examples of issues with communication that affect agile testing.

19.2 Talkin' a Lot . . . Communication Problems in Agile Testing

Good communication is essential for success in any project, whether that is written or verbal communication. IT is about information, from the conception of the initial project through to the closedown and decommissioning of the system.

The means and media of communication are different in traditional and agile projects. In traditional projects, the key communication methods and media are written or electronic documents and meetings. The communications can be slow, bureaucratic, and hierarchical in nature, although that is not always the case. For many traditional projects, hierarchical power structures supported by words on paper define "the truth." Unfortunately, much of the real truth about the project may remain hidden in people's heads; the hierarchy may inhibit communication, and documents have gaps which are filled by people's assumptions.

One reason for adopting an agile approach to projects is to speed up successful delivery into production, and this may be done by reducing hierarchy, reducing documentation, and reducing meetings. Communication is intended to be direct, honest, speedy, productive, and egalitarian. The agile project is intended to overcome communication problems. In agile projects, a typical approach might include reduced, less-formal documentation with speedy meetings and verbal decisions.

Key words for successful agile projects are team work, collaboration, communication, trust, and respect. But these qualities need to be worked for; just putting a group of people together does not make them a team. So let's start by looking at some ways that communication may go wrong.

Some People Just Prefer a More Formal Style

It might be that people have misunderstood or don't trust the agile methods; they may not realize that the agile approaches are not just an ad hoc approach but require the discipline of keeping one's teammates informed. If a team or team member is not used to working this way or if a manager is not sure how to manage an agile team, then the discipline of information exchange may be missed. People who prefer to communicate by email, written report, or formal presentation may be uncomfortable with the direct interpersonal interactions required; they may be shy, or lack confidence, or prefer to put their thoughts in writing in order to review them more easily before showing them to others. Additionally, some people want to make a statement of fact or a decision once only – they want to issue their decision (email, report) and that's it – job done! If someone feels forced to take part in agile processes against their will or disagrees about how to organize the team, then they may opt out from the collaborative process.

Some People Are Good at Talking but Not So Good at Listening

Those of us who generate ideas are often noisy and talkative, and we can dominate meetings. But sometimes we forget to listen to our quieter colleagues. We are only communicating in one direction, and our teammates cannot get us to listen. By sheer will power we move the meeting to the conclusion we want. But supposing it is the wrong conclusion? Or supposing there is more than one noisy person in the room and we don't agree with each other? Discussions may degenerate to an inconclusive argument, and the rest of the team members mentally pack their bags and leave. They no longer want to contribute.

Some People Just Don't Get On

If team members do not get on with each other, and there are personality clashes, it may become difficult to collaborate. This can be exacerbated if anyone abuses the collaborative approach – if meetings allow the "loudest voice" always to win, if there is bullying, or people fall into abusive behavior. This can happen if anyone adopts parent–child relationships in the team, as described in Abe Wagner's book *The Transactional Manager* [71]. We think we are exchanging facts, but actually our exchanges become loaded with emotions, and not always constructive ones. We end up telling each other off, or capitulating when we are challenged incorrectly. Wagner suggests that:

> We are all six people rather than just one and that some of these six "inner people" are effective in dealing with others, but some of the "inner people" are not so useful.

The six inner people or ego states Wagner identifies are as follows:

1. The natural child is an effective ego state that acts spontaneously, expresses feelings, and has need for recognition, structure, and stimulation.
2. The adult is an effective ego state that is logical and reasonable; it deals in facts rather than feelings.
3. The nurturing parent is an effective ego state that is firm with others, but also understanding, sensitive, and caring.
4. The critical parent is an ineffective ego state that uses body language, gesture, and tone of voice to "tell others off" perhaps by sarcasm, pointing the finger, or raised voice.
5. The rebellious child is an ineffective ego state that gets angry and stays angry, is very negative, does not listen, and may deliberately forget things or procrastinate.
6. The compliant child is an ineffective ego state that blames itself, uses a soft voice, whines, is very careful and self-protective.

> Communication between the effective ego states is generally useful . . . If we cross into the ineffective ego states, we will argue, whine and blame without communicating or changing anything; in fact we may make things worse [72].

People Use Information as Power

For some people, information is the source of their power. By hiding information, they maintain their power base in the organization. The mistaken belief that they are uniquely able to solve certain problems – perhaps particular system knowledge – means that collaboration will be a threat to them. They may express this by saying that no one else has the knowledge to solve those problems. Or, they may cite loss of confidentiality and security requirements as a reason to withhold information. These may in some circumstances be valid arguments, but they may be red herrings.

Methods of Communication May Be Inappropriate

The number, style, length, and recordkeeping for meetings may not favor collaboration. Recordkeeping may be inadequate or overdetailed; either extreme prevents good information exchange.

Environment Is Not Conducive to Collaboration

The project may not be sited or equipped in a way that fosters good communications and collaborative behavior. For example, if there is no team room or if the team is on a split site, this will reduce face-to-face communication. In *The Mythical Man Month* [73], Fred Brooks pointed out what a short distance away people need to be before they stop communicating well. A colleague has just observed this on a project; the developers and testers were moved to only 100 meters apart in the same open plan office, but they had reverted to communicating only by email. Attempts to run agile projects without co-located teams will require far more effort to maintain communication. Organizations attempting to run projects across split sites, multiple countries, and multiple time zones are setting themselves additional challenges for communication and collaboration. Part of the environment is the equipment available to the team; if there are problems with computer equipment, communications technology, and information storage and retrieval, the project team will not be able to communicate well.

None of these problems are unique to agile teams; the same problems apply to traditional projects. It is just that in traditional projects it might be easier to hide the consequences for longer.

19.3   Something to Say . . . Techniques to Free Communication Logjams

If the problems are the same, so are many of the solutions. The methods I am going to suggest are tried and tested inside and outside IT projects. Because all humans carry taken-for-granted assumptions about the world, it is easy to believe that our communication preferences are the correct ones. We need to understand and empathize with others; they may have different preferences. As the team interacts, it will need to build understanding between the team members to help build shared assumptions and hence trust [74].

Although many taken-for-granted assumptions are shared, there will be differences between cultures, organisations and family/friendship groups. Just because you "always do it that way" it does not mean it is the right way. One of our assumptions can be that others will share our taken for granted assumptions. If we discover that other people have different core beliefs, we are surprised and may dismiss their views as wrong – it is hard to see other people's view.

We may also assume that other people communicate in the same way as we do, that they share our sense of humour, use body language in the same way, and share our preference for written, pictorial or verbal messages. I recently had a discussion with a colleague because we could not understand each other. It turns out that we used two key phrases in opposite ways, both equally correct but meaning the opposite to each other:

- I had used "I think" to mean "I am not sure" but my colleague had used "I think" to mean "I am certain."
- My colleague had used "I feel" to mean "I am not sure" but I had used "I feel" to mean "I am certain."

These communication differences are increased by cultural differences between organisations, and between colleagues from different types of organisation, and from different countries [72].

The following sections review a couple of techniques that I have found valuable in freeing communications logjams, specifically De Bono's Six Hats in a Meeting and cause and solutions analysis with Ishikawa Fishbones.

Technique 1: De Bono's Six Hats in a Meeting

Sometimes collaboration can be held up by conflict – personality clashes, insuperable arguments, and endless, unresolved conflict. We find ourselves always contributing in the same way – pessimistically, optimistically, coldly, or emotionally! And we notice that other people are equally predictable. As a consequence, we find that the meeting dissolves into acrimonious chaos, with people no longer on speaking terms. Can we do anything about this?

Edward de Bono [75] decided that we could, and the Six Thinking Hats was the result. I first came across it as an idea for improving software projects from Jens Pas' EuroSTAR presentation and workshop [76] as a means of introducing emotional intelligence to rationally biased software projects – in other words, allowing fact-based people an opportunity to also express emotional views. The "six hats" encourages people to take different roles at their meeting. It allows them to deal with one problem at a time and to focus on resolving problems. You can refer to the hats in two ways: You can define the thinking process that's required in a given situation, or you can comment on how someone *is* communicating without appearing critical. So you might be struggling with an apparently insurmountable problem, and call on the team to put on their green hats to generate some ideas. Or you can ask someone who's getting negative to take their black hat off for a moment – this is a more neutral request!

By using the hats we set rules for behavior. Everyone wears the same colour hat at the same time, and the hats are not associated with particular people. This allows meeting members to move outside their perceived stereotypes and allows time for different, sometimes difficult types of communication. De Bono discussed the order and way the hats are used; it depends on the meeting and the problem, as well as the team's experience in using the techniques. Suppose we have a meeting to discuss a design for an interface.

We might have a meeting agenda like this:

▶ Blue hat to set the scene – why are we here and what do we want to achieve?
▶ White hat – what facts do we have that everyone can agree on?
▶ Red hat – do we like or dislike the design – what is our gut feel about it?
▶ Yellow hat – what are the good things about the design?
▶ Black hat – what disadvantages can we see?
▶ Green hat – can we identify new ideas to help us overcome the black hat points?
▶ Red hat – how do we feel now?
▶ Blue hat to close the meeting – what are the next steps?

The advantages de Bono identifies [75] are

▶ *powerful, focused working*, which is *time-saving* because the meeting is not filled by confrontational arguments;
▶ *removing of ego by removing confrontation*, allowing the meeting to *deal with one thing at a time.*

All the ideas from all the people at the meeting are treated as parallel rather than confrontational. Once a complete picture has been arrived at using the Six Hats, then it is easier for people to agree to a solution or make a decision. We can use the hats to change focus: "It looks like with the yellow hat thinking we've identified some real advantages to the approach we're discussing. Let's just try some black hat thinking – what are the disadvantages?" You can find more information about de Bono's work on thinking, including the six thinking hats, on his Web site [77].

Technique 2: Cause and Solution Analysis with Ishikawa Fishbones

Cause–effect analysis helps us look for the root causes of problems, using *cause-and-effect diagrams*, sometimes called *fishbone diagrams* because of their shape or Ishikawa diagrams after the person who first developed them, but now widely used in identifying quality and other problems [78, 79].

Put simply, this is a structured form of gathering and sharing information, either in a brainstorm meeting or as work is going on, day to day. It is used in factories, with a blank fishbone on the wall in easy reach by a production line, so that anyone can add an idea about the cause of a problem or a potential solution. Periodically, the group working on the production line will discuss the information and ideas gathered in the diagram and decide on problem solutions.

This open approach with simply documented ideas to which anyone can contribute lends itself to lean manufacturing and to agile project teams. In both cases, the teams are empowered to analyze and change their own processes to facilitate fast improvements.

The diagram is simply a means of helping us think about and classify the causes of problems and their underlying root causes. The first step is to draw a fishbone diagram with the effect (which is the problem or symptom noticed) on the head of

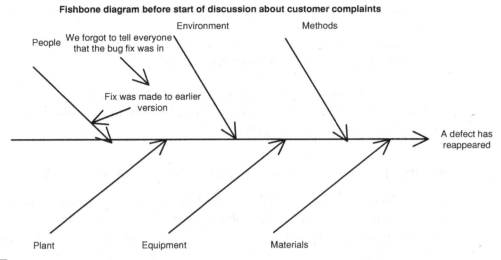

Fishbone diagram before start of discussion about customer complaints

19.1   Ishikawa fishbone diagram.

the fish. Then, label the ribs of the fishbone to show typical areas of root cause. You can choose your labels. Typical ones are "The 4 Ms – Manpower, Machines, Materials, Methods" [78] or the "PEMPEM" labels, which give People, Environment, Methods, Plant, Equipment, Materials [79], or you could make up your own labels.

In a traditional project, a brainstorming meeting would be called to generate causes for the effect, grouping the ideas on the fishbone to show how they relate to each other. In an agile team, the fishbones could be started on a whiteboard or flipchart in a brainstorming session during team meetings or between team meetings as people have problems to solve; ideas can be allowed to incubate naturally. Even for a traditional project, we would want to put the diagram on a public board so other people can see it, comment on it, and add to it, and so that the people can suggest other causes [79]. The diagram in Figure 19.1 shows the very start of a discussion of a problem: the first two ideas have been added. Notice that – because we are looking for a root cause – we are not just adding ideas at the major bones. We backtrack, adding one or more causes until we reach a root cause; a defect has reappeared because a fix was made to an earlier version, because we forgot to tell everyone that the bug fix was in, because we did not realize that other people might change this code module . . . and so on. We add ideas under each of the headings. Although a quick look tells us this is highly likely to be a configuration management problem, the breakdown helps us see whether we need to look at an improved process, tool, or education of the team as they move from a traditional approach (*only I can change this code*) to a collaborative approach (*we work on this problem together*).

We then "reverse" the fishbone, to go from a problem to a solution. To do this we draw the diagram in reverse, write our proposed solution in the box, and then under our fishbone headings discuss whether the proposed solution will work:

▶   What actions do we require under the 4 Ms or PEMPEM or our own titles to make sure the solution works? (Note: whichever titles you use, make sure you have a place to look at time, money, and staffing, which will all constrain the solution.)

▶ What advantages or positive affects will the solution have?

▶ What disadvantages or negatives can we identify?

You can use different-color pens for the advantages and disadvantages, so you could match pen colors to the de Bono Six Hats® colors, using yellow for optimistic and black for pessimistic views [72].

19.4 Something Worth Listening to . . . Understanding Each Other's Viewpoints

There are several methods of understanding viewpoints; these include psychometric methods such as the Belbin Team Roles [80, 81, 82] and the Myers Briggs Type Indicator (MBTI [83, 84, 85]). These are well explained elsewhere, so I shall only summarize them here.

Belbin discussed the way people behave when working in teams and suggested that a balance between the roles supports success.

For example, *plants* have new ideas while *completer-finishers* want to finish to fine detail. If you have too many plants in the team you'll never finish anything, but if you only had *completer-finishers*, you might not have so many new ideas. Each person in the team takes an assessment, and this provides a picture of the strengths and weaknesses of the team as a whole [72]. Most people will score to show a mix of the team roles.

In contrast, the MBTI looks at people's personalities and suggests that communication styles and preferences follow certain patterns. A person may be introvert or extrovert, for example, and that will alter the preferred amount of interaction. Another factor is the degree of analytical or empathetic approach that someone prefers. The four pairs are as follows:

▶ E and I – Extroversion (prefers social interaction) versus Introversion (quiet and private);

▶ S and N – Sensing (experience and practicality) versus iNtuition (novelty and aspiration);

▶ T and F – Thinking (analytic or critical approach) versus Feeling (sympathizing and appreciative approach);

▶ J and P – Judgement (firmness and control) versus Perception (flexibility and spontaneity).

With each person being assigned one value from each pair, this gives Myers Briggs sixteen distinct personality types. Beware of how you interpret these:

The communication preferences of these groups may be radically different. However, if you are going to look at MBTI, beware of stereotyping! It is worth noting that just because someone is in a particular job, it does not mean they are a particular type, and just because someone appears to be a particular type does not mean they will be a success in an apparently related job. Remember, if 10% of computer staff are INTJ, then 90% are not INTJ. Similarly, being a woman does not mean you cannot be an ESTJ. As with all of these types of test, make sure it is administered by someone who is suitably trained and can interpret the results properly [72].

Notice how use of the Six Hats and the Ishikawa fishbones would encourage people out of their roles as they allow everyone to contribute ideas, facts, and commentary in a controlled way that might be more acceptable to some personality types; an introverted team member could add his or her ideas quietly to the fishbone rather than having to participate in a direct discussion. The roles and latest thinking are described on the Web sites in the references. There are other useful models such as looking at attitudes to innovation [86] and learning styles [87] which are summarized in [72].

19.5 Starting the Conversation . . . and Keeping It Going

In addition to thinking about personality differences we should also consider organizational viewpoints.

Technique: Weaver Triangle

All the communication points from traditional processes – reviews, entry and exit criteria, coverage measures – still have something to offer in terms of clarifying that everyone in the agile team has the same goals for the project. To help us with this, an "on one page" method of capturing goals for a project is the Weaver Triangle. This was originally developed by Jayne Weaver for use with not-for-profit organizations, and we then adapted it for use in IT and business projects [72]. Using the triangle, the group identifies and agrees the aim of the project (why it is being done) and associated indicators of success, then the objectives of the project (what is to be done) and associated targets. This helps identify where stakeholders have different aims for the project. The form is used to encourage teams to focus on an overall aim or goal, and to show pictorially how the aims and objectives fit together.

Some ground rules of this approach are as follows (see Figure 19.2):

▶ The aim should answer the questions "why are we doing this?" and "what difference will this make?"
▶ The specific aims should break down the overall aim into a small number of detailed aims.
▶ Each specific aim also answers a "why?" and "what difference?" question.
▶ In order for the aims to be achieved, something needs to be done, so each specific aim must be associated with at least one objective that answers the question "what do we need to do in order to meet the aim?"

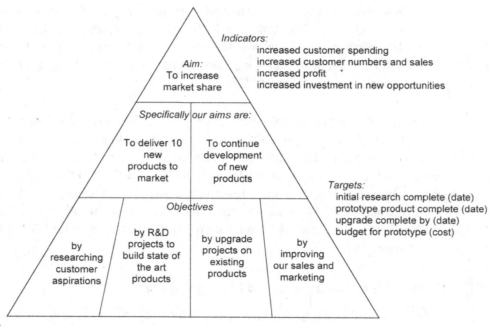

19.2   Typical Weaver Triangle.

▶ Objectives, which may be projects within a program or parts of a project, depending on their size.

▶ Each objective must be focused on achieving at least one of the aims, otherwise there is no point doing it.

▶ Aims are measured by indicators that measure whether we are making the difference we intended.

▶ Objectives are measured by delivery targets such as savings, number of people affected, and delivery dates.

▶ Indicator and target measures should be linked to measures used generally in the organization; for example, you could show how these measures link to the organization's balanced score card.

▶ Consensus is required between the stakeholders. This is not done by the managers and told to everyone else; it needs contributions and discussion from the whole team.

Technique: Think Group Viewpoints

In Reference 72, I have discussed that there are five viewpoints in any IT project: the Customer, the Manager, the Builder (including all the analysis, design, and development groups), the Measurers (including testers and reviewers), and the Supporters (including IT infrastructure). Each of these groups holds particular views about quality, has specific information for the other groups, and requires particular information from the other groups (see Table 19.1).

Table 19.1. The five IT project viewpoints

Group	Quality	Risks	Constraints	Acceptance criteria and plan are . . .	When involved traditionally	Additionally involve them in
Customer	User (fit for purpose)	Impact on organization	Business, service level, time, cost	Realistic, timebound	Preproject At go live Post go live	All project stages
Manager	Value (can we afford it?)	Impact on other projects	Cost, time, skills, resources	Realistic, timebound	Preproject Project At go live	Postproject
Builder	Manufacturing (defect and process)	Likelihood–technical	Technical skills, infrastructure	Achievable, realistic	Project Go live	Preproject Postproject
Measurer	Product (ISO 25000 attributes)	Likelihood–previous failures, predictions	Technical skills, infrastructure	Specific, measurable	Project (sometimes late) Go live	Preproject All project stages Postproject
Supporter	User (fit for purpose) Product (ISO 25000 attributes)	Impact on existing systems and infrastructure Future growth	Technical skills, infrastructure	Achievable, realistic	Go live Post go live	Preproject All project stages

19.6 Conclusion

Only by considering the communication needs of all the people involved in the successful delivery of software can the team succeed in delivering what its customer needs to meet the correct quality attributes.

For the agile team to succeed, equipment, infrastructure, approaches, and tools used in the project must support disciplined communication.

The team members need time and opportunity to understand each other's communication styles and to build trust. An understanding of how others think and feel will help team members interact more effectively, and use of techniques such as De Bono's Six Hats, Ishikawa fishbones, group viewpoints, and Weaver Triangles provides opportunities for structured interaction to improve communication. An understanding of the different viewpoints in the organization allows the team to draw the right representation into the team.

Agile teamwork is not necessarily a natural way of working for all of us, but we can all improve our communication by understanding ourselves, empathizing with others, and using techniques to structure our communication processes.

Chapter Acknowledgements

Aspects of this chapter are based on conversations with Elisabeth Hendrickson, and I also benefited from her excellent workshop at the London SIGiST (British Computer Society Specialist Group in Software Testing) event in 2007, where I was able to observe and take part in the group interactions. Figures and tables are based on [72]. Comments on communication and on agile projects from Graham Thomas and others informed my thinking.

20 Very-Small-Scale Agile Development and Testing of a Wiki

Dass Chana

SYNOPSIS

This case study reviews an agile approach to the development, testing, and delivery of a Wiki in very short timescales, with chronically low budget, and with very few resources. There were a number of potential risk issues with the project, such as difficulties with co-location of the customer and the project manager, but which were successfully mitigated by intelligent use of collaborative technologies such as instant messaging and teleconferencing.

Overall, the project was very successful, delivering precisely the system the customer needed, and with good quality. The only significant issue that could be reported was that the original delivery timescales of four weeks overran by one week, although this was actually due to deliberate enhancements requested by the customer.

I also make some suggestions for improvements to the agile development and test process that I would use on future projects.

20.1 Introduction

My name is Dass Chana and I am a computer science student. This case study describes a project I undertook as an industrial placement student working for a very large IT company. I was assigned as a resource to a large distributed team who were responsible for providing technical support to the company's business partners, and tasked with setting up and delivering a Wiki (for internal use within the team) under very challenging timescales, with extremely low budget, and with very few resources. I was given the goal of getting the Wiki up and running in just four weeks (although in the end I actually took five weeks due to enhancements to the system that were requested as the "customer" saw what the Wiki could do for them).

20.2 Overview of the Testing Challenge

At the risk of starting a circular argument, Wikipedia [36] defines a Wiki as

> a collection of web pages designed to enable anyone who accesses it to contribute or modify content, using a simplified mark-up language. Wikis are often used to create collaborative

websites and to power community websites. The collaborative encyclopaedia, Wikipedia, is itself one of the best-known wikis. Wikis are used in business to provide intranets and Knowledge Management systems.

The manager of the team I had been assigned to, as a work experience student, gave me the goal of implementing a Wiki to provide the team with a resource for posting team news and success stories. In effect my teammates were also the customers/users of the Wiki.

The inevitable requirements creep[1] would eventually lead to the purpose of the Wiki being extended to include information on best practices for the team, definition of team roles and responsibilities, team structure, and reporting/liaison lines (in effect, a process/framework definition for the team – yet another recursive aspect of the project and this case study write-up)!

Given the nature of the system I was tasked with developing, the chaotic nature of the requirements (often driven by two different managers simultaneously, plus the ad hoc requests/comments from the team; i.e., the users), the lack of available resources (i.e., low/no budget, plus limited access to other human resources), and the need to employ a formal method to develop the Wiki, I determined that adopting an agile approach would be the best solution to developing and testing the software.

Also, using an agile approach to developing and testing the Wiki seemed a particularly appropriate solution, as the origin of the word Wiki comes from the Hawaiian *wiki wiki*, which is translated as "fast."

20.3 Definition of the Agile Development and Testing Process

My agile process incorporated the following characteristics:

- ▶ *RUPesque* – Having been exposed to the Rational Unified Process (RUP [7]) at college, I employed a fundamentally RUP-like approach to the iterations (that I termed the RUPesque method). I also included elements of the V-model [4] to enable me to convince my manager that I was doing some formal planning of the project. (It seems managers like to be reassured about these things.)
- ▶ *A small team* (not co-located; see Section 20.5 for details of how I overcame the issues of lack of co-location) comprised
  - ▷ the customer/user (basically the team I had been assigned to during my industrial placement),
  - ▷ the project manager (my boss),

---

[1] In my young and innocent state, I did begin to wonder if the "Requirements Creep" might actually be a role held by one of the team members – perhaps the person responsible for coming up with new and crazy requirements.;-)

 ▷ the developer and tester (me), and

 ▷ ad hoc resources (a member of the team as and when needed for pair development and test – see later discussion).

▶ *Short iterations* (matched to a week-long cycle to coincide with and to piggyback on an existing weekly team telephone conference call on Friday afternoon to allow the users [i.e., the team members] to review the previous week's development and provide comments for the next week's work).

▶ *Agile requirements* – capture and maintenance (documented using an agile requirements tool [61]).

▶ *Rapid prototyping* – I relied heavily on a prototyping approach in which I would produce simple mock-ups (essentially just demonstrating the navigation and the basic features requested by the users) to show to the users in order to obtain their feedback on the suitability of the proposed system (formally during the Friday conference call, but also informally [but then documented in the requirement tool] via the SameTime instant messaging system [a facility available under Lotus Notes]).

▶ *Pair development* – To make particularly fast progress, I organized a number of intensive sessions where I worked with an experienced member of the team at the same workstation, bashing out code, and producing very good results (see Section 20.5). Pair development was particularly valuable where I had very challenging timescales and proved to be an excellent technique for very intensive development and testing and rapid delivery of good-quality software.

▶ *Pair testing* – Again, working with my colleague, we identified suitable test scenarios, test data (including boundary and partition values), and employed state-transition techniques to design tests to verify correct navigation [4]. I have broken this out separately from pair development, because I was so impressed by what turned out to be a particularly effective means of reducing defects.

▶ *Manual tester packs* – I don't subscribe to the popular notion that all students are lazy, fun-loving, hedonistic parasites (well, not completely). To avoid additional wasted testing effort, and to ensure I wasn't stuck in the office after 5 p.m. or (God forbid) testing on the weekend, I made sure that testing was as slick and efficient as possible. My main solution was to ensure I got maximum reuse from the tests that I (and my colleague, during pair testing) created. To this end:

 ▷ I created a simple *test script template* in the IBM Symphony word processor package and adopted a consistent script naming convention (a unique identifier formed from the iteration number, the Wiki page [and subpage], and an incremented number – e.g., *02-TeamOrgChart-01*).

 ▷ To promote *test reuse*, I ensured that all test scripts that were developed were filed (both electronically as Symphony files and as paper-based copies in my test reuse folder, which was a file box with separate tabs into which the tests for separate iterations were stored).

▷ *Regression testing* was achieved by photocopying those tests that were required from earlier iterations and including them in the testing pack for the current iteration.

▷ I employed *test refactoring* to ensure the testing load did not grow to unmanageable volumes; the earlier tests were reviewed and omitted if it was felt that that aspect of the system being tested was now stable (in practice, that there had not been a defect observed since the last but one iteration).

▷ *Acceptance testing* did involve creating some new tests (by reviewing the requirements and identifying areas that needed additional test scenarios) but also involved the reuse of a random selection of manual test scripts from the previous iteration.

▷ In retrospect, in order to save even more of my valuable time and to reduce effort, I would have used *automated testing tools* if we had had budget and/or access to them. (Ironically, I discovered a day after the end of the project, we could have obtained a thirty-day temporary copy of Rational Functional Tester [62], which would have been very useful for recording and playing back web and Java tests overnight and/or over the weekend!)

▶ *Continuous integration and code refactoring* – Although this may sound like a virtue, this was in fact a necessity. As I worked across the weekly iteration, I incorporated changes as and when they were received, and as and when I was able to make them, republishing them in the live system. In fact, as I describe later, this is one of the few areas I feel could be improved (again, perhaps by tool support), allowing me to rerun the test suite overnight following changes, or even over the weekend.

20.4 Results of the Agile Approach

The adoption and use of an agile approach to developing the Wiki proved to be very successful. In terms of the general success criteria for the project, I am able to provide the following information.

▶ *Budget* – Although there was no explicit budget to meet (except for the implicit time I spent performing the work and that of my colleague, who provided ad hoc pair development and testing support across the later weeks of the project), I needed no additional effort or resources (aka money) to complete the project. Since I had planned to complete the work in four weeks, but actually took five, you might argue that I had overrun by 25%. However, in reality the additional week was an extension that I negotiated with the customer and project manager to allow the incorporation of further features that the customer requested after seeing what the system could do for them as they observed the development of the prototypes and full functionality of the evolving Wiki.

▶ *Timescales* – As I described earlier, the initial four-week allocation for the project grew to five weeks. This is a difficult issue to deal with in this case study. For while I was delivering customer satisfaction by implementing additional features that they requested (and which I formally agreed with both the customer and my project manager), we were not really operating in a commercial environment. My time was in effect free to my boss (aka the project manager), the software I was developing was not a commercial bespoke system (in fact, it was only really intended for internal use by our team), and bottom line, was not commercially critical to the success of our company.

▶ What I can say is that, if this had been a full-blown commercial project to deliver a business-critical system, with contractually binding budgets and timescales, I would have looked to agree the requested changes from the customer with my project manager and, if appropriate, would have proposed an additional charge to the customer to cover the additional work.

▶ *Quality* – Overall, the quality of the delivered system has been good. So far there have been no serious defects identified, and five minor issues reported to me following final delivery, requiring trivial reworking and retesting of the system (about two hours in total, or about 1.85% of the total project time).

▶ I can report that, in the initial iterations of the project (when there was no pair programming and test resource available), we identified about half a serious defect per week and some six minor issues. During the last two weeks, when I was able to implement pair development and test, this fell to an average of zero serious defects per week and three minor issues. Although the sample size is a little small for formal statistics, my feeling is that we "doubled the quality" by employing pair development and test – which is also my estimate for overall productivity (i.e., more than twice the productivity compared with single-person development).

▶ *Customer satisfaction* – The delivered Wiki has been a great success, with not only my own team using the system, but with our project manager also providing links to the Wiki to the managers of other groups we work with within the organization. (There is definitely an element of showing off here, although my manager justifies sharing access to the other groups as "showcasing our capabilities.") In formal terms:

▷ The system has been acceptance tested against all of the requirements in the requirements management tool and *we can demonstrate 100% coverage against the requirements.*

▷ En route to completing the project, the use of rapid prototyping meant that *we kept closely to the needs of the users* (who could provide rapid feedback on the direction we were taking).

▷ The formal weekly testing of the system (plus regression testing) meant that *we started testing early and continued throughout the project.* I am proud to say that this approach meant that, once a defect was identified, it was fixed quickly and with thorough regression testing did not reappear again in subsequent iterations.

Lessons Learned

What Worked Well

With the project complete, the Wiki delivered and working, and having had the time to review what I did (is this what they call an agile retrospective?), I would like to report the following positive aspects of the development process:

▶ *Pair programming and pair testing* worked very well. I estimate that working alongside another member of the team in developing and testing the Wiki was more than twice as effective as working on my own (in terms of timescales and lack of reworking). The obvious and tangible benefits included:

▷ Being able to *keep each other focused on the task at hand* (made it harder for me to keep checking out my auctions on eBay or my mates on Facebook and Second Life).

▷ *Filling in for each other's knowledge gaps* – There was often something I couldn't do that my esteemed colleague did know about, and vice versa – this meant together we had a more complete coverage of the knowledge of the development environment capabilities.

▷ *Providing a testing dummy* – I have often experienced the situation where you have observed a bug, spend ages trying to understand what is going wrong, but don't seem to be able to make any progress. Then a mate comes past who you grab and ask for their help, and even though they don't really say a word, the act of explaining what is going on actually gives you the eureka moment where you spot the problem. At this point they usually stand up and wander off, feeling smug about having done so much to help you! This experience is just part of the pair development and test paradigm, and happened to us several times each session.

▷ *Solving that developer testing thing* – I find it hard to test my own work. I seem to focus on showing that the code works the way I expect it to work, rather than focussing on showing that the code doesn't work. This is a subtle difference between a developer's approach to testing compared with a tester's approach, but in practice it seems to make a big difference (more on this later). With a pair testing approach, I found that together we would come up with more test scenarios and more thorough scenarios (maybe finding more error conditions to test against, for example). The other person also keeps your testing "honest" – no cutting corners or making rash assumptions about how good your code is. Where I had tested on my own, there were always lots of issues reported by the team when they made their weekly review of the system. On those weeks where I had been able to work with a colleague on pair programming and testing, we calculated that there were only about 50% of the bugs reported.

▷ *The weekly iteration cycle* – While I don't believe this will work for large projects where they have large tasks to complete, I found this to be a highly effective technique to adopt on my project. Because we were running to a weekly cycle, everyone seemed to get into a rhythm in terms of their responsibilities and tasks:

- I knew I had to review the requirements (existing and new requirements) every Monday morning and ensure the requirements tool was kept up-to-date.
- The team knew that they would get the latest version of the system to review each Thursday afternoon, and also that they had to have their comments ready for the teleconference on the Friday afternoon.
- Similarly, I had access to the project manager (my boss) on the Friday conference call, as well as the customers/users (the rest of our team), and could take direction from them on priorities and goals for the next week, as well as, where appropriate, to make requests for additional resources (such as a pair developer and tester).
- Monday afternoon to Wednesday was development and testing time.
- That left Thursday morning to do some formal testing to ensure I had met the requirements for the week, and to regression-test the Wiki to make sure I hadn't introduced any deleterious changes; I had to be thorough and I had to make good progress to hit the Thursday lunchtime "code drop" deadline to deliver to the users.

▶ *Lack of co-location with users* – The fact was, that although we weren't physically co-located, the company we worked for provided extensive team working support facilities. I could always ping one of the team using our company instant messaging system and could always publish the latest version of the Wiki for anyone to take a look at some aspect of the functionality I was working on. I don't believe I could have developed the system as quickly, with as high a level of quality, or with as close a match to the users' needs working on my own in isolation and only having contact with the users once a week.

▶ *Lack of co-location with the project manager* – Again, although not physically co-located, I was able to quickly and easily ping my project manager using instant messaging. My feeling is that the project timescales, quality, and match to the users' requirements did not suffer through lack of face-to-face contact with my project manager.

▶ *Tool Support* – I found that having access to a requirements tool was very useful:
  ▷ It provided me with a simple and effective solution to documenting requirements.
  ▷ I could use the tool to publish the requirements to my project manager and the users so that they could review them and provide me with their comments.
  ▷ Keeping the requirements up-to-date was straightforward, and I had a built-in trace of how the requirement had changed and who had requested the change. This proved to be invaluable several times, as guilty parties in the team denied having suggested a particular change – the tool never lies.;-)
  ▷ I would have liked to have had access to testing tools as well – such as the sort that can automatically scan a web application to identify problems (such

as missing links, widows and orphans,[2] security issues). The reality was that this project was too small and had no funds to allow us to use such tools. However, having seen such tools demonstrated, I would certainly investigate their use on other projects that I may get involved in. (I am selfish, and anything that saved me time and effort on testing would be something I would be very interested in using!)

▷ And last but definitely not least – *rapid prototyping*. I found this to be a really useful means of increasing my efficiency and keeping to my timescales. Rather than just assume I knew best and spend ages developing a complete solution that it turned out nobody wanted, very quickly producing a simple, navigation-only model and running it past the team meant that if I had gotten it wrong, I had only spent a couple of hours of time on the task (and had gained the big bonus that I now understood better what was actually needed). So, prototypes are a quick, simple, and easy way to check you are developing the right thing and if not, to not waste too much time and effort, with the bonus of getting a clearer insight into what the users actually want.

What Would I Change in the Future?

Although the project completed successfully (admittedly, with a deliberate fifth iteration overrun), with the benefit of 20–20 hindsight, the one area I might change, if I was still working in the team and there was a requirement to run a similar project, would be in the area of continuous integration and refactoring.

What I would have liked to have been able to do was to undo changes I had made in a formal, safe (i.e., allowing me to restore a change), and repeatable manner. For example, if a particular request for a change had resulted in a catastrophic problem in the system, it would have been nice to have easily restored the system to its prechange working state. Also, it would have been nice to have been able to retain those successful changes that might have been made in parallel with the problem change while undoing that change.

Given the relatively low size and complexity of this project, this was in practice a relatively small problem (although I did spend several frustrated sessions in the evening, and on one occasion across a weekend, fixing such issues). However, I can see where this would be an extremely serious issue with larger and more complex applications and larger teams.

This seems to me to be largely a configuration management problem, and my solution to this issue on future projects would be to employ tool support, using either a shareware tool off the Internet for the sort of small project described in this case study or a more capable and robust proprietary product (such as [88]) for larger, industrial-strength projects.

---

[2] Widows and orphans refer to web pages that no longer have any links pointing to them, or links where the original page they pointed to is no longer present.

Perhaps the most innovative thing I might try in the future, if I was involved in a similar project, would be to use some of the new hi-tech means of online collaboration, such as team meetings in Second Life [64]. For example, I have heard of Second Life design review meetings where the team could actually walk through a 3D representation of the design diagrams and provide instant online feedback on the information displayed. While Second Life might not be a perfect solution to the problem of not being able to get together for face-to-face meetings, I really believe it is an option well worth exploring (assuming my older colleagues actually have accounts on Second Life)!

Finally, my only other wish – and again while this was not really an issue on this small project (I can see benefits for larger and more complex projects) – would be to consider automated software testing. In the case of this project, a web testing tool (to check navigation, usability, and security) might have been very useful and, for larger projects, some form of record and playback tool (such as [62]) to regression-test later builds and releases could save huge amounts of valuable tester time and effort (avoiding the unwelcome prospect of spending too much time manually testing the software in the evenings and at weekends, when I could have been out partying instead)!

21 Agile Special Tactics: SOA Projects

Greg Hodgkinson, Software Development Process Evangelist, Prolifics

SYNOPSIS

Service-Oriented Architecture (SOA) projects [89] require specific qualities in the solution that they produce around flexibility and extensibility. Most agile methods don't focus on providing method support to address these needs, or at least not to the degree required for an SOA project. This case study will describe my process configuration that borrows from the best of agile techniques and combines these with SOA development techniques to support projects that produce SOA solutions. And most importantly, this has been tried and tested on our SOA projects for many years with resounding success.

21.1 Introduction

My name is Greg Hodgkinson and I work for Prolifics, where one of my roles has been to provide leadership in software development process. It has to be said that I started with a love–hate relationship with agile methods born out of many years' experience of seeing them both being successfully used, but also (sometimes) abused; let me explain:

▶ I love some of the techniques that agile methods champion as I truly believe that they have, in their own way, had a revolutionary impact on the way the industry approaches software engineering.
▶ At the same time though, I hate seeing them being abused to excuse bad practices, or even worse as a political tool to bash other valuable practices.

So, taking a step back, it's not the methods themselves I have a problem with – far from it – but rather the blind faith from those who have jumped on the agile bandwagon without proper consideration for what they are trying to achieve.

And who hasn't jumped on a bandwagon at some stage or other? In fact I'd suggest that one of the best things about the emergence of agile methods is that it has stirred up passions for the use of software development processes as a way of improving the lot of the IT professional – fantastic!

But blindly applying agile methods without really trying to understand what problems you're trying to solve with them, and also which problems you're not relying on them for solution, can cause unnecessary problems. I'd like to start by observing three reasons why adopting methodologies sometimes goes wrong:

▶ *Good method, wrong type of project* – Some methods just do not suit certain styles of projects – period. Good luck trying to use XP (Extreme Programming [20]) "out of the box" to deliver a "system of systems" [90] style of project covering hardware and software, involving multiple large teams who are distributed around the world. No use blaming Kent Beck if it goes wrong – XP itself describes the class of projects for which it is intended.

▶ *Good method, overrelied on* – Make sure you understand the limits of the method that you are using. Scrum is not going to tell you the form that your architecture needs to take. But then, it doesn't profess to provide method support for architecture. If you need architectural guidance then you shouldn't be relying on Scrum to provide it. Some people fall into the trap of overrelying on a method to cover all their method needs. You need to have a clear idea as to what you want out of a method, and then choose the best bits from those methods that meet your needs.

▶ *Good method, misunderstood* – To illustrate, a fictitious but yet not unrealistic quote from a project manager – "I bought a really good book on Rational Unified Process [7] and I've made sure that we are applying all of its roles, work products, and tasks, and yet the team hate it and my projects are not delivering. I thought the three amigos were supposed to be process gurus!" Erm, do you know that RUP is a process framework and not a process? Guess maybe you aren't applying all of the roles, especially not the process engineer, whose role responsibilities include "tailoring the process to match the specific needs of the project" and "assisting the project manager in planning the project" [91].

So building on this, for anyone who has spent any amount of time thinking long and hard about software development methodologies, the inevitable and oft-written conclusion is that the best thing to do is to customize your own – consider the types of projects you need to run in your organization and then take the best bits of the various methods out there (as applicable) and combine them to "grow your own!"

Apply care and attention, prune where required, and over time you will end up with a mature method that perfectly fits the needs of your organization. It also helps to start with the right seeds (base methods) and cuttings (customizations). Don't get me wrong – there is no reason for the average organization to have to build a custom method from scratch. The exercise should be one of assembly rather than of build. If you're building your own from the ground up then you're doing it the hard (and expensive!) way.

This case study focuses on methods to support a specific class of project – those that produce SOA solutions. To support these projects requires "special tactics" over and above what is covered by "out-of-the-box" agile methods. This is the *raison d'être* for me growing my own method – AgileSOA, which, as the name suggests, combines the best of two classes of methods: *agile methods* and *methods used to produce SOA solutions*.

This case study is based on my experiences in applying this method to a number of significant customer projects over the years at Prolifics and at my previous company, 7irene, where this method was first formed. Any method should be judged by its performance, and we have yet to have a project use this method that has not been a success (although we have learned along the way!). I hope you find some parts of this case study useful to your own efforts to "grow your own" method!

21.2 Overview of the AgileSOA Testing Challenge

I'll start with my three favorite things about agile methods:

▶ They have improved many organizations' ability to deliver with short-term focus as they place a lot of focus on the iteration to plan the project team's work and deliver the solution incrementally.

▶ They encourage customer involvement in the process.

▶ They are relatively simple to understand and succinct to describe.

Expanding on this, one of the most tangible ways I've seen agile methods impress is in improving the amount of focus of activity to get the first release of a solution into production. This solves the problem that many organizations have, which is that their projects seem to drag on forever without actually delivering anything.

Agile methods normally achieve this level of focus by planning short-term, using iterations, and by measuring progress in terms of functionality produced by each increment. This works very well as teams are motivated by short-term success. After all, success breeds success! Also, if there are any issues with the project's delivery capability they will soon be encountered early in the project life cycle rather than being hidden until late. The sooner the issues are identified, the sooner they can be resolved.

Turning to SOA, it's important to note that many of the important benefits of SOA are realized when building "long-term IT solutions." It's fundamentally about building your software in such a way that it improves the long-term costing and flexibility of your IT solutions.[1] The following define the usage of "long term" and "short term":

▶ *Long-term IT solutions (strategic)*
  ▷ support an ongoing business function,
  ▷ have a "long" life span (5 years plus),
  ▷ are core IT systems that support the business need to be able to be extended to support new business requirements,

---

[1] It is worth pointing out that this is not to say that there are *only* long-term benefits. We've achieved many short-term benefits in building SOA solutions – less risk, more organized work effort, and improved direction, to name a few.

      ▷   have high quality requirements,

      ▷   often have a high degree of interconnection with other IT systems, and

      ▷   the consequences of failure are considerable.

   ▶   *Short-term IT solutions (tactical)*

      ▷   solve a niche problem,

      ▷   have a "short" life span,

      ▷   are often required to provide an edge over competitors,

      ▷   have lower-quality requirements,

      ▷   do not have considerable consequences of failure, and

      ▷   can sometimes be R&D-type efforts.

Agile methods have achieved huge success when approaching short-term IT solutions. However, I have seen issues arise when these same methods have been applied to SOA "long-term solutions."

This doesn't need to be the case. The challenge for our agile SOA projects is to stay simple to understand and to keep a short-term focus while adding the necessary support to plan and design SOA solutions and addressing the long-term considerations of the solutions you deliver.

Before we move on to look at my development process, I'd like to outline this challenge by mentioning some of the issues we want to avoid when building SOA solutions:

▶   *"Loose" requirements factoring results in duplication of effort and/or increased refactoring.* A requirement is "a statement that identifies a necessary attribute, capability, characteristic, or quality of a system in order for it to have value and utility to a user" [92].

     I very much like the "factory/production-line" analogy when thinking about our agile software development projects. A master list of requirements is created using one of the popular mechanisms for expressing requirements – features, use cases, or story cards, to name a few. Iteration planning will scope out a subset of this master list to be delivered by each iteration.

     The "factory" (combination of team and tools) will then continue to produce increments "production-line style" by running these scoped iterations, with each iteration producing an increment.

     As it is the requirements that define the contents of each iteration, it is important that there is no functional overlap between any of the requirements; otherwise, the result will be duplication of effort and inevitably this will result in some refactoring of previous increments.

▶   *"Fat requirements" don't fit well into iterations.* Your requirements specifications need to be structured in such a way that they fit well into iterations. If the smallest unit of requirement that you have results in two months of work to deliver, then you've got a problem as this doesn't fit well with an iterative mode of delivery.

▶   *Lack of agility in specifications.* If we take agility to mean the ability to change direction quickly, then we know that our specifications need to be able to handle two kinds of changes: (1) *changes to modify functionality* (i.e., functionality that has already been delivered) and (2) *changes to include new functionality*.

By "lack of agility in specifications," I mean specifications that are not able to quickly incorporate these kinds of changes. Otherwise we risk ending up in a situation where the specifications get sidelined and become out of touch with the solution code.

So we need to focus on producing agile specifications as we know that we're at a minimum going to encounter a lot of the second type of change when doing iterative development, as each iteration adds new functionality that builds on that delivered by previous iterations. Hopefully we'll also try and minimize the first type of change, but more on that later.

▶ *Extensibility and flexibility qualities suffer without design specifications.* Two very important qualities in a good SOA solution are its degree of extensibility and flexibility:

▷ A good SOA solution is able to incorporate functional extensions without undue effort (extensibility). Also, a good SOA solution should allow for its constituent parts to change without compromising its functionality and reliability (flexibility). This is required when the same parts are shared between multiple SOA solutions and one of the solutions requires changes that shouldn't compromise the other solutions.

▷ Extensibility and flexibility don't happen by accident. They need to be built in, either as a forethought (design specifications) or an afterthought (refactoring). There are limits to the extensibility and flexibility that you will achieve in a solution through refactoring – so design specifications are critical to achieve these qualities in meaningfully sized solutions.

▶ *Mixing requirements and design makes it harder to understand what the system will do.* Requirements specifications provide a tangible understanding of what the solution will do. As such they need to be understandable by the customer, who needs to be satisfied that what the solution is planned to do (requirements) is what they want it to do. Mixing in solution design in your requirements specifications means it becomes difficult to achieve this.

▶ *Lack of specifications means code can become impenetrable (or costly to understand).* Not only can a lack of specifications cause problems with the initial production release of the solution, but there will definitely be problems later. As we're focusing on our previously defined "long-term IT solutions" with SOA, it is inevitable that during a sizeable part of the solutions life span there will be a number of pairs of eyes that will be peering at the code and will need to understand how the solution works. Now, even with the best of intentions, there is a limit to the degree that the code for a solution can be "self-documenting." Specifications will play an important role in helping to understand the solution's requirements and design in a cost-efficient manner.

▶ *Solution costs don't end with delivery of the first production release.* It is a well-known fact that when it comes to long-term IT solutions as defined previously, the cost of producing the first release is relatively small compared to the costs over the total life span of the solution. Examples of later costs include

▶ costs associated with delivering functional extensions,

▶ costs associated with providing support to the users,

▶ costs associated with fixing defects found, and

▶ costs associated with technology upgrades.

A number of practices already mentioned contribute to minimizing these costs: up-to-date agile specifications, built-in flexibility, and extensibility through design specifications.

An overriding focus on functional delivery at the expense of these practices will mean that any "savings" made by taking shortcuts in the delivery of the first production release will be heavily outweighed by later resulting costs.

▶ *Lack of design guidance often results in technologies being inappropriately used.* An end-to-end SOA solution might end up including a number of different implementation technologies – Portlets[2] running in a Portlet engine for the user interface, an enterprise service bus to plug together the various service-oriented parts, executable business processes running in a Business Process Execution Language (BPEL) engine, messaging middleware to connect to external systems, adapters for connecting to specific external solutions. Many of these technologies are fairly specific in terms of the type of solution part they should be used to implement, which means that it takes a bit of foresight to plan to use the technologies appropriately. As an example, although you could write most if not all of your solutions logic as BPEL, is that a good idea? Probably better to only use it to write your business process logic which, strangely enough, is what BPEL was designed for.

Without a design for the SOA solution being built, it is that much harder for developers to pick and choose where to use implementation technologies appropriately.

▶ *Overreliance on refactoring to fix design problems results in projects stalling.* Agility is about being able to quickly change direction when you need to.[3] However, this doesn't mean that it is a good idea to rely on changing direction a lot to get you on the right track. This is especially true when it comes to your SOA design. Sure, you could try to "evolve" this by building the code to meet the functional requirements and then refactor later to achieve a good design for this code – but this isn't a way of working that scales well or suits SOA-style solutions. I have

---

[2] Portlets are pluggable user interface software components that are managed and displayed in a web portal.

[3] "When you need to" is an important caveat. Too much change in direction over the life span of a project can result in a large amount of avoidable cost.

seen projects where the delivery of new functionality has stalled for months while the team refactored the current solution before adding new functionality. This just isn't acceptable to the customer. Although refactoring might have its place, overreliance on it as a way of evolving the solutions design does not work when it comes to SOA solutions.

▶ *Planning and measuring just developer activities is not enough.* Our software projects consist of more than just developers. Excluding project managers and other supporting roles, they include systems analysts, architects/designers, and testers. Each of these subteams needs to be taken into account in both planning of project activities and measuring of project progress. If you're not measuring the progress of your system's analysts in creating requirement specifications, then you might miss the fact that you are running out of completed requirement specifications to hand to your architect/designers, which will have a knock-on effect on your developers and then later testers.

▶ *Relying on having the entire project team co-located is often not practical.* Having your entire project team co-located will undoubtedly have benefits in terms of improving communications. However, this is often not practical. Most of the SOA projects I've worked on have included multiple suppliers, and more often than not each of the supplier's resources is geographically distributed. Your development method cannot rely on co-location of resources to achieve good communication between team members.

21.3 Definition of an Agile Testing SOA Process

Now that we've spent some time dwelling on the challenges faced by teams producing SOA solutions, I'd like to tell you a little bit about my AgileSOA process, which we've been using for many years to deliver SOA solutions for our customers. I'll do so by describing each of the key aspects that I think have made it work for us.

Specialized Subteams in the Iteration Workflow

Using the RUP as a framework, AgileSOA has a specialization of roles in the project team. These are organized into subteams, each having well-defined work products that they are responsible for, and each having their place in the overall iteration workflow. In this way, the "workers" in the team are divided up quite sensibly (if not a bit predictably) as follows:

▶ The *requirements team* is responsible for creating specifications that describe the requirements for the software solution.

▶ The *design team* is responsible for interpreting the requirements specifications and in turn creating corresponding design specifications. This includes describing the overall architecture of the software.

▶ The *implementation team,* as any developer will tell you, is where the "real work" is done. Not only is the team responsible for creating the solution code,

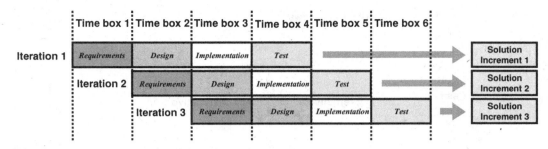

21.1 AgileSOA iterations across time boxes.

but also for producing developer tests that will live with the code to be used for regression testing.

▶ The *test team* is responsible for rooting out any defects that exist in the code produced by the developers. These defects are passed back to the implementation team for fixing.

The SOA solution is delivered incrementally using iterations, with each iteration planned as four end-to-end time boxes, with each time box being used to focus the efforts of the four subteams just described earlier. In practice this looks a bit like what is described in Figure 21.1.

The net result is that, in any given time box, each of your subteams will be working on a different iteration – each being one ahead of the other in the sequence of *requirements*, *design*, *implementation*, and *test*.

This organizes the work done as part of each of the project iterations. Note that not all the work is organized this way. As an example, you may have business modellers producing models that provide a useful business context for the solution in terms of process models and information models. This would be done in advance of your iterations. Also you will have people responsible for setting up and executing the performance and acceptance tests of the solution. Most of this happens after your iterations have executed because they need to test the entire solution (all increments) that will be released to the end users.

Structuring Requirements for Iterative Delivery

Requirements are crucial to our development process as they are used to scope out the work that the overall project life cycle needs to deliver but also to divide this work into iterations.

We use two mechanisms for scoping requirements for our SOA projects:

▶ First lightweight lists of needs/features are used to quickly produce a view of what is in scope for the project life cycle and, just as importantly, what is out of scope.

▶ Second, these features are traced to use cases, which become the primary means for structuring the project requirement specifications and scoping the contents of each iteration.

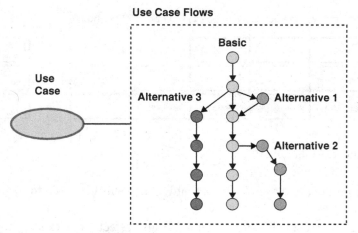

21.2 Use cases contain flows.

So why do I think use cases make such ideal units for our requirements specifications? Let's look at two useful properties:

▶ They are carefully factored nonoverlapping partitions of system functionality. Each system scenario that the system should support will end up in a single use case. This means that by choosing the use case as the primary unit for grouping our system behavioural specifications, we avoid overlap in coverage between specifications.[4]

▶ Use cases can be further divided into use case flows. Each use case has a basic flow which should describe the simple scenario. Scenarios that deviate from this basic flow are covered by describing their deviations as alternative flows (alternatives to the basic flow) – see Figure 21.2.

These two properties make use cases the ideal format for our requirements specifications. First, the fact that use cases don't overlap in their coverage of the systems scenarios means that they make good units for planning solution increments. You know that by allocating the full set of in-scope use cases to iterations you will have covered all the required functionality without any duplicated effort across iterations. Second, the fact that we can break up use cases into smaller parts means that we reduce the problem of having "fat" specifications that don't fit into a single iteration.[5] It is possible to assign a use case's basic flow to an iteration, and then assign groups of its alternative flows to later iterations.

---

4 This is not to say that the same step might not occur in more than one system use case. However, you wouldn't have entire scenarios duplicated between system use cases.
5 It is still necessary to sometimes have to take a single flow (normally the basic flow) and break it up over more than one iteration.

UC#	Use Case	Use Case Flow	Iteration
UC17.1	Capture client campaign order	Basic flow	1
UC17.2	Capture client campaign order	Order information is incomplete	1
UC24.1	Request carrier certification test	Basic flow	1
UC24.2	Request carrier certification test	Issues with certification	2
UC33.1	Make payment short code/s ordered	Basic flow	2
UC33.3	Make payment short code/s ordered	Credit card payments rejected	2
UC34.1	Note short code details	Basic flow	2

21.3 Use case plays planning example.

I define a use case play as follows. Each iteration that a use case is assigned to contains a play of that use case. That is, a use case play is one or more flows of a use case assigned to an iteration for delivery. For planning purposes, it is normally a good idea to split a use case up into multiple use case plays to manage the risk associated with delivering the use case.

For an idea as to what this looks like in practice, Figure 21.3 shows a set of use case plays from an example iteration planning work product. This example shows seven use case plays across two iterations. To understand how this works, we note the following:

▶ Iteration 1 contains two use case plays – the first contains both the basic flow and an alternative flow (order information is incomplete) of the Capture client order campaign use case, while the second contains just the basic flow of the Request carrier certification test.

▶ Request carrier certification test has two use case plays – the first is assigned to iteration 1 and contains just the basic flow; the second is assigned to iteration 2 and contains an alternative flow (issues with certification).

Specifications That Are Rich but Get to the Point

One of the popularist aspects to agile methods is the disdain with which they treat lengthy, verbose specificaton documents. And quite rightly so! Vague, ambiguous specifications defeat the purpose of putting together specifications. Worse still is when the specifications attempt to make up for quality with quantity!

Specifications need to be concise, clear, and unambiguous for them to have value. But also they must be easy to change – and this would suggest that they are no more "wordy" than they need to be.

In the AgileSOA process, the focus is on a key set of work products that attempt to achieve clarity and unambiguity while being as concise as possible. This is achieved by making the semantics of the specifications as rich as possible so that much can be said with little effort.

For SOA solutions, the key thing that we need to specify is the individual service contracts that are consumed by the various service consumers, and provided by the service providers.

Figure 21.4 shows a set of work products that contributes to our goal of creating quality service contracts:

▶ The *domain model* is probably the simplest and yet most widely used of these work products. It provides a structured view of the business information in the business domain. This is important as our service contracts will need to pass information around, and it is crucial to understand how this information is structured for you to have a good-quality set of service contracts.

▶ The domain model is coupled with the *business process model*, which describes the flow of the business processes. This is important as the services that you produce are internal aspects of a solution that needs to support a business. Any flaws in the understanding of the business and its processes can have a knock-on impact on the solution requirements, which in turn will have a knock-on impact on the service contracts.

▶ Having taken a look at the in-scope features for the SOA solution, a set of use cases is created in the *use case model* (i.e., System Use Cases), which provides a factored view of the requirements expressed by these features. The use cases should be cross-referenced against both (1) the business domain types in the domain model, so it is clear what business information they will act upon, and (2) the tasks in the business process model, so it is clear what business tasks they will automate. *Use case specifications* provide us with descriptions of what solution needs to do, and the service contracts will be the focus points of the collaborations that provide this behavior.

▶ The *external systems model* contains specifications of any systems that are external to your SOA that your SOA solution needs to interface with. The use cases in the use case model should identify which use cases these systems are involved in; that is, the system actors (as opposed to human actors) in your use case model should have corresponding external system specifications in the external systems model. Certain service contracts in our solution will have their behavior provided by service providers that integrate with these external systems. Therefore, an understanding of these external systems is crucial to ensure that the service contracts for these service providers are suitable for their integration.

▶ The *service model* is where the design for your service-oriented solution is captured [93] and is ultimately where the service contracts live. The service contracts are specified using service specifications, which define the interface points between service consumers and service providers. These are organized into service-oriented systems. The behavior of these systems is described using service interaction specifications, which are organized into service collaborations that match the use cases one-to-one.

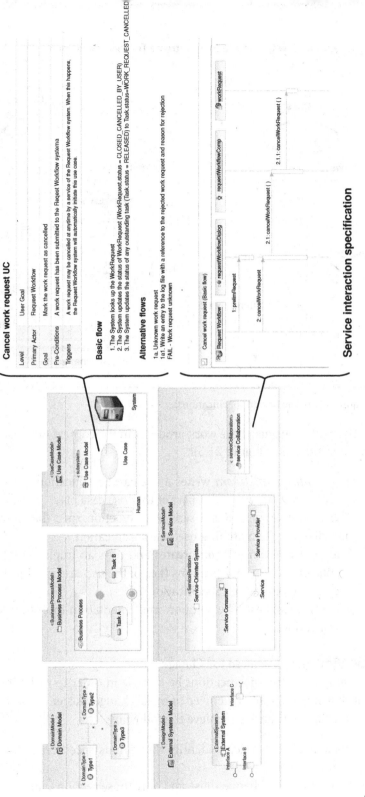

Use case specification

Cancel work request UC

Level	User Goal
Primary Actor	Request Workflow
Goal	Mark the work request as cancelled
Pre-Conditions	A work request has been submitted to the Request Workflow system
Triggers	A work request may be cancelled at anytime by a service of the Request Workflow system. When this happens, the Request Workflow system will automatically initiate this use case.

Basic flow

1. The System looks up the WorkRequest
2. The System updates the status of WorkRequest (WorkRequest.status = CLOSED_CANCELLED_BY_USER)
3. The System updates the status of any outstanding task (Task.status = RELEASED) to Task.status=WORK_REQUEST_CANCELLED

Alternative flows

1a. Unknown work request
1a1. Write an entry to the log file with a reference to the rejected work request and reason for rejection
FAIL. - Work request unknown

Service interaction specification

21.4   Key AgileSOA specification work products.

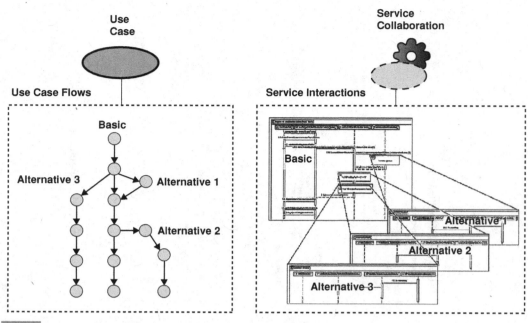

21.5   Requirements and design specifications.

Let's briefly consider these work products in the context of the subteams working in our iterations (see Figure 21.5):

▶ The *requirements team* writes a use case specification[6] describing the steps in each of the flows that are a part of that use case play.
▶ The *design team* writes a service interaction spec that provides the behavior described by the matching use case specification.
▶ The *implementation team* creates and tests an implementation of the requirements and design specifications (i.e., of the use case specification and the matching service interaction specification).
▶ The *test team* tests the solution implementation to ensure that it matches the specifications.

Specifications Structured for Change

Not only must the specifications be concise in order to make them easy to change, but they must also be structured to make changes easier. In order to do this, for any given change we have to achieve the following:

▶ make it easy to quickly identify the various specification sections that need to change,
▶ make it easy to change those and only those sections, and
▶ avoid having to make the same change in multiple places.

---

6   Depending on the project these are normally supplemented by other requirements specification work products such as screen mock-ups.

Some examples of this structuring follow:

▶ Each use case specification is clearly divided up into each of the basic flow and alternative flows. Once it is known which flows are affected by a change, it is clear exactly where in the document these changes should be made. Use case flows can be inserted by reference instead of by copy-and-paste.

▶ The interactions in the service interaction specifications match these flows exactly – there is a separate service interaction diagram for each use case flow. This means that, for any given use case specification change, it is easy to see exactly which matching parts of the service interaction specification need to change. As with use case flows, service interactions are inserted by reference instead of copying and pasting.

▶ Each service consumer and service provider lives in its own package, and these are separate from the service-oriented solutions that use these. This means that the consumers, providers, and systems can all be modified and pop in and out of existence individually. Also, service specifications are used by reference and therefore changes are automatically reflected in the service interactions they appear in.

Workflow Tooling to Help Track What's Going On

Most of our projects consist of hundreds of individual use case flows. According to the process, there are four high-level pieces of work to do for each of these use case flows – requirements, design, implementation, and test.

That means that, for a 200–use case flow project, there are at least 800 individual pieces of work that need to be done. As there are sequencing dependencies between these 800 individual work items (requirements needs to be done before design, design before implementation, and implementation before test), it's crucial for a project manager to know what the status is of each of these work items so that any bottlenecks or other planning problems can be spotted.

We use workflow tooling to help out here. This has two main benefits:

▶ It's easier to track progress for the individual, the subteam, and the project team as a whole.

▶ It's easier for each person to know what work is currently on their plate and what is coming down the line.

Handle Change While Avoiding Unnecessary Change

Being agile is about being able to handle change well when required. However, we still want to avoid unnecessary change as much as is possible as it causes unnecessary expense.

Two types of change exist:

▶ *extension* – it already does X and Y. Now need to also make it do Z.
▶ *modification* – the way it does X is incorrect. We need to change it.

Now the first kind of change is unavoidable in our iterative development world. And this isn't a bad thing. Each iteration will be adding new functionality to what was produced by the previous iteration.

However, we want to avoid as much of the second type of change as possible. I'll subdivide this modification type of change into

▶ *modifications to the requirements* – changing the way the solution behaves, and
▶ *modifications to the design* – not necessarily changing the way the solution behaves, but rather changing the shape of the implementation.

We avoid unnecessary modifications to the requirements as follows:

▶ Create a shallow but complete view of the requirements early on, and refine that later during the iterations. This means that all requirements have at least been considered before worrying about detailing any of the requirements.
▶ Cross-reference requirements against the business domain model and business process models. This is a useful exercise to pick up issues.
▶ Tackle difficult use cases in early iterations. These are the use cases that are most likely to have a knock-on effect on other use cases once you get into the detail.
▶ Showcase increments to end users as soon as you have working increments. Anything learned from these showcases can save time for those use case plays that haven't been assigned to the requirements team yet.

We avoid unnecessary modifications to the design as follows:

▶ Create a shallow but complete view of the design early on and refine during the iterations. This mean the overall architecture can be assessed before any of it gets refined.
▶ Build prototypes early on to validate the design.
▶ Design focus should follow requirements focus. Focus your design work on those parts of the solution where the requirements are most solid.

Risk Mitigation on Integration Projects

With any software development project there are the risks that the solution might not do what the end users want, that it might not do it in a way that suits their pattern of working, or that the technology that you're using to build the solution doesn't really suit the solution. But integration projects bring along a whole new bag of risks.

To provide a few examples:

▶ What if the mainframe application experts we've been provided don't understand their own applications as well as they tell us they do?
▶ What if the route planning software that we've bought doesn't actually work the way that the Application Programming Interface (API) says it does?
▶ What if the interface specifications that we have for our accounting package aren't up to date or complete?

These are the kinds of risks that, if they materialize, can bring an integration project to its knees.

For our projects we try and achieve two things:

▶ Let's make sure that we have a clear description of what the system does.
▶ Let's make sure that what it actually does matches this description.

For the first of these we use the previously mentioned external systems model. In this we capture a concrete view of the interfaces that we need to interact with and the information that the system holds. This will ensure that the way that we plan on integrating with the solution will work and also that it can be described to the developers.

Second, before we try and design against these interfaces, we write tests that verify that the system works the way we think it works. It doesn't help to put in design effort against an interface specification that is incorrect. A large amount of the risk is taken out of integration projects by creating interface verification tests early on in the project.

Usage of SOA Design Patterns to Ensure Extensibility and Flexibility

The success of your SOA solutions over time will be measured by how well these solutions handle change. How easy is it to add new functionality to the solution? What impact does this have on other solutions? Does change cause a reduction in the quality of service offered by your solutions? Does it compromise their behavior?

The key to ensuring this success is good design. And one of the keys to good design is to have a good set of design patterns that are consistently used across your solutions.

An example list of these is provided in Figure 21.6.

Estimation and Planning

To make our iteration planning effective, we ideally need an estimate for each of the work items on the project. By our previous calculation, a project of 200 use case flows will have an estimated 800 work items. We need a way to quickly get useful estimates for each of these 800 work items!

The procedure we follow is a simple one:

▶ For each use case flow, the team places it into one of the categories of complexity shown in Figure 21.7. The factor to the right is used to adjust estimates. So a Complex is seen to be twice as much work as a Medium Complexity, a Simple is half as much work, and so on.
▶ We then have some basic estimates (in ideal days) for the work of each of the subteams in order to deliver a Medium Complexity use case flow (Figure 21.8).
▶ The result is a set of estimates for each of our work items (Figure 21.9).

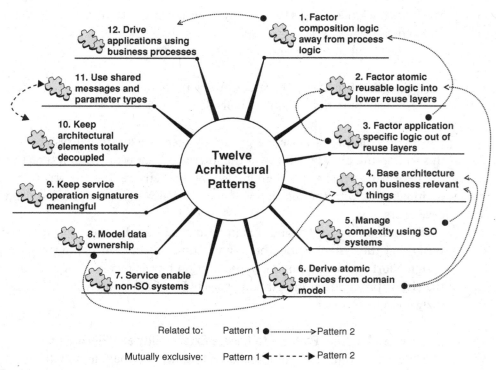

Related to: Pattern 1 ●·············▶Pattern 2

Mutually exclusive: Pattern 1 ◀ - - - - -▶ Pattern 2

21.6 Example of SOA design patterns.

▶ The use case flows (row in Figure 21.10) are each assigned to an iteration. In doing this we can assign each of the work items to a time box. So if UC17.1 is assigned to iteration 1, then the requirements work for it is assigned to time box 1, the design work to time box 2, the implementation to time box 3, and the test to time box 4. Similarly, if UC18.1 is assigned to iteration 3, then the requirements work will be in time box 3, the design in time box 4, the implementation in time box 5, and the test in time box 6.

▶ This allows us to quickly sum up how much effort is required in each time box for each team and, therefore, how many resources are required in each team.

Using this simple mechanism, the planning factors of number of resources, number of time boxes, and amount of in-scope work can be adjusted until the best plan is found.

Very Complex (VC)	4
Complex (C)	2
Medium Complexity (MC)	1
Simple (S)	0.5
Very Simple (VS)	0.25
Very Very Simple (VVS)	0.1

21.7 Complexity ratings.

Requirements	1
Analysis & Design	1
Implementation	4
Test	1.25

21.8 Estimates for iteration work items.

21.4 Results of an Agile Approach

Having applied the process for a number of years, there has been a lot of opportunity to work out what works well and what doesn't work so well. Let me share some of the results with you:

▶ We've used this process on projects that included multiple vendors working in multiple geographies and the process allowed the necessary collaborations to take place in a predictable and efficient way.

▶ Using design to guide the development teams has improved the usage of implementation technologies and has allowed specialist implementation teams (e.g., Portal, BPEL, integration connectors) to work effectively together as a team.

▶ The consistent view of the design across multiple technologies from different suppliers makes the overall solution easier to understand.

▶ The process has made it possible for teams to leverage design parts built by previous teams to produce new solutions.

▶ Quality issues are caught early by our projects due the fact that QA testing kicks in from the very first iteration.

▶ Our early showcases to the end users prove very effective at both getting useful feedback and making end users feel an integral part of the process.

▶ Doing proper progress tracking based on plans that are well thought out to start with reduces the amount of shortcuts required later.

▶ Having a continuous build and test in place is very important for developer productivity.

▶ Missing or bad design puts pressure on the development team, who end up releasing bad-quality code, which then puts further pressure on the testers.

▶ Tracking change is crucial to ensuring the team's ability to execute the plans. If changes are "slipped in" without planning updates, then the plans become unachievable and meaningless.

UC#	Use Case	Use Case Flow	Complexity	Requirements Days	Design Days	Implementation Days	Test Days
UC17.1	Capture client campaign order	Basic flow	S	1.11	1.11	4.44	1.39
UC17.2	Capture client campaign order	order information is incomplete	VS	0.56	0.56	2.22	0.69
UC17.3	Capture client campaign order	Exception flow	VS	0.56	0.56	2.22	0.69
UC18.1	Log in to Portal account	Basic flow	S	1.11	1.11	4.44	1.39
UC18.2	Log in to Portal account	Login failure	S	1.11	1.11	4.44	1.39
UC18.3	Log in to Portal account	Exception flow	VS	0.56	0.56	2.22	0.69
UC19.1	Manage client Portal account updates	Basic flow	MC	2.22	2.22	8.89	2.78
UC19.2	Manage client Portal account updates	Exception flow	VS	0.56	0.56	2.22	0.69
UC24.1	Request carrier certification test	Basic flow	C	4.44	4.44	17.78	5.55

21.9 Estimated use case plays.

Timebox	Start	End	Requirements Planned			Analysis & Design Planned			Implementation Planned			Test Planned		
			Available # Days	Required Days	Adj. %	Available # Days	Required Days	Adj. %	Available # Days	Required Days	Adj. %	Available # Days	Required Days	Adj. %
					Total			Total			Total			Total
E1	25-Jun	13-Jul	1.00 10	9.8		0	0.0		0	0.0		0	0.0	
E2	16-Jul	3-Aug	1.00 10	10.0		1.00 10	9.8		0	0.0		0	0.0	
C1	6-Aug	24-Aug	1.00 10	10.0		1.00 10	10.0		4.00 40	39.1		0	0.0	
C2	28-Aug	14-Sep	1.00 10	10.0		1.00 10	10.0		4.00 40	40.0		2.00 20	19.6	
C3	17-Sep	5-Oct	1.00 10	9.4		1.00 10	10.0		4.00 40	40.0		2.00 20	20.0	
C4	8-Oct	26-Oct	1.00 10			1.00 10	9.4		4.00 40	40.0		2.00 20	20.0	
C5	29-Oct	16-Nov	1.00 10			1.00 10			4.00 40	37.8		2.00 20	20.0	
C6	19-Nov	7-Dec	0	0.0		1.00 10			4.00 40			2.00 20	18.9	
C7	10-Dec	28-Dec	0	0.0		0	0.0		1.00 10			2.00 20		
C8	31-Dec	18-Jan	0	0.0		0	0.0		0	0.0		1.00 10		

21.10 Work items assigned to time boxes.

▶ Velocity and other progress tracking mechanisms allow for mature conversations with customers and other suppliers. It helps to be able to discuss progress in black-and-white terms.

21.5 Lessons Learned

Succeeding in applying software development process requires continually learning and improving. These are a few lessons learned that are worth sharing:

▶ *Keep an eye on whether everyone is playing by the rules.* Sometimes you need to make sure that other process participants are playing by the rules. Does the code being produced meet the design specifications? Are specifications complete? It's no use having a group of suppliers sign up to a process, only to then go ahead and completely ignore the process. I've worked on a project where this has happened as the other supplier felt under pressure to say that they were following the process. They had a requirements team writing use cases and a design team working on design. At the same time, though, they had a large development team ploughing ahead, writing code before specifications were even in place. The net result was that the project nearly ground to a halt when they had to spend a lot of time reworking the solution, and solution quality took a hit as software was delivered to the test team late, which placed them under a lot of pressure.

▶ *Watch the defect count!* One of the advantages of using iterations is that it allows you to learn from your mistakes. If iteration 1 testing has a 90% failure rate on its use case plays, it doesn't help if iteration 2 implementation is focusing all of its effort on releasing another set of use cases instead of addressing the current problems. Delivering loads of new use cases when the ones that you've already delivered are full of bugs is a strategy that is going to end in tears. While it might look like the team is making progress, having a big backlog of defects is just asking for trouble.

▶ *UAT is not QA.* There is often a temptation to go ahead and start user acceptance testing (UAT) for a solution before QA has signed off that all the defects have been fixed. This is likely to cause delays in UAT as this phase of testing is not meant to root out defects in the code but rather to check that the solution does its job in the hands of test end users. Rather it would be better to arrange another time box to sort out the remaining defects before starting UAT.

▶ *Increased automation.* It would be useful to make use of increased automation to check things such as whether the code matches the design or to check whether the design adheres to the design patterns.

22

The Agile Test-Driven Methodology Experiment

Lucjan Stapp, Assistant Professor, Warsaw University of Technology, and Joanna Nowakowska, Rodan Systems S.A.

SYNOPSIS

This case study describes a research project to determine the differences between one group of subjects following an agile testing method and another group of subjects following an ad hoc approach to testing. Results showed that the use of an agile approach improved defect detection by some 50% with just a 10% increase in test effort over the control group.

22.1 Introduction

My name is Lucjan Stapp and I work as an Assistant Professor at the Warsaw University of Technology. This case study describes research conducted at the Warsaw University of Technology, Faculty of Mathematics and Information Science, to determine the differences between one group employing an agile testing method and a control group using an ad hoc approach to testing.

22.2 Overview of the Testing Challenge

Agile approaches are often proposed as a solution to improving a number of characteristics of the testing process; typical improvements are claimed in speed and cost of testing, but many of these claims are only backed up by qualitative or anecdotal evidence.

This research was conducted to try to quantify the benefits of agile versus ad hoc testing approaches.

Teams and Exercises

To check the cost of using test-driven methodology, we have created two groups with the same knowledge of programming in Java:

▶ the test group, later called the TDD team (using test-driven development [TDD] methodology), and
▶ the control group, which, traditionally, does not have unit tests built in.

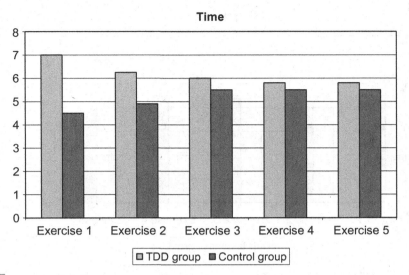

22.1 Time needed for preparation of application.

Both groups have made the same, rather simple applications (about 6 hours of coding for a three-person group). For these two groups we have prepared six exercises.

Programming and Test Environment

Both teams work in the same environment:

▶ Eclipse SDK 3.0.2 with
  ▷ built-in JUnit[1] for unit tests and
  ▷ built-in Hammurapi[2] for code review; and
▶ EMMA[3] for code coverage.

22.3 Experiment Results

Time Results

In Figure 22.1, we present times needed for preparation of the given application. As you can see, at the beginning, the TDD team needs much more time (about one-third more) than the control group, mostly for getting used to new tools (JUnit and Hammurapi – in our experiment EMMA was used only to check the predetermined level of test coverage). After the time needed for training (i.e., the first two exercises), this difference is not so significant; the TDD team needs about 7–10% more time to build the application.

[1] www.junit.org.
[2] www.hammurapi.org.
[3] emma.sourceforge.net.

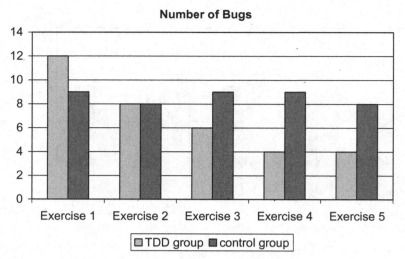

22.2 The number of defects.

Number of Defects in the Applications
In the next figure (Figure 22.2) one can see the number of defects that were found during the test process.[4] As one can observe, in the beginning period (i.e., the first exercise) the control group obtained the better result (produced fewer defects). In our opinion, it is the result of the additional stress on the TDD group and poor (not enough) knowledge of using tools by members of TDD group.

Quality of Source Code
In the last figure (Figure 22.3) we present the results obtained after checking the quality of the source code (using Hammurapi) – as one can observe, the TDD group created code that was much more coincident with coding standards than the code presented by the control group.

22.4 Lessons Learned

Summarizing this simple experiment, one can find that, using the agile TDD methodology in development and testing:

▶ Not much additional cost is incurred; when the developing teams are familiar with methods used, the extra time needed is rather small (less than 10%).
▶ Substantially (about 50%) fewer defects are found in the source code.

Also important is that the prepared code is amenable to refactoring. Analyzing the Hammurapi reports, one can find the proper scheme for code development.

---

[4] These tests are done by an independent experienced test team, which used white box and black box techniques to test applications.

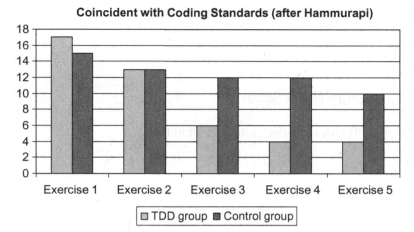

22.3 Coincident with coding standards.

On the other hand, we also want to underscore some weaknesses of the TDD method:

▶ When we used the TDD method, the rule *everything or nothing* stands – if we break before finishing all tests (e.g., because there is no more time), we do not obtain anything; the module does not exist.

▶ TDD does not replace unit testing – if we are working to a contract that states that unit testing has to be completed, we are obliged to prepare and execute these tests in addition to the TDD tests.

▶ It is an agile methodology; hence, some organizations reject it.

The last remark is at least controversial; the first two are much more important.

However – in our opinion – the gain (a greater than 50% reduction in defects with only 10% additional time) is an interesting argument for using this method.

23

When Is a Scrum Not a Scrum?

Dr Peter May, Technology Consultant at Deloitte

SYNOPSIS

This chapter presents a case study in which a large project was managed with Scrum by splitting the deliverable into three separate parts. Each part was assigned to a separate development team and the project was run as a "Scrum of Scrums." The case study focuses on one of these teams, describing how they followed the Scrum methodology closely to build and system-test their part of the deliverable. It then examines a few of the reasons for the exceptional outcome achieved by this team: zero code bugs in their first live code release.

The chapter closes with a look at common deviations from the prescribed Scrum methodology, and whether a project that deviates in any of these ways can still be considered to be following Scrum.

23.1 Introduction

My name is Peter May and I have worked for Deloitte as a technology consultant for the past six years. During this time, I've been involved in a number of agile projects in various roles, including developer, test manager, and latterly, as a project manager. Each of these agile projects has used the Scrum project management approach, but each has deviated from the "pure" Scrum approach to a greater or lesser extent.

In the case study that follows, I look at a model example of how Scrum, when implemented in a form close to its "pure" form, can lead to the production of very-high-quality software artifacts. I describe the testing challenges and how these were overcome, but I also consider the wider development aspects.

I have also worked on a number of other projects where pragmatic deviations from the prescribed Scrum methodology were made, to satisfy client or wider project needs. To close this chapter, I consider some of these deviations and discuss whether a project that deviates from Scrum's prescribed approach in these ways can still be considered to be following Scrum.

23.2 Overview of the Testing Challenge

Although I've worked on a range of Scrum projects, with a range of technologies (including SOA-based projects), the testing challenges have, by and large, always been the same:

▶ Frequent releases of the software product have been required, requiring stable software each time. This puts immense pressure on the test team within the Scrum to not only thoroughly system-test the functionality developed during the sprint but also to execute an ever-increasing amount of regression testing.

▶ The detail of how pieces of functionality will be implemented is not known before the sprint starts, so test scripts cannot be written in advance.

▶ Frequent releases typically means that the code has to be branched. This of course means additional work for the testers.

▶ In larger projects (>10 developers), it is good practice to split the team into two or more separate Scrums, then run the project as a "Scrum of Scrums." This can be very effective, but it does create the additional challenge of a cross-supplier integration test phase before integration testing with existing business systems can commence.

▶ The volume of testing resource required is frequently underestimated, causing a great deal of stress for the testers and impacting on quality. (As a rule of thumb, I would recommend two testers for every four or five developers.)

23.3 Definition of an Agile Testing Process

The first Scrum project I was involved with (my role was test manager) was the project that was able to follow the principles of Scrum most closely.

The client was a large U.K.-based organization that was interested in developing a new delivery channel for its products. The process (and technology) required to achieve this aim could be split into three distinct segments. Thus, the client decided to assign development of each of these segments to a separate Scrum team and then to run the project as a Scrum of Scrums. I was test manager for the Scrum team responsible for one of these segments.

My team followed Scrum's methodology by

▶ *completing all system testing (as opposed to cross-supplier integration testing) within the sprint*, ensuring that each sprint ended with the production of a working piece of software – a release candidate.

▶ *co-locating developers and testers in the same area.* We couldn't get a closed room, but we did get our own area. To ensure that the testers knew exactly what the developers were developing (and, hence, what they had to test), we initially tried inviting the testers along to the development design meetings that followed on from the sprint planning meetings. This tended to bore and confuse the testers, so we soon switched to an alternative approach whereby the development lead would brief the testers on the detailed design for a user story, once the developers had agreed the design.

▶ *encouraging frequent interaction between developers and testers* – including through table tennis!

▶ *estimating pieces of functionality in terms of user story points.* This was hard at first, but got easier as time went on. We used this to calculate a sprint velocity and hence to estimate when the product backlog (as it stood at any given time) would be finished. Crucially, we ensured that testing effort was taken into consideration during estimation.

▶ *having stand-up briefings every day* and ensuring that people turned up! We also ensured that they were kept brief.

▶ *frequent unit testing.* An automated set of unit tests ran every night to make sure that recent code changes had not broken previously developed functionality.

▶ *keeping the sprints short.* The client suggested four-week sprints, but we opted for two-week sprints as we knew that the client's development priorities would change rapidly. We were proven right and two weeks proved to be the optimum sprint length.

▶ *starting each sprint with a sprint planning meeting*, which would be in three phases:
   1. Sprint review: The output of the last sprint was demonstrated to the product owner (see later).
   2. Sprint retrospective: The team discussed which behaviors they should start doing, which they should stop doing, and which they should continue doing (and positively reinforce) to help make future sprints more successful.
   3. Sprint planning: The team received candidate user stories from the product owner and committed to develop and system-test some or all of these during the sprint.

▶ *not defining requirements too tightly.* We had a product backlog of user stories and we had a solution architecture that described the basic components required in the system. Beyond that, it was up to the development team to decide how to implement requirements. Where clarification on technical issues was required, these would be taken to a fortnightly Design Authority meeting with the customer and the other suppliers. Once the development team had decided how to implement a user story, they would brief the testers, who could then start preparing test scripts.

▶ *having a Scrum board,* on which was posted the product backlog, the sprint backlog, the burndown chart, and the latest "start–stop–continue" list.

▶ *insisting that we be left alone during a sprint to complete the tasks that we had been set.* We reminded the customer that a sprint could not be altered – only abnormally terminated. One abnormal sprint termination did occur just after the sprint had started.

▶ *not having one Scrum team with thirty or so members*, but splitting this into a "Scrum of Scrums." A central Scrum master coordinated our work with that of the other Scrum teams to ensure that we developed functionality in a coordinated fashion and were able to put releases into cross-supplier integration testing at the same time.

My team differed from Scrum's methodology by

▶ *using a "proxy" product owner.* The development and test team were 30 miles away from the customer, so the business analyst represented the customer in sprint planning meetings. To make this work, the business analyst would spend two days per week with the customer, getting to know and understand the customer's requirements.

▶ *developing a back-end system, which helped* (i.e., without a user interface). The customer, therefore, didn't need to see frequent demos: evidence from integration testing that what we were building was working was enough.

23.4 Results of the Agile Approach

The Scrum approach was remarkably successful: each user story was thoroughly system-tested as soon as development finished. As a result, the first code release made it through cross-supplier integration testing, user acceptance testing (UAT), and into live with zero code defects. (There were a few configuration problems in each environment, but the code itself was faultless.) Future releases also had a low code defect count.

A further success was that the Scrum team worked "sensible" hours, by and large. This was a result of the Scrum estimation process and the calculation of sprint velocity, which allowed us to set expectations with the customer about what was deliverable in any given sprint. Indeed, the customer was often able to work this out for themselves.

That the development cycle ran so smoothly is, I believe, for the following reasons:

▶ *The customer was 100% behind Scrum.* Indeed the decision to use Scrum was taken by the customer, who then requested that we use it. The developers and testers were also open-minded – indeed excited – about trying out Scrum for the first time.

▶ *We had a right-sized test team.* To compliment our five developers, we had two testers (plus a test manager). This allowed the user stories developed in each sprint to be fully system tested before the sprint was complete.

▶ *Testers and developers enjoyed good relations,* fostered through the collegiate spirit that arises from co-location and augmented by social activities (including pub lunches and frequent games of table tennis!).

▶ *The daily stand-ups proved their worth.* Initial skepticism about the value of these meetings quickly gave way to a firm belief in their benefit, after early identification of issues saved a lot of time for both testers and developers.

Note that we did not run integration testing and UAT as sprints – we found it was much easier to run these in "classical" fashion. Where fixes were required, those that were nonurgent were added into the current sprint (time was set aside for this), then deployed to integration/UAT with the rest of that sprint's code. Where the fix was urgent, we would branch the code and patch the fix straight in.

23.5 Lessons Learned

From this initial experience of Scrum, the main lesson learned was that, when properly applied, Scrum is a very effective project management methodology for software development.

However, I have also worked on a number of other projects where pragmatic deviations from the prescribed Scrum methodology were made to satisfy client or wider project needs. In what follows, I consider some of these deviations and whether a project that deviates in these ways can still be considered to be following Scrum. Test-specific considerations are examined first, followed by general considerations, which affect testing and development equally.

▶ *System testing not carried out during the sprint.* For system testing to be successfully conducted within a sprint, a "sprint test" environment is required in addition to the developer sandbox environment. The sprint test environment should be a "private" environment, for the sole use of the Scrum team. It should be possible to make frequent deployments to the environment at short notice. Without this environment, Scrum cannot function. (Note that system testing is distinct from cross-system integration testing, UAT, nonfunctional testing, and operational acceptance testing. These types of testing are not normally carried out within the same sprint – indeed they may not be subject to sprint discipline at all.)

▶ *Testers and developers not co-located.* Communication is key to Scrum, and this includes communication within the Scrum team. Sprint testing relies on the testers enjoying good relations with the developers, talking to them frequently to understand the detailed design that the development team has chosen to implement to satisfy a given user story. If testers and developers are not sitting right next to each other, the frequent informal discussions (and more formal meetings) required for (1) the testers to understand what the developers are building and (2) the developers to understand why the testers have raised a particular bug cannot happen. This leads to the breakdown of effective testing and is a frequent cause of testing failure in an agile environment.

▶ *No requirements at all.* It's a common misconception, but in fact agile (and Scrum) does need requirements to function. Without requirements, the project would be chaos. The requirements should take the form of "user stories" – descriptions of the functionality that the system should offer to users. They should be worked out by a business analyst, in consultation with the "product owner" and other key stakeholders.

▶ Additionally, agile can often benefit from a solution architect – someone who maps out the high-level components that are required to make the solution work and to make it reusable. The solution architect should have visibility of existing systems (or anticipated future systems) in the organization and so will be able to put together a high-level design that integrates well with these existing systems or makes integration with anticipated future systems straightforward. (Note that the solution architect should not attempt to specify the technical details of how systems interact – this should be left to the development team or technical architect.)

▶ *Highly detailed requirements.* Agile does not specify up front the detail of how to implement a piece of functionality; it expects the developers to work this out for themselves. This is based on the notion that no one will have a better idea about exactly what will and won't work than the developers. A project that tries to specify requirements to a deep level is by definition not an Agile project (see also *"No requirements at all"*).

▶ *Some projects need highly detailed requirements.* A good example would be a project to implement a new piece of regulation. The regulatory requirements are fixed: there is no room for manoeuvre here. This sort of project would not be suitable for an agile approach, but would be well suited to a waterfall approach.

▶ *Team is not left alone during a sprint.* A fundamental principle of Scrum is that, during a sprint, the Scrum team is left alone to complete the workload it had agreed to at the start of the sprint. The Scrum team can only do this if they are not interrupted by changes to the user stories agreed at the start of the sprint or by requests for new user stories to be added to the sprint. Note that this does not mean that there is no interaction between the team and the product owner during the sprint: the product owner should be on hand to answer queries from the developers and to adjudicate on "bug versus feature" disputes as required.

▶ *Long sprints.* A "sprint" is a short development cycle. The most popular sprint lengths are two and four weeks [94]. Sprints of longer than six weeks tend to defeat the purpose of Scrum – short development cycles and frequent reviews of the software product with the product owner are key to making a success of Scrum.

▶ *Stand-up meetings that take too long.* A stand-up meeting should be short (maximum fifteen minutes). To encourage this, it should be held standing up. If it's taking longer than fifteen minutes, it's not adhering to the principles of a stand-up meeting. Instead, it's probably become a design discussion or a debate about how best to fix a particular problem. This is all very well, but not a discussion that should keep the whole team back from continuing their work. The alternative explanation is that too many people are talking at the meeting.

Remember that, while anyone is welcome to attend, only members of the Scrum team (i.e., developers, testers, business analyst) can speak.

▶ *Customer demands fixed scope and fixed time or price.* It's not that unusual for a customer to demand fixed scope and fixed price or time, but it is certainly not agile! Agile was founded on the philosophy that scope cannot be fixed, as change is inevitable. Time and price certainly can be fixed; however, agile states that when time or money runs out, the software artifact that exists at that point should become the live system (subject to successful integration testing, UAT, and operational acceptance testing, of course).

PART THREE

AGILE MY WAY: A PROPOSAL FOR YOUR OWN AGILE TEST PROCESS

> A very important lesson to be learnt is that there is always another lesson to be learnt; the goal of fine-tuning our processes continues today, and will continue into the future.
>
> **Tom Gilb**

This section of the book provides an analysis of the agile case studies presented in Part 2 and draws upon the material from Part 1 to make a series of proposals about what components might be used to generate your own successful agile testing approach:

▶ Chapter 24, Analysis of the Case Studies, examines in detail the agile case studies presented in Part 2, identifying particularly successful agile techniques, common themes (such as successful reusable templates), as well as those testing approaches that were not successful and which may need to be treated with caution.

▶ Chapter 25, My Agile Process, draws on the information covered in the earlier chapters of this book and on the information provided in the case studies and their analyses to make a series of proposals for how you might set up and run your own practical, effective, and efficient agile testing process.

▶ Chapter 26, The Roll-out and Adoption of My Agile Process, provides advice and guidance on how to successfully introduce, roll out, and drive the use and adoption of your agile process within your own organization.

24 Analysis of the Case Studies

> If you plan to run a test more than ten times, it's cost effective to automate it.
> If you don't automate it, it's unlikely that you'll run it more than once!
>
> **Jon Tilt**

24.1 Introduction

This chapter examines in detail the agile case studies presented in Part 2, identifying particularly successful agile techniques, as well as those testing approaches that were not so successful and which may need to be treated with caution. The next chapter, Chapter 25, makes a number of proposals based on the analysis in this chapter for agile practices that you could reuse as part of the process of setting up your own agile method, while Chapter 26 provides a series of recommendations on how you might manage the roll-out and adoption of your agile method.

In addition to the case studies that made it into this book, I was lucky enough to have had offers of roughly the same number again, and I am very grateful to all those agile practitioners whose work helped to inform the material in this and the following chapters.

I have also been fortunate enough to be able to draw upon a rich vein of agile material from a number of other sources, including:

▶ my association with the British Computer Society Specialist Group in Software Testing (the BCS SIGiST), a number of whose members have been kind enough to submit agile cases studies;

▶ I am also indebted to those SIGiST members with whom I have discussed and corresponded with on the subject of agile testing and who have helped drive and define the material in this chapter;

▶ my work on the committee of the Intellect[1] Testing Special Interest Group, where I have been very pleased to have been asked to promote the cause of testing best practice and process;

▶ the academic community where, both through my early career on the teaching staff at the Open University and later as part of my own research activities in

---

[1] The organization whose goal it is to represent the U.K. technology industry (formed from the merger of the Computing Services and Software Association and the Federation of the Electronics Industry).

support of my doctorate, I have been involved with a wide range of academics working at the cutting edge of agile research;

▶ and last but not least, The Day Job, where I have been fortunate enough to work on a daily basis with agile development and testing best practices, and with colleagues who are not just inspired by and evangelical about agile, but who also work in real-world agile projects delivering genuine value to their customers.

This chapter is structured in the following manner:

▶ Sections 24.2 to 24.7 of this chapter review a series of agile best practices that the case studies have highlighted as being particularly valuable from a software quality perspective and are organized under the following headings:

   ▷ Agile Development and Testing,
   ▷ Agile Process and Project Management,
   ▷ Agile Requirements Management,
   ▷ Agile Communications,
   ▷ Agile Meetings, and
   ▷ Agile Automation.
▶ Section 24.8 provides a summary of the findings of this chapter.

Wherever appropriate, references from the case studies are used to support the findings in this chapter. In the couple of instances that a reference has been sourced from one of the case studies that did not make it into the body of the book, this is made clear in the text.[2]

Where the case studies have flagged some cautionary aspect of a particular practice, the issues raised are discussed and appropriate suggestions for mitigating the issues are provided.

Finally, while I use the term "analysis" for the method by which I have reviewed the case studies and collated the agile best practices, I must make it clear that I have not used any formal specific statistical method to arrive at the conclusions. Rather, this is more of a qualitative "9 out of 10 cat owners who expressed a preference said . . . " style of treatment of the material provided in the studies and other sources. Although the overall number of case studies submitted represents a very substantial body of agile work, the sample size and structure of the submissions make it difficult to perform any statistically significant analysis.

24.2   Agile Development and Testing

This section reviews a number of agile development and testing practices that the case studies have highlighted as being particularly valuable from a software quality perspective. I have deliberately not separated the development and testing practices

---

[2]   In such cases, I would be very pleased to supply the original material to anyone that drops me an email.

into two separate sections; I believe making this distinction is both artificial and injurious to the cause of developing and delivering quality software (as supported by numerous case studies in this book).

Iteration

Iteration – this tried and tested agile development practice provides a powerful means of bringing testing into the development life cycle as early as possible and ensuring testing continues frequently throughout the project. The early identification of defects ensures that the software can be corrected in a timely manner, avoiding the typical problems of late delivery and cost overruns normally associated with late discovery of serious defects.

The downside of iteration, from a testing perspective, is that functional tests and regression test suites grow continuously from iteration to iteration, causing an increasing testing load that if not managed effectively can cause an overload in terms of overall testing effort (see Tilt, Chapter 18, for example) – particularly toward the end of the project. Use of good test management techniques – such as reuse packs and targeted test execution – can be of value. Test automation through capture–replay tools (see Phillips, Chapter 12, for example) is another solution that should be considered. Both the practices of identifying targets of test and the use of capture–replay tools are discussed in later sections of this chapter.

Pair Testing

Many of the case studies confirm the positive benefits of the well-established agile practice of pair programming (e.g., Thomas, Chapter 6; Cassidy, Chapter 11; and Evans, Chapter 17) and support the view that, performed correctly, a pair of developers working together is more productive than if both developers were working in isolation. A number of the case studies (that of Thomas, for example) report the need to beware of resistance to this technique by "traditional-style" management on the grounds that it ties up two programming resources whose time might be better spent doing tasks separately.

Analogous to the practice of pair programming, the pairing of test resources with developers has also been reported to be a valuable practice in a number of case studies (see, e.g., Sewell, Chapter 5; Thomas; Kingston, Chapter 15; and Chana, Chapter 20). The benefits include testers providing valuable quality assurance input to unit test specification, development, and execution, ensuring that developers follow software quality best practices, and acting as a sounding board for developers to discuss development and testing ideas (Thomas, for example). A number of the case studies (Chana, for example) report measurable improvements in the quality of the delivered code using this practice.

As a cautionary note, you must avoid the perception by developers that the testers are there as the Quality Assurance Police (Sewell). One solution is to pair developers and testers but to have the tester review the developers' work at the end of the day, for example.

Involve Test Resources at All Stages

The practice of involving test resources at all stages is similar to pair testing but ensures that a test practitioner is available at all stages of the development life cycle. Sewell (Chapter 5), for example, describes a project in which a dedicated test resource worked alongside the analyst and the customer during the requirements analysis phase, generating test cases directly based on the elicited use cases [8]. This approach was seen to deliver a number of quality benefits:

▶ The tester was available to directly advise on the testability of any given requirement (to clarify with the customer how they would verify that a particular requirement had been met by the code during testing, for example), allowing any changes that were necessary to be made while all the relevant stakeholders were still on hand.

▶ The tester was able to improve the quality of the requirements by highlighting missing, contradictory, or duplicate requirements, using their quality assurance experience.

▶ In parallel with the creation of the use cases, the tester can also review and agree the suitability of the test case design directly with the customer.

In practice, involving test resources in the project as early as possible provides a highly effective means of driving testing into the project life cycle at an early stage.

Test-Driven Design and Development

Test-driven design and development (TDD) is a technique that appears to have been widely adopted in the case studies (for example, Sewell, Chapter 5; Cassidy, Chapter 11; and Kingston, Chapter 15). The success of TDD has also been demonstrated through research (Stapp and Nowakowska, Chapter 22). Ensuring that developers specify how they will verify that their code has met its requirements and performed correctly – before they write the code – means that the developer gains a much greater understanding of the requirement and what the corresponding code needs to do to meet it. Since the developer would have needed to have written the test at some point anyway, the overall time taken to complete development and testing of the code is about the same, with the added bonus that the requirements are better understood and implemented, that the test is more closely aligned to the requirement, and that the test is more effective at verifying the correct working of the code. This technique can be particularly effective when used in conjunction with pair testing.

Fix All Defects Immediately

It is a well-established testing fact that finding and fixing defects early in the project life cycle save substantial time and effort, reducing the risk of late detection of bugs, the high cost of correcting them, and the likelihood that the project will miss critical deadlines [4].

A number of the case studies (Phillips, Chapter 12; and Evans, Chapter 17; for example) describe projects that enforce this principle strictly; if defects are detected, development is halted until they are fixed. By using continuous integration techniques plus automated testing, defects are quickly localized to the most recent code change, allowing the developers to quickly focus on correcting the error and getting the project back on track.

In combination with agile practices that allow the team to visualize the real-time status of the project (such as the red and green lava lamp solution that automatically flags a build containing a defect, described by Evans), fixing such a defect becomes a matter of team pride, and there is a determined effort from the team to get the green lava lamp back on again!

Continuous Integration

Continuous integration is another practice that appears to have been very widely used in the case studies (Gilb and Johansen, Chapter 4; Thomas, Chapter 6; Knowles, Chapter 10; Wilson, Chapter 14; and Kingston, Chapter 15; for example). Used in combination with an automated build tool, and incorporating automated unit testing, the code can be automatically tested to quickly identify quality issues associated with that unit.

Where the automated tests fail, following submission of a new component, it is reasonably clear where the fault must lie, and the development process can be halted while the defect is investigated and fixed. Used in combination with some automated and highly visual means of showing that the build is broken, the issue can be quickly highlighted and other project tasks can be suspended while the team concentrates on fixing the defect.

Tilt (Chapter 18) takes this process a step further and describes a project where automated continuous build practices had been adopted that not only automatically executed unit tests, but also functional and regression tests (implemented in a capture–replay tool), providing very thorough test coverage of the application under development. Wilson further proposes the inclusion of code coverage and code complexity analysis as part of the automated continuous integration and build process.

Test Refactoring

Many case studies (Wilson, Chapter 14; Hodgkinson, Chapter 21; and Stapp and Nowakowska, Chapter 22; for example) report benefits from the established agile practice of code refactoring, particularly where a well-experienced agile team has embraced a culture of joint code ownership. Code refactoring can be particularly successful if conducted in concert with the use of an automatic build tool [95], which can also execute associated automated unit tests [50].

Although generally considered a positive technique, Hodgkinson advises that projects should not overrely on code refactoring (particularly when it is used to address design problems), since in his experience this is likely to result in projects failing to make progress.

The use of configuration management tools can also be of significant value in code refactoring, allowing the changes to be undone in a controlled and accurate manner if necessary.

A number of case studies (Cassidy, Chapter 11; Tilt, Chapter 18; and Chana, Chapter 20; for example) also describe a testing practice that is analogous to code refactoring but involving the tests comprising the test suite. Using test refactoring, test scripts may be changed for the purposes of making them more efficient and/or more effective, or even removed from the test suite (and stored separately for potential future reuse). This process is considered distinct from test maintenance, where a test may need to be changed to reflect some deliberate change to the application under development.

Particular benefits can be gained from using test refactoring on projects where the test suite is very large. Tilt (Chapter 18) describes a project involving some 35,000 test scripts, where the regression suite took up to ten days to complete. Test refactoring (which included editing existing scripts to make them more efficient, as well as omitting scripts that were no longer needed), in combination with "laser-guided testing" (see the next section, Identify Targets of Test), allowed this project to reduce the test suite execution time from ten days down to less than a day!

Test refactoring should be conducted with caution, and tests should only be altered if there is some pressing need for change (such as to make them execute more quickly when overall test suite execution time becomes an issue). As with code refactoring, the use of a configuration management tool is of value to allow changes to the test suite to be undone in a controlled and accurate manner where necessary.

Identify Targets of Test

The practice of identifying the targets of test is of particular value in large-scale projects involving large volumes of test scripts (Tilt, Chapter 18, for example), where it may become impractical or even impossible to run or rerun the entire test suite because of lack of time or resources. In such cases, it is necessary to target a specific subset of the overall test suite to execute in the allotted time. Typically, an informal approach is used that is based on the tester's experience, omitting scripts that address "tried and tested" aspects of the system under test, selecting a subset of the overall set of partition test cases, and making "guestimates" about which parts of the developing system may have been impacted by the most recent code changes.

A risk always exists, when omitting test scripts from a functional or regression test, that apparently innocuous changes to one part of the system under development will have completely unpredictable effects on a seemingly unrelated part of the system, and the decision to omit specific test scripts from a test must be balanced by the potential impact of failing to detect such a situation.

Test automation should be considered as one possible solution to enable large numbers of tests to be executed quickly and accurately (and also to execute overnight or over the weekend to fit additional testing into project timescales using unattended-testing techniques).

Test analysis techniques (such as Jon Tilt's "laser-guided testing" approach, Chapter 18) can be used to provide a formal and rigorous means of selecting subsets of tests to execute and should also be considered.

Code Coverage

Code coverage metrics may also be of value in the process of identifying the targets of test (to make sure that, in selecting a subset of tests to run, you ensure good coverage of the underlying code base). Code coverage tools (such as EMMA – see Evans, Chapter 17) are also a useful facility to assist you to measure the effectiveness of your testing (and of automated testing tool use).

However, just because you are generating code coverage metrics, do not be lulled into a false sense of security about your code quality; code coverage figures on their own do not improve quality – actions based on them can (Tilt, Chapter 18).

Rapid Prototyping

Rapid prototyping is another traditional agile practice (although one that is not without its detractors) that has been highlighted as being of benefit in a number of case studies (that of Chana, Chapter 20, and Phillips, Chapter 12, for example). The generation of simple prototypes prior to generation of full parts of the system under development can have a number of benefits:

▶ It helps the developer explore and understand the requirements in more detail.
▶ It provides a practical means of verifying the requirements with the customer.
▶ It provides a powerful and effective means of obtaining customer feedback on the functionality, look and feel, and usability of the proposed system.

However, in practice, a significant number of prototypes are abandoned, and the actual system is recoded from scratch; in these circumstances, it could be argued that the development effort on the prototype was wasted. Before adopting a development and testing style based on prototyping, the benefits must be weighed against the effort involved in developing additional code that is unlikely to be used in the final system. Another useful approach is to ensure that the prototypes are deliberately developed in such a manner that they can be reused in the final system.

Agile Exploratory Testing

A number of the case studies make a strong argument for the role of manual exploratory testing. Evans (Chapter 17), for example, highlights the value of employing a tester to perform the role of a "skeptical" user, creating unusual usage scenarios for the application under test in order to expose defects that automated tools and methods would be unlikely to uncover.

The downside of this approach in an agile project is that it can be an open-ended exercise, with an almost infinite number of possible scenarios that could be explored. Evans' solution is to engage an experienced and imaginative tester who could fit a set number of effective and efficient tests into the exploratory testing time box. In practice, caution must be taken to ensure a balance; Stephen K. Allott (Chapter 13) argues that the restrictive timescales in an agile approach to testing may stifle the imagination of exploratory testers and reduce the effectiveness of such testing.

24.3   Agile Process and Project Management

This section reviews a number of agile process and project management practices that the case studies have highlighted as being particularly valuable from a software quality perspective. The role and use of agile meetings are not covered in this section but is given a section of its own due to the importance of meetings in agile projects.

The agile process and project management best practices highlighted by the case studies include the following.

Don't Throw the Baby Out with the Bathwater

A significant number of the case studies (Thompson, Chapter 9; Allott, Chapter 13; Denning, Chapter 8; Evans, Chapter 17; and Chana, Chapter 20) make a very strong case for considering the reuse of traditional project management practices in agile projects:

- ▶ For example, V-model has been cited as having been used successfully to help structure the overall approach to the management of testing of an agile project (Thompson).
- ▶ Similarly, the use of PRINCE2 has been shown to be of value in the management of agile projects (Denning, Chapter 8) in terms of having formally defined and documented roles and responsibilities, having agreed and signed off terms of reference for the project, and having been tasked by a project steering committee to deliver against agreed plans.
- ▶ Formal process improvement schemes, such as the Capability Maturity Model (CMM [37]), have also been discussed and employed in a number of case studies (Warden, Chapter 16, for example) to provide a more formal approach to gaining long-term benefit from the lessons learned on previous agile projects.

It could be argued that agile projects employing these traditional methods are only "agile-esque" – that they haven't genuinely embraced an agile approach properly, and that the same project could have been completed faster, cheaper, and with better quality using a purist Scrum approach, for example.

However, my personal feeling is that you should make use of whatever tools you find that are able to bring you tangible benefits and that you ignore tried and tested project management solutions at your own peril; if it works for you – reuse it.

Well-Bounded Iterations

Many of the case studies have reported the benefits of arranging the iteration interval around some "naturally" occurring time span, such as a one- or two-week period (Kingston, Chapter 15; Gilb, Chapter 4; Tilt, Chapter 18; Hodgkinson, Chapter 21; and Chana, Chapter 20; for example).

Where it is possible to fit an iteration into such a period, it appears that the natural rhythm of working in a predictable weekly cycle helps to keep the team members focused on their tasks. For example, in Tom Gilb's case study, developers, testers, managers, and the customer all know that they will be preparing for and performing some specific activities on each day of the week.

One potential downside of this practice is that certain activities (and typically, testing) may be squeezed out of the iteration due to lack of time – for example, where a time-box approach is being used, if the time allocated to development overruns then the time allocated to testing is likely to be eaten into. One suggestion to ensure testing is not missed out is to give the testing task its own separate time box (Kingston).

Agile Estimation

Estimation is a critical aspect of both agile and traditional software development projects. Historically, estimation has been a commonly cited area for concern in traditional projects, with cost overruns and failure to deliver on time or to budget being a common experience.

Although the majority of the case studies did not raise agile estimation as an issue, some notable concerns were raised: Kingston (Chapter 15), Warden (Chapter 16), and May (Chapter 23) all reported challenges associated with agile estimation.

Warden reports that, on a Scrum project he was involved with, there were consistent problems with estimation (and particularly with accurate completion dates). The metrics and estimates displayed on the burndown chart would appear to be static across the majority of an iteration but would then suddenly slip toward the end of the iteration. Since a key reason for employing Scrum is to quickly identify project slippage, this phenomenon was a cause for concern. This issue appeared to be associated with accurate calculation of velocity; Warden uses the following analogy to illustrate the problem:

> The on-board computer in my car has to solve a similar problem to predict the range of the car. It knows how much petrol is left in the tank and the past fuel consumption. The question is how do you use past consumption in a predictor algorithm? Do you take the last 25 miles driving as representative, or 50 or 75? Likewise do you take the last Scrum cycle or use more? Furthermore, how do you normalise story counts so they are comparable across cycles, as stories ranged in size by a factor of 10?

Another issue with agile estimation that Warden identifies is what he terms "sucking the pipe-line dry at the end of a cycle." To maximize velocity, staff would be allocated to clear as many user stories as possible, including QA team members who would be pulled off testing duties. As a result, although the velocity metrics improved, this approach was storing up problems for later in the project, where there would be reduced timescales and resources, with the inevitable time-scale compromises for testing the software.

In terms of the former estimation issue highlighted by Warden, metrics can play an effective role in addressing the reliable and accurate calculation of velocity. Keeping historical data provides the means of normalizing estimation data and also allows the optimistic and pessimistic reporting styles characteristic of different team members to be recognized. A number of products are available that allow estimated and actual effort to be automatically collated and which can even adjust different practitioners' estimates based on previous data (see [60, 63], for example).

In terms of the latter observation, ensuring that testing plans and resources are ring-fenced is an effective solution to ensuring testing practitioners are not pulled off their quality assurance task and onto project fire-fighting tasks. Approaches used by Sewell (Chapter 5), Thomas (Chapter 6), and Phillips (Chapter 12), for example, have also promoted the idea that having testers involved throughout the project life cycle, and of closer working practices with developers, may actually act to prevent the situation Warden described happening in the first place.

May (Chapter 23) identifies the difficulties of estimating the time and effort required to produce the code to implement user stories as a challenging exercise, particularly for practitioners new to agile methods. The information was used to calculate sprint velocity and, hence, estimate when the product backlog would be finished. Increasing experience with estimation and the use of metrics collected during previous sprints meant that subsequent estimates became increasingly more accurate. May also cites that keeping the sprints short (of two weeks' duration in this case study) was of benefit in keeping progress on track.

Finally, Kingston reports issues with estimation on an offshored agile project. In this instance, the problems with compiling accurate progress estimates from the offshored development team was attributed to problems with time zone differences, the difficulty with convening ad hoc offshored meetings, lack of formal cross-geo reporting tools, and the challenge of not having face-to-face communications when the weekly telephone conferences were held. Kingston observes that the use of an agile approach actually highlighted these issues much more acutely than a traditional project approach would have done.

The solutions to these issues that Kingston identifies include improving communications with the offshored team, firmly but politely challenging all estimates, being sensitive to possible language and culture differences, focusing on better communications infrastructure (such as instant messaging and Internet telephony systems), the use of Web 2.0 applications (such as holding virtual meetings in Second Life [64]) and videoconferencing technologies, adopting tools that support 24×7 working and process enactment (such as [63, 65]), improving the working time overlap across time zones (such as getting one team to start and finish work thirty to sixty minutes earlier each day while the other team starts and finishes thirty to sixty minutes later each day), and, last but not least, getting a member of the offshore team to co-locate with the onshore team to help address language and culture differences (these points are expanded upon in Section 24.5).

Progress Measurement

The ability to measure progress in software development projects is a key aspect of their successful management, allowing actual progress against plans to be compared and remedial action taken where problems are identified.

Frequently progress is assessed by collating the estimates of individual progress from the members of the team. However, this approach is notoriously difficult to perform accurately; individual developers and testers may report their own progress optimistically or pessimistically (or may even be "economical with the truth" about what they have or have not done). In small co-located agile projects, this is less likely to be an issue, because frequent contact between the project stakeholders, plus practices such as pair programming, all act to ensure the availability of more accurate progress information.

On larger agile projects, or where the stakeholders are not co-located, this may be an issue. Kingston (Chapter 15) and Evans (Chapter 19), for example, describe the challenges of collecting accurate progress estimates from offshore team members where time differences, cultural differences, and just simply the lack of confidence that face-to-face communication provides can cause significant errors in estimating progress. A number of simple solutions can be effective in addressing this issue:

▶ Project managers or team leaders should use simple, clear, and unambiguous language when discussing progress and should not be afraid to challenge any estimates with which they are not comfortable. The estimates should be fed back to the team to ensure that the team agree with them.

▶ Find other solutions for "face-to-face" communication with offsite or offshore team members such as videoconferencing or webcam technologies, or perhaps by using a tool that can support a virtual meeting, such as Second Life [64].

▶ Ensure you collect metrics on estimates and actuals and use these to "normalize" future estimates (in effect, balancing optimistic and pessimistic reporting styles).

▶ Use one of the so-called process enactment tools [63] that ensure developers and testers follow a defined agile process, and where data are automatically collected on planned and actual timescales as the team members plan and execute their tasks (even automatically adjusting estimates for optimistic and pessimistic workers).

Progress Visualization

On a topic related to progress measurement, a number of the case studies have reported the benefits of publishing or displaying the project progress (often in real time) to the project stakeholders. Examples have included the following:

▶ Publish quality metrics, such as the breakdown of where defects are found in the project life cycle (Tilt, Chapter 18) to encourage healthy competition between stakeholders in the project (all project metrics were displayed graphically for all stakeholders to see, which was found to be "a great motivator").

▶ Publically display project burndown charts (Warden, Chapter 16; Phillips, Chapter 12; and May, Chapter 23) to ensure all stakeholders are able to review the progress information (but ensure the data are accurate and up to date).

▶ Wilson (Chapter 14) describes a very effective approach in which code complexity and code coverage information are shown to the users as color-coded graphics to display the results of tests executed automatically using his continuous integration, build, and test architecture.

▶ Evans (Chapter 17) describes an automated system where a broken build detected during the continuous integration process would cause a green lava lamp to be turned off and a red lava lamp to come on. It became a matter of significant pride for the team to ensure that the red lava lamp was switched off before the wax could become liquid and start to flow!

Availability of Agile Process Guidance

A number of the case studies stress the importance of providing simple and effective access to agile best practices for the team members. Sewell (Chapter 5), for example, describes the benefits of the use of process summary cards from the Essential Unified Process [34], whereas Hodgkinson (Chapter 21) and Chana (Chapter 20) discuss the role of the Rational Unified Process [7], with its distributed delivery of best practices via a web browser interface.

Although availability of agile best practice guidance on a project is important, the availability of an easily accessed and used source of such information should not be used as a substitute for thorough and effective training in the use of the agile method. Many of the case studies emphasize the importance of well-planned and delivered training in the success of agile projects (Gilb, Chapter 4; and Phillips, Chapter 12; for example).

In a similar manner, where standard reusable agile templates (such as test script templates) are available for use on a project, these should also be widely accessible and easily customized. Watkins [4], for example, provides access to downloadable and customizable testing templates, and Appendices E through G of this book provide templates for a number of agile testing artifacts.

Role and Use of Metrics

A number of case studies describe the use of metrics on agile projects and their benefits (Norman, Chapter 7; Wilson, Chapter 14; Phillips, Chapter 12; and Tilt, Chapter 18; for example). These can include

▶ gaining a quantitative means of assessing the success of some activity – for example, having the data available to know that the adoption of a particular practice (such as pair testing) has reduced the number of defects detected prior to release of the software by N%;

▶ being able to publish or make information available to the other stakeholders to allow them to see the state of the project, to encourage practitioners to improve their performance (perhaps competitively against their colleagues), and to manage the customers expectations;

▶ refining the process of estimation. Metrics can be used to compare planned or estimated timescales, cost, and effort with actual figures. This sort of analysis can be used to refine future estimates and plans;

▶ being able to report gains in productivity, reductions in cost, and reductions in delivery timescales achieved by adopting a particular agile method to senior management;

▶ being able to publish gains in productivity, reductions in cost, and reductions in delivery timescales achieved by adopting a particular agile method to other interested parties in your organization (via newsletters, your intranet, or by lunch and learn presentations);

▶ supporting a process improvement program (covered in more detail later in this chapter).

While there are undoubtedly very good reasons for setting up and administering a metrics program, there are a number of important things to consider in setting up such a scheme:

▶ Make sure you understand why you are interested in metrics – what do you plan to do with the data (such as improving productivity, reducing defects, and/or process improvement)? This will influence which data you need to target and collect.

▶ Understand your current baseline; you cannot make statements about how your software development process has changed unless you have a quantitative view of where you were before you introduced your agile approach. In practice, this means collecting data as early as is practically possible and requires a great deal of foresight. In some organizations, you may be lucky and data (such as time sheet information) may already be routinely collected.

▶ Be inclusive rather than exclusive in terms of the data you collect; later on in the project, it is very difficult go back in time and collect some specific data that you suddenly discover would have been useful to have collected.

▶ Collect metrics on the time, effort, and cost of setting up and administering the metrics program – you should know how much metrics are costing you.

▶ Finally, be aware that the activity of collecting metrics can alter the value of those metrics that you are collecting (known as the Hawthorne Effect [96, 97]).

Watkins [4] provides detailed information on the setup, roll-out, adoption, and ongoing maintenance of a metrics program.

The adoption of a metrics program on an agile project must be balanced by the cost of setting up, administering, and maintaining such a program. Wherever possible, make use of tools that automatically collect, analyze, and report on metrics for you – such as integrated test management tools that can automatically produce reports on test case design versus requirements coverage, for example. Similarly, process enactment products (see [63]) are able to collate developer estimates on both task completion times and the actual values.

Also remember that the activity of collecting metrics itself is not necessarily useful, but that taking action based on the metrics is where the value is obtained (Tilt, Chapter 18).

Process Improvement

The ability to fine-tune your agile process, to learn from successes and failures, and to apply the lessons learned to future projects can be of great value. Many case studies (Gilb, Chapter 4; Allott, Chapter 13; Kingston, Chapter 15; Warden, Chapter 16; Evans, Chapter 17; and Tilt, Chapter 18) advocate the use of process improvement in their agile projects, and many of the established agile methods incorporate process improvement in their practices, such as Scrum's Sprint Retrospectives and Evo's Key Process Principles.

Metrics is a subject closely related to process improvement; if you don't have the data to verify that a particular strategy for improving some aspect of your process has been successful, it is difficult to substantiate claims that there have been improvements. If you intend your agile approach to incorporate effective process improvement, you must seriously consider the role metrics can play in such a scheme.

As a final thought, a number of the agile case study authors hold strong views on formal process improvement methods; Gilb, for example, has been heavily involved with the Capability Maturity Model (CMM [37]), and Warden discusses the role of CMM on agile projects in his case study.[3] Although such a formal approach to process improvement, involving significant time, effort, and cost to implement, may seem to be at odds with the goals of agile methods, many organizations derive benefits and value from these schemes.

Everyone Is a Software Engineer

It is one of software development's oldest clichés that there are frequent project tensions between testers and developers; developers have often perceived testers as either

▶ the people who were far too meticulous, found defects that the developers had to fix, made delivery of the software late, and made the developers look bad; or

▶ the people who didn't do enough testing, allowed code to be delivered that still contained defects, and made the developers look bad!

As clichéd as this view may appear to be, there are still many case studies in this book that demonstrate that this "us and them" tester–developer issue is still prevalent.

Denning (Chapter 8), for example, describes a particularly extreme example of this situation, where the developers and testers were in a virtual war with each other, in which the developers actively looked for opportunities to make the testers look bad to justify their cut of the bonus payment cake!

More enlightened practitioners (including Sewell, Chapter 5; and Phillips, Chapter 12) describe agile projects in which the developers, testers, and other stakeholders

---

[3] Although Richard Warden does highlight issues where the flexibility and responsiveness of agile approaches are at odds with the goals of predictability and repeatability that the CMM scheme seeks to identify in projects.

are all encouraged to take personal responsibility for software quality. Phillips takes this one step further and describes a project where the developer and tester roles are subsumed under the title of software engineer.

Other agile practices can also help challenge these negative prejudices; many of the case studies describe an approach termed pair testing (Sewell, Chapter 5; and Kingston, Chapter 15; for example). In this practice, developers and testers are paired (in a manner analogous to pair programming) to work together on software quality aspects of the development. This approach appears to have been particularly beneficial; in one such scheme, Thomas (Chapter 6) reports that developers even began to actively seek out testers to bounce development ideas off them and to get their feedback.

24.4 Agile Requirements Management

Without requirements how do you know what it is you need to develop and how do you prove the software does what it is supposed to do? These question are as relevant to agile projects as they are to traditional projects, except that the requirements elicitation process on traditional projects is often a long, complex, and notoriously difficult task to achieve; it is estimated that as many as 75% of all projects fail because of issues with requirements [98].

The time taken to elicit requirements combined with the copious amounts of documentation that commonly need to be created and maintained seem completely at odds with the goals of agile development. This section discusses a number of best practices employed in the case studies that enable requirements to be managed in an agile manner.

The Role of Use Cases and User Stories in Test Case Design

A large number of the case studies (Sewell, Chapter 5; Wilson, Chapter 14; Kingston, Chapter 15; and Warden, Chapter 16; for example) report the benefits of use cases [8] and user stories [20] in eliciting the customer requirements for the system. These approaches elicit simple and easily understood examples of how the user interacts with the system that is to be developed (or that is in the process of being developed) to produce some outcome of value to the customer.

From a quality management perspective, the scenarios documented using these practices are not only useful in assisting the developers understand what they need to produce but also map very naturally into test cases. Sewell, for example, describes how involving the testers in the requirements analysis alongside the analyst and customer representative enabled accurate and effective tests to be designed in parallel with use case capture, driving testing earlier into the project life cycle and ensuring that the customer was satisfied with the correctness of the resulting test case.

Reducing Requirements Documentation Overload

Keeping documentation and the need for document maintenance to the minimum level possible is a well-established agile principle, and a number of the case studies

(Sewell, Chapter 5; and Evans, Chapter 19; for example) describe specific practices that they have employed to achieve this.

A great deal of documentation on projects is used for communication, such as passing requirements information to developers, testers, and other stakeholders. Sewell describes the value of daily stand-up meetings in improving communications and reducing documentation to manageable levels on a large agile project; the overhead of documentation is avoided because the team members are able to talk to each other about important issues, rather than having to type the information into an email or a change request tool, and can ensure that it is distributed to the people who need to know about it.

Sewell also describes the benefits of having all the stakeholders co-located from the start of the project, and in particular the benefit of having testers work alongside the analyst and customer representative during the requirements elicitation task. In effect, this short-circuits the need to provide long, complex, and potentially out-of-date requirements information to the test team.

Evans (Chapter 19) describes a number of techniques for improving communications that can provide direct, honest, speedy, and productive information exchange with the goal of producing fewer and less formal documents (such as the Weaver Triangle [72]). The techniques that Evans describes can also be usefully applied to the process of requirements elicitation itself.

Denning (Chapter 8) makes an important point about the role of formal documentation in commercial projects, where it proved essential for a company contracted to perform a large and complex testing task on a commercially critical system to document the roles, responsibilities, and terms of reference for the project. Without this documentation, issues about the scope of the project and the responsibilities of the staff performing the work could have potentially put the profitability of the contract at risk.

From a review of the case studies and the very different perspectives on the role and use of documentation that they provide, a useful approach is to not be dogmatic about documentation but to look for strategies to reduce the project documentation capture and maintenance load. Automation, such as requirements management tools, for example, could provide such a solution.

Look Beyond Requirements to Real Customer Needs

Gilb (Chapter 4) makes the case in his Evo method [32] for delivering customer value rather than sticking slavishly to traditional requirements elicitation practices. A key principle of Evo states that you cannot know all the customer requirements in advance, but that you discover them more quickly during the process of delivering valuable working software.

Ensure All Requirements Have Tests

Except on the most trivial of projects, without requirements how do you prove the software does what it is supposed to do? Good testing practice demands that it should be possible to show that each requirement has one or more tests designed and implemented against it.

Even though agile development best practice mandates that all units have unit tests associated with them, Sewell (Chapter 5), Cassidy (Chapter 11), and Kingston (Chapter 15) extend this view by ensuring that any and all requirements can be shown to have tests written against them.

Tilt (Chapter 18) describes an approach used on a very large project in which rigorous test metrics and their statistical analyses were employed to formally demonstrate complete code and requirements coverage.

Similarly, Wilson (Chapter 14) describes an agile continuous integration and build approach that uses tool support to automatically verify test coverage combined with a powerful graphical display to highlight areas of concern to the project stakeholders.

Chana (Chapter 20) also describes the value of tool support in providing automated requirements management as well as the benefits of traceability that such products can provide (to determine who proposed and who authorized particular requirements or changes to requirements, for example).

Role and Use of Requirements Tools

As discussed in the previous sections, a number of the case studies (Wilson, Chapter 14; and Chana, Chapter 20; for example) describe the value of using tool support for requirements management.

Chana describes the use of a commercial requirements management tool [61] to document, manage, and maintain rapidly changing requirements on a small-scale agile project. Traceability is a key benefit that Chana reports, allowing him to quickly and easily use the change history facilities of the tool to identify who had requested and authorized a particular requirement or change to an existing requirement. Other stakeholders were able to review and provide comments on the requirements through a web-based user interface, allowing non-co-located team members to be closely involved in the requirements process.

Wilson describes the role of requirements coverage as part of the wider tool support for a continuous integration build and testing process that he developed. In addition to being able to provide a graphical color-coded display of the underlying code coverage metrics, a specific benefit of this approach is to establish confidence in the testing for any given build or release; as Wilson puts it, "It is better to have an 80% unit test pass rate on 95% of the code, than to have a 100% pass rate on 5% of the code."

As with any tool, care must me taken by the project manager or team leader to avoid letting the tool become the focus of attention, rather than the task the tool has been acquired to achieve; I have seen far too many technical people become obsessed with fiddling and fine-tuning the features and facilities of a tool instead of focusing on the purpose of the tool – to save time and effort, and improve the quality of the delivered product!

24.5 Agile Communications

Good communication is a fundamental principle of successful agile projects, and I would argue that the majority of agile best practices are communications-oriented. The following sections review some of the communications best practices highlighted in the case studies as being of particular benefit, including advice on offshored or distributed agile projects.

Co-location of Stakeholders

Co-location of stakeholders is a traditional and universally supported agile best practice throughout the case studies. Even the authors of those case studies (such as Thomas, Chapter 6; Kingston, Chapter 15; and May, Chapter 23) where there are issues about lack of co-location of staff accept that, in the ideal situation, the teams should be working together in the same place at the same time. A number of the case studies describe specific quality management benefits associated with co-location:

▶ Norman (Chapter 7) reports that, where developers and testers are co-located, developers are able to gain an understanding and appreciation of the tester role and even develop a professional respect for testers and testing.
▶ Sewell (Chapter 5) reports that the availability of testing practitioners at all stages of the project has been highly beneficial. For example, involving testers with the users and analysts during requirements elicitation has enabled the testers to challenge the testability of particular use cases – asking questions like "how would you verify if that (feature) works?"– with the result that the overall quality of the requirements has improved. Similarly, pairing developers and testers has enabled the testers to review unit test designs and provide their feedback to the developers, with the result that the effectiveness of unit testing has improved.
▶ Thomas (Chapter 6) also reports the benefits of co-locating developers and testers in terms of the closer working relationship that he saw forming, in his case study; in a number of instances, developers were observed to actively seek out testers to obtain their views on new ideas that the developers were working on.
▶ Co-locating the customer or users with testing practitioners also has benefits, such as allowing test analysts to speak to the users to clarify some aspect of a use case or user story during test case design, for example.

Non-co-located Teams

Although co-location of the stakeholders in an agile project is the ideal goal, a couple of the case studies (such as Thomas, Chapter 6; and Kingston, Chapter 15) describe projects where necessity (and the goal of saving costs) meant that some members of the team were offsite.

Thomas describes a project where most of the development was carried out in North America, with testing and release management in the United Kingdom. While Kingston describes a project that was U.K. based (management, design, and the higher levels of test), the majority of the code development was offshored to India and the customer perspective was provided by a small team in the United States.

The case studies describe some very valuable best practices for improving the communications of non-co-located teams trying to work in an agile manner.

▶ Set up and use an effective project communications and working infrastructure, such as
  ▷ videoconferencing facilities in combination with tools to share and remotely operate workstations (Thomas);
  ▷ Web 2.0 social networking products (Chana, Chapter 20), including instant messaging and virtual meeting tools (such as Second Life [64]); and
  ▷ the use of distributed process enactment tools (see [60, 63]) to support distributed collaborative development (Kingston).
▶ Harmonize offshore time zones – adjust the working-day start and end times (by perhaps thirty to sixty minutes in each location) to improve the overlap of the working hours between the different time zones (Kingston).
▶ Be sensitive to different cultural and language differences between different sites (Evans, Chapter 19); use simple and clear vocabulary, avoid using idiomatic phrases and/or colloquialisms, and don't be afraid to repeat, reword, or stress some important point that needs to be communicated.
▶ Consider having a representative from the offshored team co-locate with your local team; Kingston reports that this is a valuable approach to use in building a trusting relationship with the remote group. The local representative can also help address the language and cultural differences that can become amplified through poor remote communications.

Improving Interpersonal Communication

In addition to having the opportunity to communicate, a number of the case studies address the issue of the quality of communication (Evans, Chapter 19; Kingston, Chapter 15; and Evans, Chapter 17; for example). That is, how can you ensure that all participants in a meeting are able to contribute to the success of the meeting? Holding a retrospective to discuss the lessons learned on the last iteration or on the project as a whole is likely to be less than successful if the person who knows the most is the least talkative, or the meeting is hijacked by someone who wants to tell everyone about their fantastic new sports car!

The following communications practices provide a valuable means of ensuring you get the most from your agile meetings:

▶ Evans (Chapter 19) describes a technique called de Bono's Six Hats in a Meeting [77], in which the members of a meeting are encouraged to "wear different hats," each of which denotes some particular mode of thinking – for example, the Black Hat might represent a critical viewpoint, whereas the Green Hat might represent a lateral-thinking, brain-storming perspective. "Putting on a hat" allows an individual to move outside their perceived stereotype, perhaps allowing a very factual person to express emotional views, for example. The hats also provide a less personal metaphor for communicating; it may be easier and sound less critical to tell someone that they sound like they have their Black Hat on rather than telling them not to be so negative about something.

▶ A number of the case studies (May, Chapter 23, for example) highlight the issues that lack of focus in agile meetings can cause. A particular technique covered in Evans' case study that can help address this is that of Ishikawa fishbones [78, 79]. This graphical cause-and-effect analysis technique provides a highly focused approach for drilling down to the root causes of problems. The term *fishbones* refers to the graphical structure[4] that is created as the technique proceeds; team members add their ideas (perhaps as part of a brain-storming exercise) to the diagram, creating what looks like a fishbone (see Figure 19.1). Evans also describes the role of this technique to move from the problem space to a solution by "drawing the diagram in reverse."

▶ What happens in an agile meeting (such as an application design workshop [18]) where active and effective communication is essential, but where the facilitator is finding it difficult to get the design discussion started or to keep the process running? Evans describes a technique termed a Weaver Triangle [72], which can be used to assist a team to focus on an overall aim or goal. This graphical technique is structured using a triangular diagram (see Figure 19.2), which establishes a particular goal or aim at the top of the triangle. Through discussion, this high-level goal is broken down into more specific goals, each of which are documented on the diagram under the top-level goal. Finally, specific objectives that will allow the goals to be achieved are discussed and documented at the base of the triangle. This analysis provides a team with a powerful technique to proceed from the specific (a high-level objective or goal), through clarification of the high-level objective into subgoals, and finally into specific objectives to achieve the subgoals and, hence, the overall objective.

If you would like to understand how to improve the quality of communications on agile (and traditional) projects in more detail, I wholeheartedly recommend you obtain a copy of Isabel Evans' book [72].

24.6 Agile Meetings

Having established that a very large part of the success of agile projects is associated with effective communication, this section focuses on a particular set of activities in agile projects where communication is conducted in a more formal manner – agile meetings.

---

[4] This technique could be of particular benefit on a co-located agile project; the fishbone diagram could be set up on a whiteboard or wall in a location where all team members can review the diagram and add their input.

All agile methods stress the importance of regular, structured face-to-face meetings involving the project stakeholders, and this is certainly supported by virtually all of the case studies.

A wide range of reasons for and styles of meeting are advocated in the various agile methods, and range from simple fifteen-minute stand-up meetings to review progress, agree next tasks, and identify risks and barriers to achieving those tasks (as seen in Scrum projects), to several days for joint application design workshops (such as those held in RAD projects).

This section provides best practice guidance on agile meetings distilled from the experiences described in the case studies and other sources.

Agile Project Start-up Meetings

Project start-up meetings are an essential best practice in many of the existing agile methods (forming part of the preproject phase in DSDM, for example). A number of the case studies also cover the role and use of start-up meetings in the projects that they document.

Kingston (Chapter 15), for example, describes the value of holding an initial project start-up meeting to introduce the stakeholders, confirm roles and responsibilities (and lines of communication), review and agree the tasks and overall timescales (at least at a high level), and to plan and prepare for the first iteration.

Denning (Chapter 8) reports the value of employing traditional project management approaches to agile testing projects and describes how PRINCE2 [22] project management controls, including a formal start-up meeting, were used to provide an appropriate approach to kicking off an important commercial project. In this case study, Denning's company was contracted as a third-party testing partner, and it was commercially expedient to formally identify the project sponsor and have the terms of reference agreed and documented.

To ensure that all participants who are permitted to speak at an agile start-up meeting are given an equal opportunity to participate, and to ensure that those less extrovert members of the meeting are still encouraged to provide their valuable contribution to the proceedings, consider using the agile communications techniques described by Evans (Chapter 19) in her case study.

Agile Iteration Start-up Meetings

The established agile methods, such as Extreme Programming (XP) with its iteration planning meetings and Scrum with its sprint start-up meetings, all promote the role and use of formal start-up meetings for each iteration. These meetings are used to agree the tasks to be worked on (selecting user stories in XP, for example) and their timescales, to agree how the tasks are assigned, and to identify risks and discuss their mitigation.

A number of the case studies (Kingston, Chapter 15; and Phillips, Chapter 12; for example) also include a checkpoint in iteration start-up meetings to review and, where appropriate, incorporate the lessons learned from previous iterations. Phillips reports that reviewing the lessons learned has been particularly beneficial in terms of keeping the project testing processes as up to date as possible and ensuring their relevance to the project testing requirements.

Kingston explicitly includes the discussion and agreement of the test plan for the iteration, plus any specific timescales, resources, and/or staff that are needed to support the iteration test plan in the iteration start-up meeting agenda.

Daily Meetings

Both Scrum and XP promote the use of short daily stand-up meetings (typically limited to fifteen minutes). The purpose of these meetings is specifically to talk about what was achieved the previous day, what is planned to be worked on today, and what risks or barriers there might be to achieving these goals.

Such meetings are highly focused on the work at hand, even to the extent of only permitting certain team roles to speak while others attend simply to listen to the proceedings (such as the pig and chicken roles in Scrum projects). In XP, an interesting incidental goal of the daily meeting is to reduce the need for other meetings that might take place through the day.

Sewell (Chapter 5) reports that the benefits of holding daily stand-up meetings have included helping to reinforce the concept that effective testing is the key to delivering higher-quality code and also in breaking down the "us and them" issues many projects observe between developers and testers.

May (Chapter 23) provides a cautionary warning that overrunning, poorly focused, and poorly facilitated stand-up meetings are likely to be a symptom that an agile project is failing to be run in an agile manner. May urges that teams adhere closely to the duration and principles of the stand-up meeting and observes that where such meetings overrun or are ineffective, it is likely to be because the meeting has been hijacked to discuss design issues or to debate how best to fix a particular problem.

Interim Iteration Meetings

Gilb (Chapter 4), Chana (Chapter 20), and Kingston (Chapter 15) all report significant benefits of working to a "natural" iteration period (such as a one- or two-week iteration interval).[5] These authors also discuss the role of regular interim iteration meetings and their benefits in ensuring that good progress is maintained, specifically in the iteration but also in the project in general.

Gilb describes the benefits of such meetings in providing an additional opportunity for the project manager and customer to review progress against the iteration plan and for the customer to review and approve the tasks and associated design for the next *tranche* of development and testing activity.

Chana reports the benefits of integrating a weekly iteration meeting into an existing regularly scheduled team telephone conference call. In the case of his project,

---

[5] See the Timeboxing topic under the earlier Agile Process and Project Management section for more details.

Chana was able to provide progress updates to his project manager during the course of the call and obtain feedback from the users (his teammates) on the state of the developing system (a team Wiki) as well. Chana cautions care in piggy-backing on an existing meeting and recommends that the agile review items are formally included in the meeting agenda and covered off early in the meeting.

Kingston describes the benefits of such a regular meeting on an offshored agile project. Specifically, a weekly telephone conference call with the developer team in India was employed as an additional project control to confirm that the tasks in the current iteration were on track and that there were no risks or dependencies that might cause the team to fail to meet its deadlines. Kingston does advise caution in obtaining progress report information outside of a face-to-face meeting environment and recommends that all estimates are firmly challenged (often with the same question being repeated in a slightly different manner) to avoid any misunderstandings due to language or cultural differences.

Agile Retrospectives

Gilb (Chapter 4) makes the important observation that a very important lesson to be learned is that there is always another lesson to be learned. A key practice in his Evo method [32] is to continually fine-tune the agile best practices by capturing iteration and project lessons learned and acting on them.

In an agile project environment it is particularly important that the agile process and practices being used on the project are, and remain, as effective and efficient as possible. Sewell (Chapter 5) makes the point that during the course of a single project (even of moderate duration) it is possible for testing best practices to change, for new techniques to be published, or for new tools to become available (or even new releases of existing tools with new functionality). Being receptive to such changes and, where appropriate, adopting and using them can help fine-tune the effectiveness of an agile project.

Phillips (Chapter 12) describes the use of a testing specific retrospective at the end of each iteration in which the lessons learned in the previous iteration are reviewed and, where appropriate, actions are put in place to improve the testing process and/or keep it up to date with respect to new best practices or tools that may have become available since starting the project.

In agile retrospectives it is particularly important that all members of the team are encouraged and given the opportunity to contribute their views, and the techniques for improving communication between team members described by Evans (Chapter 19) are particularly appropriate to these meetings. Another valuable perspective on agile retrospectives, and techniques for making them successful, that I recommend you look at is provided by Ester Derby in her book [99].

Workshops

Although many of the more recent agile methods emphasize the benefits of short, sharp, and highly focused meetings, there may be project tasks that must be accomplished that do not lend themselves easily to a fifteen-minute stand-up meeting. RAD and DSDM, for example, both include guidance on running longer sessions, such as RAD's joint application design workshops. Where complex issues need to be discussed, where important decisions need to be agreed upon, and where key project artifacts (such as the business requirements document or the project test plan) need to be generated, a longer style of meeting may be necessary.

Denning (Chapter 8) emphasizes the role of more traditional project management approaches to running agile projects, including the role of longer meetings where necessary and their success in managing customer expectations.

May (Chapter 23) makes a case for "extended meetings" on projects where the customer and development team are not co-located to ensure the developers have gained a thorough understanding of the customer needs as well as an appreciation of the customer culture and preferred means of working. In practice, these meetings could be scheduled across a number of days to achieve their goals.

Agile Project Closedown Meetings

With the emphasis the case studies place on learning from experience in agile projects (Gilb, Chapter 4) and process improvement (Tilt, Chapter 18, for example), an agile project closedown meeting can provide an excellent opportunity to reflect on the lessons learned throughout the project.

Kingston (Chapter 15) describes the successful use of such a meeting and its value in providing an opportunity to harvest the lessons learned from all of the previous project meetings.

Meeting Focus: A Final Thought

As a final thought on the subject of agile meetings, I offer a particularly embarrassing moment from my own career, which emphasizes the need for good focus in meetings as well as the need for a strong facilitator.

I still cringe when I recall a project meeting I attended in my younger days, which was being chaired by a formidable project manager, a lady named Ruth Woodhead. In what I thought was a slack moment in the meeting, and while Ruth had to take a short but important phone call, I began to chat with a colleague about the recent rugby success that Wales had been enjoying. The next thing, Ruth was asking me conversationally – "John, do you like the radio quiz show 'Just a Minute'?" "Definitely," I answered enthusiastically, thinking I could earn some brownie points (and not spotting the trap); "DEVIATION," she said simply, instantly taking back her iron grip of the proceedings, and leaving me blushing acutely! Suffice it to say, I have never forgotten the lesson.

24.7 Agile Automation

This section provides best practice guidance on the use of automated software tool support for agile methods. Automation has the potential to save significant time, effort, and cost on agile projects, but, where selected or used poorly, it can also cost a project time, effort, and money!

As Jon Tilt (Chapter 18) puts it, "There is always the temptation to architect yet another automation framework at the start of the project. Don't! Look around at the simple tools that already exist and build on them as required. Developers and testers are much more likely to use something simple that is quick and easy to use."

In addition to quality management and testing products, this section discusses agile best practices relating to other tools such as requirements management, configuration management, build management, and process enactment tools.

Select a Tool in Haste, Repent at Leisure

Phillips (Chapter 12) reports that the agile project he worked on was forced to change tools several times during the course of the project; the time and effort needed to select a replacement tool, plus the nugatory effort expended on gaining familiarity with the previous tool, and wasted effort using it, can all jeopardize the success of an agile project, where the goal is typically to reduce the effort and cost of delivering the product.

Prior to starting an agile project there are a number of things you can do to try to avoid making poor automation decisions:

▶ Determine whether there are company standards in place for tool use (but don't follow these slavishly if they are clearly wrong for your project).
▶ Discuss the need for tool support with knowledgeable colleagues and consider the wider networking opportunities of attending appropriate special interest group events.
▶ Be aware of the need for a particular product to integrate with other tools (either in place or planned to be acquired).
▶ If the project is large enough, of sufficiently long duration, and with available resources, consider conducting a formal evaluation of tools (particularly if they are products you will need to purchase). A tried and trusted tool evaluation scheme that can be used to ensure formality in any evaluation you undertake is given in [4].

Static Analysis Tools

These products typically allow the source code to be inspected to highlight quality issues without executing the code (some are even customizable to allow company coding standards and house coding style issues to be detected). Arguably, these relatively simple but highly effective tools should be another tool in the developers' toolbox and should be used on a frequent basis to check recently written or modified code.

As with many of the products discussed in this section, static analysis tools can be particularly effective when used in conjunction with an automated build and testing approach. For example, Evans (Chapter 17) describes a system that combines continuous integration and build management tools to automate the creation of a new build of the software. During this process, automated unit, functional, and static analysis tests are run against the code to determine whether the build is a success. Should the build fail due to defects being identified, the build is rejected, and the defects are corrected before rerunning the build process once more.

Automated Unit Test

The use of automated unit test tools (such as [50]) appears to be an agile practice adopted in almost every case study (Cassidy, Chapter 11; Wilson, Chapter 14; Kingston, Chapter 15; Warden, Chapter 16; Tilt, Chapter 18; and Stapp and Nowakowska, Chapter 22). These simple and effective tools allow unit tests to be compiled in concert with code development and executed to ensure the code meets its requirements and performs as expected.

Although a wide range of unit test products are available to purchase or download as open-source tools, many developers also write their own unit test tools. Whatever solution is adopted, you should take into account support issues, the availability of practitioners who are familiar with the tools, and the need to maintain and update these tools.

Combined with test harness tools (used where the unit under test needs to interact with components that have not yet been coded) such as mock objects (Cassidy, for example), automated unit tests provide an inexpensive and effective means of initially testing a component as well as continuing to test the successful functioning of the component following a new build, release, or other changes to the software (such as code refactoring).

Finally, employed in concert with continuous integration and automated build tools [95], automated unit tests become a highly effective solution to accelerate development through continuous code quality assessment.

Test Harness Tools

It is often the case, particularly in the early stages of development, that code will be written that needs to interact with other components that may not have been developed at that point in time. Under such circumstances a typical solution is to employ a test harness to simulate the operation of the missing component(s).

It is not unusual for developers to spend some of their time writing and testing their own test harnesses (or reusing those generated by colleagues). Although of value in supporting more efficient unit testing, creating these test harnesses inevitably expends time, effort, and expense in generating a temporary tool that almost certainly will not have any purpose once the current project is completed.

To increase the productivity of developers and to save them the time and effort of building their own test harnesses, a range of open-source test harness tools have been developed that are available for use in unit testing. Evans (Chapter 17), for example, describes his experiences in using the so-called mock framework test harnesses and their role in automated build and test, while Cassidy (Chapter 11) describes how his project began by using a number of freely available mock frameworks (such as EasyMock [50]) and then went on to develop its own generic reusable mock framework – SevenMock [51].

Functional Testing Tools

Functional testing tools, such as the classic capture–replay tools, allow testers to capture user navigation against the application under test and any specific verifications (that a particular window has appeared, or some specific calculation has been made correctly, for example) in the form of an automated script. This script can be replayed against later builds or releases of the software to ensure the functionality has not changed and that the new changes have not introduced any bugs.

The benefits of the use of such tools on an agile project are clear:

▶ Automated test scripts can be scheduled to run overnight or over the weekend, allowing additional unattended testing to be performed, increasing confidence in the software.

▶ The more often you reuse the automated scripts to perform regression testing of new builds and releases, the more time, effort, and cost you save the project.

▶ Unless you are dealing with an extremely large suite of automated test scripts and are facing very long test suite execution times, you do not have to take the risk of having to pick and choose which scripts to execute – you simply run them all.

▶ Automated capture–replay tools do not get tired, do not become bored or careless, and will continue to replay the test scripts and report on the results in a thorough and repeatable manner.

A number of case studies report significant benefits from the adoption and use of capture–replay tools for functional and regression testing (such as Denning, Chapter 8; Cassidy, Chapter 11; Phillips, Chapter 12; and Tilt, Chapter 18) and variously cite reductions in testing time, effort, and cost, as well as improvements in quality through their use.[6]

However, such tools are not a universal panacea, and a number of case studies report issues with using such tools. Knowles (Chapter 10), for example, reports that well-managed manual testing delivered excellent results on the migration project described in his case study. In this instance, capture–replay tools were rejected on the grounds that the solution was too expensive to maintain in a rapidly changing development environment, with high cost and effort involved in maintaining the scripts.

Phillips (Chapter 12) cautions against underestimating the time and effort required to develop and maintain a test automation infrastructure and particularly one where the capture–replay tool has to be integrated with a number of other products.

---

[6] Interestingly (in light of the listed benefits for capture–replay tools), Jon Tilt reported that the test suite on his project had grown to an extremely large size (35,000 tests with an execution time of some ten days) and describes the use of a "laser-guided" solution to select an effective subset of tests to run.

The characteristics of those projects that seem to be particularly suited to the application of capture–replay tools are as follows:

▶ A stable user interface (Phillips) should be available – the screens in the application under test should not be in a constant state of change (such as that caused by user interface requirements churn). Under such circumstances, the cost of maintaining the automated test scripts may well outweigh the cost of manual testing.
▶ There should be numerous and frequent builds and releases of the application under test. Under such circumstances, thorough and extensive manual testing becomes unrealistic, and an automated solution is much more appropriate (Tilt). A further benefit of frequent builds and releases is that each time the automated test suite is reused, the overall return on investment in the tool is improved.
▶ The application under test is complex, involving numerous screens and complicated navigation and with a large amount of functionality to test. Where the software is relatively simple, more cost-effective manual testing may suffice.

As a final thought, if you combine the introduction of capture–replay testing tools with your metrics program, you will be able to work out the precise benefits obtained from using the tool and make an informed decision on whether it is of value to your project.

Requirements Management Tools

A number of the case studies report the benefits of using tools to document and maintain requirements (Kingston, Chapter 15; and Chana, Chapter 20; for example).

From a quality management perspective, the ability to provide up-to-date requirements information to test managers and test analysts for test planning and resourcing, and test case design purposes were commonly cited uses of such tools. Kingston makes a strong case for the use of such tools to demonstrate formal test coverage against requirements, while Chana describes the value of the change history supported by such tools in providing a useful source of traceability (allowing the persons who requested, reviewed, and authorized a particular change to the code base to be easily identified, for example).

Kingston makes a further point about the utility of such tools on agile projects where not all the stakeholders can be co-located; the ability for remote stakeholders to access the requirements tool via a web-based interface enabled the offshore staff to work more closely with other members of the team and allowed all stakeholders (irrespective of where they were based) to contribute to the requirements elicitation and documentation process.

Sewell (Chapter 5) and Hodgkinson (Chapter 21) both describe the value of automated support in requirements elicitation, specifically in documenting and analyzing use cases within the EssUP [34] and RUP [7] frameworks, respectively.

Build Management Tools

A large number of the case studies document the benefits of adopting a continuous build or integration approach (Gilb, Chapter 4; Thomas, Chapter 6; Knowles, Chapter 10; Wilson, Chapter 14; and Evans, Chapter 17).

Unless the project is of trivial size and complexity, a build management tool must be considered for use in starting and running the build process (see [95], for example). Many of the case studies (such as Evans; Phillips, Chapter 12; Wilson, Chapter 14; and Tilt, Chapter 18) also report the benefits of integrating other automated tools (such as unit test, functional test, and code analysis tools) with the build management tool to ensure that those builds that contain defects are rejected.

Configuration and Change Management Tools

Configuration and change management are well-established best practices in both traditional and agile software development projects, and many of the case studies report the value of using them (Thomas, Chapter 6; and Cassidy, Chapter 11; for example).

Numerous configuration and change management tools are available, including commercial products, open-source tools, and those developed in-house (see [61], for example), that can be employed in agile projects. In selecting such a product, you should be aware of support issues, the availability of practitioners who are familiar with the tools, and the need to maintain and update these tools.

Finally, be aware of the need for the configuration and change management tools you select to integrate with other tools that you are already using on a project or those that are planned to be acquired.

Process Enactment Tools

A number of the case studies emphasize the importance of providing good process guidance to the stakeholders involved in developing and testing the software (Sewell, Chapter 5; Kingston, Chapter 15; and Hodgkinson, Chapter 21; for example); if you want your agile project to be successful, it is essential that the practitioners working on the project understand and are able to employ agile best practices.

Several of the case studies also provide cautionary tales about projects that claimed to be following an agile approach, but which in reality were not using agile best practices (Thompson, Chapter 9; Allott, Chapter 13; Warden, Chapter 16; and May, Chapter 23; for example). The reasons for this can be diverse:

▶ Thompson suggests in his case study that a company made claims about their agile credentials to win a development contract, but that in practice there was very little evidence that the company had used an agile approach.
▶ Allott suggests that an agile project needs particularly well-trained and experienced agile practitioners if it is to be successful, otherwise weak or poorly trained staff will fall back on more familiar (nonagile) practices.

▶ Warden highlights a litany of examples where an agile approach was shoehorned into a project, but where true agile practices were not actually adopted (such as the failure to ensure that the end users performed the sprint QA/sign-off, instead of this step being performed by the analysts who wrote the specifications).

▶ Similarly, May documents a number of departures from agile (in this case Scrum) practices, which jeopardized the success of the project he was involved in, including poor user stories, interrupted sprints, excessively long sprints (greater than six weeks), failure to co-locate stakeholders, and poorly focused stand-up meetings of too long a duration.

There are a number of options for addressing these issues:

▶ Ensure that you employ experienced agile staff who have a good track record of using agile practices successfully.

▶ Provide staff with appropriate training on the agile method being used and its practices before you begin the agile project.

▶ Provide easy access to agile best practice guidance – such as practice summary sheets (Sewell) or easily accessible online process guidance [7].

Another possible option that has become available recently is to deploy a so-called process enactment tool (see [63, 65], for example). Such tools provide a rich integrated development environment in which the use of agile best practices is enforced by the tool itself. For example, such tools can

▶ allow the addition of new team members to a project using standard templates for roles and responsibilities, with defined lines of reporting, privileges, and permissions;

▶ provide defined workflows within which tasks can be assigned to other team members, which can then be accepted and worked on, with the developer entering estimates of the time and effort required to complete them as well as the ability to update the task with the actual values;

▶ provide real-time reports on individual and project progress and generate accurate estimates, such as the timescales required to complete a particular task; and

▶ be customized to match the specific agile practices of a particular agile method. For example, MacDonah [100] describes the implementation of the EssUP process in a commercial process enactment product [101].

24.8 Summary

This chapter has provided a detailed analysis of the agile best practices documented within the twenty case studies appearing in Part 2 of this book with particular emphasis on quality management.

From these twenty case studies, more than fifty separate examples of specific agile best practices are documented under the headings of agile process and project management, agile development and testing, agile requirements management, agile communications and meetings, and agile automation.

I believe that the agile best practices documented in this chapter will be of genuine value to existing agile developers and testers and to any practitioners who are new to agile. However, it is undoubtedly the case that not every agile practice covered in this chapter will be universally applicable to all sizes, types, and styles of agile project.

The next chapter, Chapter 25, makes a number of proposals for how different practitioners involved in different sizes and types of agile project might make use of the best practices described in this chapter to compile their own agile process.

25 My Agile Process

> The easiest way to get any agile process to fail, is to expect too much from it.
>
> **Ryan Concannon, Scrum Master**

25.1 Introduction

This chapter draws upon the information provided in the cases studies and their analyses to make a number of proposals for how you might set up and run your own practical, effective, and efficient agile testing process. Using the set of agile testing practices highlighted during the analyses, this chapter provides a series of proposals, allowing you to pick and mix from these practices to create an agile method tailored to your own particular development and testing requirements.

In providing a valuable source of real-world development and testing practices, the case studies reinforce the idea that each project is unique. Each project is of different size and complexity and, in reviewing the agile practices, you need to consider what will work for you. To simplify this task, the practices in this chapter are organized around four stereotypical projects, and you should make an assessment about which one best matches your own agile requirements. Try not to use the information provided dogmatically; look at the proposed agile practices critically and decide if you think they would work for you.

As a final thought, whatever set of practices you pick will probably not be perfect, so make sure you follow the advice provided on process improvement: keep doing what works for you and challenge the use of, or modify, those practices that do not.

This chapter is structured as follows. Section 25.2 provides guidance on those agile practices that have been found to be successful in the majority of case studies and in the other sources of agile methods described in the previous chapter. These practices can be viewed as providing a solid foundation on which you can build your own agile process by adding those practices from the following sections that best match your own agile requirements.

Section 25.3 provides guidance on those agile practices that have been shown to provide value on *small agile projects*,[1] characterized by having a team size of up to

---

[1] Although in practice, everyone will disagree with the fine detail of what constitutes a small, medium, and large agile project, the definitions used in this chapter provide a pragmatic solution to the organization of the agile best practices described in Chapter 24.

eight staff members, with low complexity (that is, involving a co-located team, low budget, small timescales, and, in technical terms, a relatively simple development environment).

Section 25.4 provides guidance on agile practices that have been shown to provide value on *medium-sized agile projects*, characterized by having a team size of between nine and twenty staff members, with moderate complexity (that is, involving a co-located team, possibly with some offsite members; moderate budget; moderate timescales; and, in technical terms, a moderately challenging development environment).

Section 25.5 provides guidance on those agile practices that have been shown to provide value on *large-sized agile projects*, characterized by having a team size of greater than twenty staff members, with challenging levels of complexity (that could include a co-located or partially co-located team, large budget, large timescales, and a technically challenging development environment).

Section 25.6 provides guidance on those practices that have been shown to provide value on agile projects characterized as having a large *offsite or offshore* aspect to their organization.

Section 25.7 provides a summary of the agile process proposals made in this chapter.

To obtain further information on each of the agile practices described in this chapter, refer back to the relevant section in Chapter 24, where each practice is described in more detail and which can also be traced back to the source case study using the references that are provided. The format used to organize the best practices in this chapter mirrors that used in Chapter 24; the practices are grouped together within the following sections under the headings Agile Development and Testing, Agile Process and Project Management, Agile Requirements Management, Agile Meetings and Communication, and Agile Automation.

25.2 Foundation Agile Best Practices

The best practices documented in this section have been shown to have been used successfully in the majority of the case studies. These practices can be viewed as providing a solid foundation on which you can build your own agile process, by adding those practices from the following sections that best match your own agile requirements.

All agile projects should strongly consider the use of the following practices.

Agile Development and Testing

▶ *Iterative development* – This fundamental agile practice is valuable from a software quality perspective because it allows testing to begin as early in the project as possible and to continue frequently throughout the project. In addition to allowing early and frequent testing, this approach also provides value in terms of allowing early versions of working software to be shown to the customer, obtaining valuable feedback, clarifying the requirements, and also managing the customers' expectations of the final delivered software.

▶ *Well-bounded iterations* – Time boxing, sprints, and other techniques for bounding agile development tasks are tried and tested agile best practices. From a software quality perspective, it is recommended that the planned testing element of such iterations be strongly protected to ensure adequate testing occurs. In projects where the testing time within an iteration is habitually eaten into, strongly consider creating a ring-fenced iteration (such as a testing time box) explicitly for testing. Where appropriate, look to fit iterations into naturally occurring intervals, such as one- or two-week periods.

▶ *Early involvement of test resources* – Look for opportunities to involve testing practitioners as early as possible in the project and continue to involve them throughout the project life cycle. For example, involving a testing analyst or designer in the process of generating use cases or user stories alongside the analyst and customer has been shown to be of significant value by allowing the test analyst to review the requirements for testability, to help ensure there are no errors in the requirements (such as duplications, omissions, or contradictions), and to create the test cases in parallel with the use cases and user stories.

▶ *Every day is test day* – In addition to implementing practices to drive testing earlier into the project life cycle, encourage a culture that is aware of the need to test the code as frequently as is practical. Unit testing tools can be valuable in supporting this approach in the early stages of code development. In terms of looking for additional solutions to increase the amount of testing completed on the project, unit testing tools can be combined with continuous integration, build management, and capture–replay tools to allow testing to be run unattended (overnight or over a weekend, for example).

▶ *Test-driven design* – In addition to being a key best practice in a number of agile methods (such as XP), the case studies have shown that where developers review the requirements and generate the unit test before coding begins, they gain a much clearer understanding of the requirements, produce better quality code, and don't spend any additional time overall completing the task. In fact, because of the benefits of gaining a better understanding of the requirements and writing high-quality code, this practice arguably saves time and effort that otherwise might have been spent rewriting and retesting code containing defects.

▶ *Fix all defects immediately* – A number of the case studies describe a practice in which, as soon as a defect is detected, all development halts while the defect is fixed. This approach has very significant benefits in terms of avoiding late detection of defects, and the cost and time-scale implications this has for the project. Combined with some of the practices allowing for the real-time visualization of the status of the project (such as the lava lamp solution covered later in this section and in Chapter 17), fixing defects can become a matter of both urgency and pride, with the team working hard to achieve a "green lava lamp state" again.

▶ *Collective code and test ownership* – Collective code ownership is another best practice that a number of the agile methods promote (such as XP). From a software quality perspective, a number of the case studies describe the benefits of the analogous practice of collective test ownership and its role in encouraging test refactoring (that is, all members of the team have the opportunity to modify contents of the test suite for the purposes of improving the quality of the tests and/or their efficiency). Where this practice is adopted, consider the role of change and configuration management tools to trace the changes and to allow changes to be undone where necessary.

▶ *Agile exploratory testing* – This is a valuable addition to other testing practices being used on a project. An experienced test practitioner will frequently find defects that a developer or testing tool cannot, using their knowledge of the sort of errors developers often make (such as incorrectly coding logical boundary conditions), knowledge of how users often abuse systems (such as performing unexpected navigation or entering inappropriate values), and that mystical tester ability termed error-guessing [4].

Agile Process and Project Management

▶ *Co-location of project stakeholders* – This fundamental principle of agile development and testing is the ideal solution for organizing an agile project team. Co-location of the project stakeholders supports the practices of early involvement of, test resources, as well as pair testing (see Section 25.3) and early test case design. Although an essential agile best practice, this approach becomes increasingly difficult to employ where team sizes become very large, or impossible where it is necessary for some of the team to be at a different site or even offshore. Advice and guidance on what to do under these circumstances is provided in Sections 25.5 and 25.6, respectively.

▶ *Agile estimation* – Estimation is a key aspect of agile projects, and methods for estimating project and iteration velocity are well understood and used. Although most projects employ estimation successfully, a number of the case studies reported issues with agile estimation and stressed the importance of employing previous experience; the most accurate estimates for any particular project are made with the assistance of metrics collected previously on that project. For example, metrics collection and analysis can help a project leader identify resources who regularly overestimate or underestimate the effort involved in a particular task.

On larger projects, with longer timescales and/or the additional challenges of not having a co-located team, there may be value in employing automated distributed support for estimation (such as [63]).

▶ *Progress measurement* – Typically calculated agile metrics such as velocity are a valuable source of information for stakeholders to be able to understand project progress. Many of the case studies also report the value of collecting and measuring a number of quality management metrics as well. Examples include test case coverage versus requirements, defect detection and distribution rates, code coverage, and code complexity metrics. The availability of such metrics can be used to improve the effectiveness of the testing process, such as identifying which aspects of the application are more prone to defects, which testers are most effective at finding bugs, and supporting the comparison and analysis of historical and current data.

On the smallest agile projects with relatively simple tasks, daily stand-up meetings can be a particularly effective means of reviewing such data. With growing team sizes and increasing project complexity, more formal means of obtaining estimates of productivity and calculating progress are needed. While spreadsheets may provide a simple and frequently used solution to recording the estimates and actual effort needed to compete a task, larger and more complex projects may need to employ tool support (such as [60, 63]) to collate such data.

▶ *Progress visualization* – Although it is important for the project leader to have access to accurate and up-to-date project data, there is also a great deal of value in displaying progress information to the wider project stakeholders. Examples of progress visualization solutions drawn from the case studies include traditional approaches such as pinning up project burndown charts in shared project areas and using distributed electronic data (such as the graphical code coverage and complexity information provided through the continuous integration and build solution described in Chapter 14).

Visualization of project data means that the project stakeholders can make use of this information to make decisions about how to improve their performance. For example, in the case study described in Chapter 18, displaying a chart showing the breakdown of defects detected versus the testing phase in which they were found provided developers with the encouragement to improve the effectiveness of unit testing. Similarly, the automated switching on of the red lava lamp when a build failed due to detection of a defect provided a massive motivator for the team to fix the problem and get the green lava lamp back on before the red wax became hot enough to melt and flow!

▶ *Process improvement* – While process improvement should apply to all agile projects, the scope of this activity will change depending on the size, duration, complexity, and importance of the project. For small projects, agile retrospectives held at the end of each iteration/sprint (and particularly heartbeat retrospectives [54]) may be sufficient. As project size, duration, and complexity grow, more formal approaches to process improvement may be appropriate; for large, long-duration, and complex projects, or projects being run within an organization that has corporate interests in process improvement, a scheme such as CMMI [37] might be employed.

▶ *Everyone is a software engineer* – To avoid the adversarial mindset that is frequently reported between developers and testers, a number of the case studies reported the benefits of replacing the titles of those practitioners responsible for development and testing with the title of software engineer. This practice was shown to provide benefits in one of the case studies by improving productivity and lowering quality issues through closer working, and in another by encouraging those staff performing development tasks to seek out staff with quality assurance skills for advice. Combined with the notion that software quality is everyone's responsibility, this practice can lead to significant improvements in the quality of the delivered software.

Agile Requirements Management

▶ *Use cases and user stories* – Strongly consider having a test practitioner work alongside the analyst and customer during the process of requirements elicitation to review the requirements for testability, to help identify errors in the requirements, and to create the test cases in parallel with the use cases or user stories. Designing test cases based on use cases is a very natural process, because the use cases which describe a series of actions leading to a specific outcome map very easily into test scenarios, which specify the navigation that needs to be performed to produce some expected result.

▶ *Look beyond requirements to customer needs* – This practice provides valuable guidance about what to focus on when trying to understand precisely what the customer needs. An overly formal approach to requirements elicitation may under certain circumstances miss those aspects of the proposed software system that will deliver genuine value to the customer.

Being aware that you cannot know all the customer requirements at the start of the project and adopting an approach in which you refine the customer needs at each iteration will help address this issue. The feedback obtained using a rapid prototyping approach may also help in further understanding the customer needs.

▶ *Ensure all requirements have tests* – To ensure complete test coverage of the requirements, each requirement must have one or more associated tests. On smaller agile projects, simple tool support may be used (such as a spreadsheet that lists the requirements, with a corresponding column to show the associated test case). For larger agile projects that have access to requirements management and testing tools, you should look for integrated solutions that are able to map test cases back to specific requirements to demonstrate test coverage.

Agile Communication and Meetings

▶ *Agile project start-up meetings* – Agile projects should begin with a start-up meeting in which issues such as the team structure, project planning, risks and dependencies, architecture, and product release planning are discussed and agreed. Ensure quality management issues such as testing roles and responsibilities, test planning, and test resourcing are also covered in this meeting.

▶ *Agile iteration start-up meetings* – Each project iteration should begin with an agile start-up meeting, whose agenda should include a discussion of the priority of the features that should be implemented within the iteration, agreement on the iteration plan, discussion and agreement of the success criteria for the iteration, and identification of any iteration-specific risks and dependencies. On a Scrum project, for example, this is analogous to a sprint planning meeting.

▶ *Daily stand-up meeting* – During the course of the iteration, the project team should get together for a short (typically fifteen-minute) stand-up meeting for the purposes of discussing three things: (1) what progress they made the previous day; (2) what they plan to achieve today; and (3) what issues, problems, risks, or dependencies might prevent them from achieving their plans.

▶ *Agile retrospectives* – Retrospectives should be held at the end of each iteration to ensure that the lessons learned during that iteration are discussed and recorded.

These could be as short and simple as heartbeat retrospectives [54], or more formal (perhaps following the guidelines provided in [72, 99]). Ensure quality management issues are covered in the meeting, for example, by reviewing the success of automated testing tools, highlighting lessons learned in trialing some new testing technique, or reviewing how well testing plans were adhered to during the iteration.

An agile retrospective should also be held at the end of the project to ensure that the lessons learned on the project are discussed and documented. This will be particularly useful if there are likely to be similar or related follow-on projects with the same customer.

Agile Automation

▶ *Automated unit test* – From the analyses of the case studies, automated unit testing is a universally successful agile practice; all developers should be provided with access to automated unit testing tools (such as [50]). Such tools are simple to use, provide good results, and can be easily integrated into automated continuous integration and build solutions, where the unit tests can be automatically run to verify the quality of the code. For small- to medium-sized projects, free open-source unit test tools may well be suitable. For larger projects, review the needs of unit testing tools to integrate with other tools and/or test harnesses being used on the project and consider the purchase of commercial products if appropriate.

▶ *Automated configuration management* – All agile development projects should consider the use of configuration management tools as a general best practice. For small- to medium-sized projects, free open-source configuration management tools may well be suitable. For larger projects, review the needs of configuration management tools to integrate with other tools being used on the project and consider the purchase of commercial products if appropriate.

25.3 Agile Best Practices for Small-Sized Projects

The best practices documented in this section have been shown to have value when used on small agile projects. Combine the agile practices documented in the following sections with those described in Section 25.2 to provide a set of best practices for use on small projects.

Agile Development and Testing for Small-Sized Projects

▶ *Pair testing* – Where there are sufficient resources on the project, consider the value of pairing a testing resource with a developer to provide software quality advice and guidance during development. Be careful not to give the impression that the tester is performing a "quality police" role. This practice works particularly well if you have avoided the "us and them" issues often seen between developers and testers by encouraging these practitioners to view themselves as software engineers.

▶ *Continuous integration* – Although this practice works particularly well where there are a number of developers writing and testing code, its value on smaller agile projects, perhaps used in combination with tool support, should also be carefully considered.

▶ *Rapid prototyping* – Consider the role of this practice on small agile projects but ensure that, if used, the prototypes are developed in such a way as to maximize their potential reuse in developing any deliverable code produced as a result of the prototyping exercise; that is, be careful not to waste time writing code that isn't actually used in the final system.

Agile Process and Project Management for Small-Sized Projects

▶ *Metrics* – There may be some value on a small agile project in collecting simple metrics to support the analysis of quality management information, such as defect detection rates. Without having such metrics available, it will be very difficult to measure the benefits of any test process improvements one might make.

   Since the activity of collecting and analyzing metrics involves time and effort, the use of metrics on a small agile project must be carefully considered. In the event that collecting and using metrics is thought to be of value, any metrics scheme should be very clear about the purpose the metrics are being collected for and should be focused on collecting just the data required for that purpose. The benefits of any adopted metrics scheme should be reviewed during agile retrospectives.

Agile Communication and Meetings for Small-Sized Projects

▶ *Improve interpersonal communications* – Even on small, co-located agile projects, effective interpersonal communication is essential to the success of the project. In fact, in small teams, poor communications problems can have a disproportionately high impact. For example, it is possible for one particularly forceful personality to dominate meetings. Similarly, it is quite possible for the least assertive member of the team to have the most important contribution to make but not be given the opportunity to make it! Make use of the communications techniques described in Chapter 19 (as well as in [72, 99]) to significantly improve the quality and effectiveness of communications in small agile projects.

▶ *Interim iteration meetings* – Although of more value in medium and large agile projects, in projects involving longer iterations, or where some important stakeholder cannot be co-located, there may be some value in holding a meeting midway through an iteration or at some other appropriate point(s) to review progress, review risks and dependencies, and/or discuss lessons learned.

Reasons for holding such a meeting might include the availability of a particular stakeholder (such as a non-co-located project sponsor) at a specific point in the iteration, the occurrence of some event external to the project that may impact project progress, or the detection of some significant risk or dependency that needs to be reviewed. However, the scheduling of additional meetings should always be challenged on a smaller agile project, since it is quite possible that the daily stand-up meetings will be sufficient.

▶ *Agile project closedown meetings/extended retrospectives* – Consider holding a brief agile project closedown meeting if there are outstanding items not covered in the agile retrospective. If this is likely to be the case, consider combining the retrospective and closedown meetings into a single meeting that includes the agenda items from both.

Agile Automation for Small-Sized Projects

▶ *Role of static analysis tools* – Consider the use of one of the open source static analysis tools that are available to check the quality of the code generated in the project. These tools can be used to detect issues or errors in the code that need to be addressed prior to execution, with a number of these tools also capable of being customized to check project or organization issues, such as adherence to a particular coding standard or company style.

▶ *Test harness tools* – Where a significant need exists to test software components that interact with other components that have not yet been developed, the potential use of test harness tools should be considered. In addition to tools that may have been developed in-house, there are a number of free test harness tools available (e.g., [51]) that can save the project time and effort.

▶ *Requirements management tools* – The majority of small agile projects employ simple, cheap (or free) solutions to record and use project requirements; very often, a simple spreadsheet will suffice. Where more rigor is required on a project – to formally document a customer's requirements or to be able to trace the origin of some specific requirement, for example – a more robust and reliable solution many be required. The use of a commercial requirements product should be considered carefully on a small agile project, because such tools may need to be purchased and, even where free, are likely to incur training and familiarization costs.

25.4 Agile Best Practices for Medium-Sized Projects

The best practices documented in this section have been shown to have value when used on medium-sized agile projects. Combine the agile practices documented in the following sections with those described in Section 25.2 to provide a set of best practices for use on medium-sized projects.

Agile Development and Testing for Medium-Sized Projects

▶ *Pair testing* – With increasing numbers of staff on the project, there is increasing value in pairing a testing resource with a developer to provide software quality advice and guidance during development. This practice will work particularly well if you have adopted the approach of encouraging developers and testers to see themselves as software engineers, avoiding any "us and them" issues. Where you do observe push-back from developers who perceive the tester as being a member of the "quality police," consider involving the test resource in a reviewing role toward the end of the workday.

▶ *Continuous integration* – As the number of developers on the project team increases, this practice becomes increasingly valuable with individual developers submitting completed code to the growing code base. Using tool-based continuous integration, it is not only possible to automate the build process, but it is also possible to automatically run other tools, such as unit test, code coverage, code complexity, and functional/regression testing tools.

   Combined with innovative techniques for visualizing the results of a build, such as the graphical code coverage and complexity information provided through the continuous integration and build solution described in Chapter 14 and the practice of fixing all defects as soon as they are found, this becomes a highly effective and efficient means of building defect-free software.

▶ *Test refactoring* – Where the testing suite becomes large and complex, difficult to manage, and/or takes an unacceptably long time to execute, you should consider the value of test refactoring. Removing test scripts from the test suite (but not deleting them, so that they can be reused later in the project if required) and/or editing or modifying them can result in a leaner, meaner, and more effective test suite. Care must be taken to target only those tests that are no longer being used, that are out of date, or that test low-risk or tried-and-tested elements of the code base. Combined with the practice of identifying targets of test, test refactoring provides a valuable solution for improving the efficiency of your test effort.

▶ *Identify targets of test* – In the event that the suite of test scripts becomes sufficiently large that there are difficulties in completing functional and regression testing within allocated timescales, you should consider the use of this practice to assist you in selecting an effective subset of tests to run that will still provide you with good results from a quality perspective. Chapter 18 provides excellent advice and guidance on this best practice.

▶ *Code coverage metrics* – Consider the use of this practice as part of the process of ensuring good test coverage of the software. Where there are large numbers of tests to run and the application under test is large and/or complex, you should consider the use of a code coverage tool. Such a tool can also be of value in assisting you to identify targets of test (see previous section) as well as assisting you to target additional testing effort in those areas of the software where more thorough testing is needed. Combined with the automated build process and sophisticated graphical solutions for visualizing code coverage described in

Chapter 14, this practice can quickly and easily highlight code coverage issues before they seriously impact the project.

▶ *Rapid prototyping* – This practice can be of great value in exploring the customer requirements, gaining valuable feedback, and ensuring that the final system matches the customer needs. Where used, ensure that the prototypes are developed in such a manner to maximize the reuse of the code in developing the final system; that is, don't waste time and effort writing code that isn't actually used in the final system.

Agile Process and Project Management Practices for Medium-Sized Projects

▶ *Be receptive to the reuse of traditional testing techniques* – With increasing project size and complexity, the benefits of traditional project and test management practices should be considered. For example, there are a couple of case studies in which the V-model [4] has been shown to have helped with test planning in agile projects, and where elements of PRINCE2 [22] have been of value in agile project management. Where you have very experienced testing staff involved in your agile project, be receptive to any suggestions they may have about traditional practices that may benefit the current project.

▶ *Availability of agile process guidance* – On a medium-sized agile project, with a moderate team size, where team members leave and/or join the team frequently or one that involves new and inexperienced agile practitioners, you should strongly consider the need to make formal guidance on the agile process being used on the project available to the team members. Effective solutions can include distributing process summary cards as and when needed [34] and publishing the process guidance online [7], for example.

▶ *Metrics* – Metrics can be used for a variety of purposes in medium-sized agile projects, such as fine-tuning estimates, publishing data on some aspect of the project, and supporting process improvement. Because the activity of collecting and analyzing metrics involves time and effort, the use of metrics on a medium-sized agile project should be considered with care. Any metrics scheme that is implemented should also collect data recording the time and effort expended on metrics collection, and this information should be used in agile retrospectives and iteration start-up meetings to determine the benefits of, and the continuing role and use of, metrics on the project.

▶ *Reduce documentation overload* – As agile projects increase in size, it is very likely that the amount of documentation used on the project will also grow. The time and effort taken to compile, distribute, maintain, and make use of these documents have significant implications for the agility of the project. In medium-sized projects where the volume of documentation is likely to be an issue, strategies should be investigated for managing the problem. Daily stand-up meetings have been proposed as one solution to communicating information that might otherwise have been typed into memos and/or emails; automation can offer another (requirements management tools allow information on the customer needs to be recorded once and accessed many times, for example).

▶ *Co-location of project stakeholders* – Although co-location is the ideal option for organizing the team in a medium-sized agile project, as the team size grows, ensuring their co-location becomes increasingly challenging. This will be particularly true where the customer representative is an important individual whose time is valuable and who has commitments involving them in other roles outside the agile project. Where it is not possible to ensure all members of the team are co-located, other strategies for improving communications should be considered (this subject is covered in greater detail in Section 25.5).

Agile Communication and Meetings for Medium-Sized Projects

▶ *Improve interpersonal communications* – Good interpersonal communication is essential to the success of agile projects, but with increasing project size, larger teams, and the potential for some of the stakeholders to not be co-located for part of the project, maintaining good communication becomes increasingly challenging. During meetings and in other project communication, techniques to encourage all members of the team to participate must be used, because all members of the project have a valuable perspective and must be given the opportunity to contribute. The communications techniques described in Chapter 19 (as well as in [72, 99]) can all be used to significantly improve the quality and effectiveness of communication in medium-sized agile projects.

▶ *Interim iteration meetings* – For medium-sized agile projects there may be value in holding a meeting midway through an iteration to discuss progress, review risks and dependencies, and review outstanding tasks. This would be particularly appropriate where one or more key stakeholders are not co-located but could make time to be present for such a meeting. One of the case studies describes the benefits of scheduling such a meeting to coincide with another regular event or meeting to enable particular staff to attend both events (Chapter 20). On a Scrum-style project, this goal might be achieved through a Scrum of Scrums (in effect, a higher-level meeting where the attendees are representatives drawn from other Scrums), scheduled at some convenient point during the iteration.

▶ *End-of-iteration retrospective* – These longer meetings (of up to four hours' duration) provide an opportunity for the team members to reflect on what worked well in the iteration, what could have been done better, and to document the lessons learned as part of the task of process improvement. Ensure that quality management topics are on the agenda at such meetings and that effective communications techniques are employed [99].

▶ *Agile workshop meetings* – As the project size expands, team numbers grow, and the complexity and duration of the project increases, there is likely to be a requirement for larger and more formal meetings. For example, RAD includes the notion of the joint application design workshop, which is attended by customer and developer representatives, chaired by a facilitator, and documented by a scribe. While such workshops can last up to five days for particularly demanding tasks in large and complex projects, clearly the smaller the agile project, the greater the drive for more focused meetings of shorter duration.

The role of such workshops in medium-sized projects can be of significant value as an intensive means of discussing and documenting an important aspect of the project, but their duration must be challenged in order to ensure they do not adversely affect project progress. Techniques exist to focus the meetings (such as the fifteen-minute and 80/20 rules [102], and these can be used to ensure such meetings do not exceed the time allocated to them.

▶ *Agile project closedown meetings* – With increasing project size and growth in team numbers, there may be significant value in holding a project closedown meeting above and beyond the end of iteration retrospective meetings. An agile closedown meeting can be of value by allowing the lessons learned from earlier iteration retrospectives to be collated, providing an overall project perspective on what worked well and what could be improved (Chapter 15). From a Scrum perspective, such a meeting could be supported using a Scrum of Scrums approach, with one or more representative from each retrospective providing their input on the key lessons learned.

Ensure quality management issues are covered in the meeting, such as reviewing the success of automated testing tools, highlighting lessons learned in trialing some new testing technique, or reviewing how well testing plans were adhered to during the iteration.

Agile Automation for Medium-Sized Projects

▶ *Tool selection process* – For those medium-sized agile projects where there will be significant requirement for the use of automation, it may be necessary to undertake a formal tool selection process. This process should be as lightweight as possible and could rely heavily on the previous experience of the team members, who may already have preferences for particular tools. Any tool review, evaluation, and selection process must take into account the integration and interoperation needs of other tools already selected or in the process of being selected for use on the project.

Although open-source products may be acceptable on small-sized agile projects, their use may need to be challenged on medium- or large-sized projects. In particular, issues such as availability of support, experienced users, training, upgrade, and maintenance should all be considered when making any decisions about a particular tool. Company standards and guidelines on tool selection and use may also need to be considered. Jon Tilt (Chapter 18) offers this advice on tool selection:

> There is always the temptation to architect yet another automation framework at the start of the project. Don't! Look around at the simple tools that already exist and build on them as required. Developers and testers are much more likely to use something simple that is quick and easy to use.

There may be some benefit in terms of reduced time and effort in using the tools evaluation framework presented in [4].

► *Static analysis tools* – While the use of one of the free static analysis tools should be considered to check the quality of the code generated in the project, the use of more professional commercial static analysis products should also be investigated, particularly if the tool needs to integrate with any existing or planned tools in use on the project.

► *Test harness tools* – Where there is a significant need to test software components that interact with other components that have not yet been developed, the potential use of test harness tools should be considered. In addition to those tools that may have been developed in-house, there are a number of free test harness tools available (e.g., [50]) that have been reported to save the project time, effort, and money.

► *Functional test tools* – For small agile projects it is likely that the volume of functional and regression testing can be satisfied using a manual test approach. As the project size increases, it may still be possible to manage the increasing manual testing load using good test management techniques (such as reusable test scripts and test packs). At some point, however, when the duration needed to execute the manual test suite no longer fits into the planned timescales, when there are frequent builds and releases of the software, and/or when the maintenance of the manual test suite becomes an issue, it may be necessary to consider the use of a commercial capture–replay tool. Such tools record the navigation and verifications employed in a manual test in the form of an automated test script that can be replayed against later builds and releases to perform regression testing (see [62], for example).

► *Requirements management tools* – Although small agile projects may be able to employ in-house or open-source requirements management tools, medium-sized projects are more likely to require an increasingly rigorous, robust, and reliable solution. A number of commercial products are available (see [59], for example) that provide facilities for documenting, utilizing, and maintaining project requirements. In selecting such a product, be aware of company standards and guidelines, the knowledge and advice of colleagues, and the need for the tool to integrate with existing or planned project tools. For example, a requirements product may need to integrate with a test management tool for test planning and design purposes.

► *Build management tools* – Build management tools automate the process of generating a build, bringing together the units and components required to assemble the application under development. Used in combination with a continuous integration approach and potentially incorporating automated testing, these tools can provide a powerful solution to building and testing the software being developed. While the use of one of the open-source build management tools may be an option to consider in relatively small agile projects, as the project size, number of developers, and complexity of the software increase, there is a growing need to consider employing one of the more robust and reliable commercial build management tools.

▶ *Change management tools* – Where agile teams are relatively small and co-located, simple communications between the stakeholders may well be sufficient to ensure that requests for changes to the software being developed are implemented. With increasing team size, complexity of the system under development, and potential lack of co-location of key stakeholders, the role and use of a change management tool becomes more compelling. On small agile projects, in-house or open-source configuration management tools may be an option, but as the project size increases, the use of more robust and reliable commercial products (such as [95]) needs to be considered.

▶ *Defect tracking tools* – Having spent significant amounts of time, effort, and money tracking down bugs in the software, it is essential that these defects get fixed. Similarly, when customers report defects in the software following its release, it is important that these are fixed by a patch or in the next release of the software. To ensure the formal logging of defects, their correction, and retest, some form of defect tracking mechanism must be employed on the project.

In a small agile project with co-located stakeholders, which employs an approach where all defects are fixed immediately, the use of a commercial defect tracking tool may be unnecessary. However, as project size increases – with growing numbers of developers and testers, a large code base, and corresponding defect reports – a rigorous commercial solution (such as [52]) will become increasingly necessary.

Often, change management tools will also be used for defect tracking (since a defect is arguably a special case of a change request). Whatever defect tracking solution is selected, ensure it integrates with the functional, regression testing, and test management tools already being used or planned for use in the project.

▶ *Process enactment tools* – For larger agile projects, particularly those involving new or inexperienced agile practitioners or where project stakeholders are distributed across a number of separate sites or even offshore, it may be a challenge to ensure that all stakeholders follow the chosen process correctly.

Process enactment solutions (see [63], for example) provide an integrated development environment in which the users are constrained to follow agile practices. Such environments typically incorporate sophisticated facilities to promote effective communications across the project (which can include the offsite and offshore team members). Developer estimates and actuals can also be captured in real time to enable the project leader to accurately report on project progress.

25.5 Agile Best Practices for Large-Sized Projects

The best practices documented in this section have been shown to have value when used in large-sized agile projects. Combine the agile practices documented in the following sections with those described in Section 25.2 to provide a set of best practices for use in large-sized projects.

Agile Development and Testing for Large-Sized Projects

▶ *Pair testing* – In combination with the practice of involving testing practitioners as early as possible in the software life cycle, strongly consider pairing testing resources with developers to provide software quality advice and guidance during development. Combined with the practice of encouraging developers and testers to see themselves as software engineers, pair testing can be a particularly effective practice to improve the quality of delivered code. Where you do observe push-back from developers who perceive the tester as being a member of the "quality police," consider involving the test resource in a reviewing role toward the end of the workday.

▶ *Continuous integration* – The practice of continuous integration becomes increasingly valuable with a large team of developers writing and submitting completed code in parallel with the growing code base. A tool-based continuous integration solution should be adopted to automate the build process and also run other tools such as unit test, code coverage, and functional/regression testing tools to verify the quality of each build as it is generated.

Combine continuous integration and automated build with innovative techniques for visualizing the results of a build, such as the red–green lava lamp solution described in Chapter 17 (where a red lava lamp would come on if a build failed). Ensure all defects that are highlighted through this approach are fixed as soon as they are found to support the process of building defect-free software.

▶ *Test refactoring* – For a large agile project, with a large team and a complex application, there is also likely to be a large and complex test suite. With good test management practices, the test suite may be well structured, perhaps involving subsuites linked to particular functional areas of the application under development, or associated with testing code developed within a specific iteration. However, if the test suite is not well structured, or there are difficulties in completing the regression testing within acceptable timescales, test refactoring must be considered. Removing tests[2] that cover some aspect of the application under test that you have a high level of confidence in, or modifying existing tests, may improve the efficiency of the regression test. This practice should be combined with the practice if identifying targets of test.

▶ *Identify targets of test* – In the event that the suite of test scripts becomes sufficiently large that there are difficulties in completing functional and regression testing within allocated timescales, you should consider the use of this practice to assist you in selecting an effective subset of tests to run that will still provide you with good results from a quality perspective. If you have a well-structured test suite – perhaps involving subsuites linked to particular functional areas of the application under development, or associated with specific iterations – it may be possible to simply leave a particular subsuite out of the current regression

---

[2] Ensure the scripts are removed, but not deleted; they may need to be reused in a later testing phase.

test (particularly if the tests are associated with a tried and trusted part of the application under test). More rigorous approaches are also possible for selecting the individual scripts to omit from any particular test, involving code coverage metrics and statistical calculations (see Laser-Guided Testing in Chapter 18, for example).

► *Code coverage metrics* – When running a large test suite against a complex application under test, it is very difficult to have confidence that each and every code statement has been covered in the test, that all subroutines have been tested, or that all possible logical paths through a conditional statement have been exercised. The use of code coverage tools and the metrics they produce will give you an accurate picture of just how thorough your testing has been. Such tools can also be of value in assisting you to identify targets of test (see previous section).

Combined with the automated build process and sophisticated graphical solutions for visualizing code coverage described in Chapter 14, this practice can quickly and easily highlight code coverage issues before they seriously impact the project.

► *Rapid prototyping* – The practice of rapid prototyping can be of major value in a large agile project – exploring the customer requirements, gaining valuable feedback, and ensuring that the final system matches the customer needs. It is important to make sure that the prototypes are developed in such a manner that maximizes the reuse of the code in developing the final system; avoid wasted time and effort writing code that isn't actually used in the final system. In a large agile project, also look for opportunities to share the use of a particular prototype with other developers, who may be able to reuse the code in the completion of their tasks.

Agile Process and Project Management for Large-Sized Projects

► *Be sensitive to the reuse of traditional testing techniques* – In large agile projects, with large (and potentially distributed) teams and involving complex software development, you must consider the value of reusing traditional development and testing techniques where appropriate. V-model [4], for example, is a tried and trusted solution to organizing testing plans that has been shown to have benefits when used in agile projects, and particularly when applied to test planning in longer iterations.

Many agile methods reduce the number of testing phases used in a traditional test process (such as XP), but, depending on the project, it may be necessary to increase the number of testing phases. For example, in developing an application that needs to integrate and interoperate with other existing systems, you may have to consider introducing a systems integration test phase to ensure these requirements are properly tested.

Similarly, with increasing project size and complexity, the benefits of traditional project and test management practices should be considered. For example, elements of the PRINCE project management method [22] have been shown to have been of value in agile project management. Where you have very experienced testing staff involved in your agile project, be sensitive to any suggestions they may have about traditional practices that may benefit the current project.

▶ *Progress measurement* – For large agile projects with large teams and extended timescales, the availability of accurate information on progress is of essential importance, particularly where timescales and budgets are likely to be tight and meeting planned milestones and delivery dates are critical. Add to this the likelihood that it may not be possible for the whole team to be co-located on a large project, and collecting and analyzing progress data quickly becomes a major challenge. While simple fifteen-minute stand-up meetings may be sufficient in small agile projects to discuss progress, such techniques can become unwieldy and inefficient in large projects.

The role and use of tool support must be considered in large projects. While simple tools, such as spreadsheets, may provide a practical and inexpensive (in terms of tool acquisition costs) solution to collecting and recording estimates of the time and effort to complete a task and the actual time expended on the task, they must rely on timely and accurate reporting of progress and estimates for completion. Commercial products are available that automatically collect data on estimates and actuals as tasks are planned and completed. These products do not have to rely on the vagaries of optimistic or pessimistic estimates or on the need of the developer to submit these estimates; they can provide the project leader or manager with an accurate view of the state of the project in real time (see [63, 65], for example).

Ensure that effective progress measurement is combined with effective methods for progress visualization.

▶ *Progress visualization* – In addition to the importance of making project progress information available to the project leader, it is essential that all the stakeholders on the project have access to key project information. With increasing numbers of staff working on a larger agile project, and with the likelihood that not all of the stakeholders will be co-located, providing accurate and effective information to the team is challenging. Project and/or iteration burndown charts that are attached to the wall in a shared project area are unlikely to be effective under such circumstances, and more sophisticated means of sharing project data are needed.

Consider publishing project information via the Internet or a local intranet, particularly if the tools that have been selected for use on the project have a web interface, which allows stakeholders to remotely access requirements information, for example (see [61]). Other tools can be used that allow the setting up of a project portal, where customized views of project data can be displayed [103] and could also be adopted as a means of delivering agile process guidance to the stakeholders. This is an area where thinking out of the box can bring significant results, such as the more unusual display methods described in the case studies, such as the solutions described by David Evans in his case study (Chapter 17) that were used to show the quality results of the code integration process.

▶ *Availability of agile process guidance* – A very significant number of the case studies point to agile project success being linked to the availability of well-trained, well-motivated, knowledgeable, and experienced agile practitioners. It may be a relatively simple task to obtain the small numbers of such individuals for modest-sized agile projects, but trying to staff a large agile project entirely with such superdevelopers and testers would be both a major recruitment challenge and have serious cost implications for the delivery of the project (although it could be argued that a large project staffed entirely with the cream of agile practitioner-hood would be bound to complete early and under budget – if we ignore the issues of obtaining such a team in the first place).

The reality on projects of any significant size is that they will almost certainly be staffed with a mixture of experienced practitioners and less-experienced staff. Also, over the course of an extended project, it is very likely that staff will leave or join the team fairly frequently. Under such circumstances care must be taken to ensure project staffing is organized in a way that ensures a good mixture of experienced and inexperienced staff on tasks, and to encourage skills transfer and mentoring. It is also critical to have good agile process guidance readily available to the team for reference and for skills enablement purposes.

Effective solutions can be as simple as providing process guidance on ready reference sheets (such as those used with [34]). Internet-based portal solutions can also be used to deliver process guidance to the team via web browsers [103]. In large agile projects that are staffed with a high proportion of new or inexperienced agile practitioners and/or those that involve offsite or offshore teams, there may be value in using a process enactment–style product that provides a customizable agile development environment, and which itself embodies and enforces the principles and practices of whatever agile approach has been selected for use on that project ([63], for example).

▶ *Metrics* – It is strongly recommended that a metrics scheme be set up and run for a large agile project. A metrics scheme can provide value to the project in a number of areas, including assisting with more accurate estimation, supporting process improvement, and feeding information to the project portal (or other means of distributing key project information). Given that there is already likely to be significant project activity associated with collecting information about estimates and actuals, productivity, defect detection rates, code coverage, and so forth, the additional effort expended in ensuring that this information is reused in a wider metrics scheme should not result in a large overhead.

When deciding what metrics to collect, first make sure you are clear about the goals of the scheme and precisely what it is you intend to investigate or analyze, since this will guide your selection of data. Make sure that the effort expended collecting and analyzing the metrics is recorded in the metrics scheme (to determine how much time and effort it costs to run the metrics scheme).

Review the benefits of the metrics scheme in the project retrospectives and challenge the value of continuing to run the scheme and, where appropriate, change how the scheme is run. Consider the role and use of tool support for the scheme, particularly if an existing product that is being used on the project can provide access to the data needed. [4] contains comprehensive guidance on setting up and running a metrics program.

▶ *Reduce documentation overload* – The time, effort, and cost required to compile, distribute, maintain, and make use of documents on a large project have significant implications for the agility of the project. Also, paper-based solutions are notoriously error-prone, involving the potential loss of critical project information.

While daily stand-up meetings may be a solution to communicating information that might otherwise have been typed into memos and/or emails for small and even medium-sized agile projects, such techniques can become unwieldy and inefficient in large projects.

Information that might, in traditional projects, have been recorded and distributed using paper-based solutions, such as project progress information, process guidance, and reports, can all be managed using appropriate tools. Requirements management tools provide a thorough and effective means of documenting and maintaining project requirements, while a web-based project portal [103] can be used to provide real-time graphical displays of project progress and instant access to agile process guidance, as well as graphs, bar charts, and pie charts showing defect rates, code coverage, and metrics revealing where in the project life cycle the most defects are being detected.

▶ *Co-location of project stakeholders* – Although this is the ideal option for organizing the team in small- and medium-sized agile projects, as the team size grows, ensuring their co-location becomes increasingly challenging. This will be particularly true where the customer representative is an important individual whose time is valuable and who has other demands on her or his time.

For those large projects with stakeholders that are offsite, effective solutions need to be found to ensure that they are able to communicate with other team members who are co-located as efficiently as possible. A range of solutions can be investigated, such as simple instant messaging systems; Internet telephony, with or without webcam technologies; full-blown videoconferencing facilities; or even use of Web 2.0 technologies, such as virtual project meetings in Second Life [64]. This subject is covered in greater detail in Section 25.5.

Agile Communication and Meetings for Large-Sized Projects

▶ *Improve interpersonal communications* – Good interpersonal communication is vital to the success of large agile projects; but with increasing project size, larger teams, and the potential for some of the stakeholders to not be co-located for part or all of the project, maintaining effective communications becomes increasingly challenging.

In meetings and other project communication, techniques to encourage all members of the team to participate must be used; all members of the project have a valuable perspective and must be given the opportunity to contribute, and instances of where dominant personalities may hijack meetings or where knowledgeable but less extroverted individuals are prevented from contributing must be avoided. Similarly, when important issues need to be discussed, techniques for keeping all members of the team focused on the task at hand are key in facilitating larger meetings.

Make good use of the communications techniques described in Chapter 19, as well as in [72, 99], to significantly improve the quality and effectiveness of communications in large-sized agile projects.

▶ *Interim iteration meetings* – For large-sized agile projects involving relatively long iterations, there is likely to be value in holding a meeting at the midpoint (or more frequently if the iteration is particularly long) to discuss progress, review risks and dependencies, and review outstanding tasks. This is particularly appropriate where one or more key stakeholders are not co-located but are able to make time to be present for such a meeting. One of the case studies also describes the benefits of scheduling such a meeting to coincide with another regular event or meeting so that particular staff can attend both events (Chapter 20).

On a Scrum-oriented project, this goal might be achieved through a Scrum of Scrums (in effect, a higher-level meeting where the attendees are representatives drawn from other Scrums). In particularly large Scrum projects, this might even be achieved using a Scrum of Scrum of Scrums [104].

▶ *Agile workshop meetings* – As the project size expands, as team numbers grow, and as the complexity and duration of the project increase, there is likely to be a requirement for longer and increasingly formal meetings that involve more stakeholders. In RAD projects [18], joint application design (JAD) workshops are attended by customer representatives, developers, and project administrators and can last up to five days for particularly demanding tasks in large and complex projects.

Where such meetings are necessary, the proposed duration of the event must be challenged to ensure it does not adversely impact project progress. Additionally, make good use of techniques to control the duration and focus of the meetings (such as the 15-minute and 80/20 rules [102]) as well as using the communications best practices described in Chapter 19 and in [72, 99].

▶ *Agile project closedown meetings* – For large projects with extended timescales and a large number of stakeholders, there may be significant value in holding a project closedown meeting above and beyond the end of iteration retrospective meetings. Such meetings can be of value by allowing the lessons learned from earlier iteration retrospectives to be collated, providing an overall project perspective on what worked well and what could be improved (Chapter 15). From a Scrum perspective, such a meeting could be supported using a Scrum of Scrums approach, with one or more representative from each retrospective providing their input on the key lessons learned.

Agile Automation for Large-Sized Projects

▶ *Tool selection process* – On large-sized agile projects where significant use of automation is likely, or where an automation architecture is planned or in the process of being set up, it may be necessary to follow a formal tool selection process. This process should be as lightweight as possible, and could rely heavily on the previous experience of the team members, who may already have had exposure to particular tools.

Any tool review, evaluation, and selection process must take into account the integration and interoperation needs of other tools already selected, or in the process of being selected, for use on the project, as well as company guidelines on tool selection. Also, investigate what tool skills are available within the team; decisions involving the selection of a product that nobody knows about, in preference to one that members of the project team already have experience of using, should be challenged.

Also challenge the use of open-source products; although their use may appear to offer cost savings, issues such as availability of support, experienced users, training, upgrade, maintenance, and scalability should all be considered in making any decisions about a particular tool. Similarly, the need for a particular candidate tool to integrate and interoperate with existing or planned products needs to be carefully considered.

To save time and effort in evaluating products, and to adopt a formal rigorous approach, consider using the tools evaluation framework presented in [4].

▶ *Static analysis tools* – Strongly consider the use of a commercial static analysis tool to check the quality of the code generated in the project. For large projects with many developers, these tools can be used to ensure that a consistent approach to development is maintained. Examples of these tools exist that can also be used to verify that code conforms to project or company coding standards.

▶ *Test harness tools* – In a large project there is likely to be a significant need to test software components that interact with other components that have not yet been developed. Under such circumstances, the use of test harness tools should be strongly considered. Although individual developers may generate their own test harnesses, to encourage standardization and reuse, you should strongly consider the use of the open-source test harness tools available ([50], for example) to save the project time and effort and reduce cost.

▶ *Functional test tools* – For larger agile projects involving many developers, with substantial code generation, and a complex application involving frequent builds and releases, there is likely to be significant value in using a capture–replay style functional and regression testing tool. Such tools are able to record the navigation and verifications employed in a manual test in the form of an automated test script that can be replayed against later builds and releases of the software to perform regression testing (see [62], for example).

Although they are of value to many projects, capture–replay tools are not the panacea for all software quality issues; they work best with reasonably stable software systems (where the user interfaces are not subject to frequent change), they should be used in combination with integrated requirements management and defect tracking solutions, and you should consider the value of using an integrated code coverage tool.

Although such tools are valuable in allowing testing to be conducted in significantly shorter timescales than equivalent manual testing, and to support additional unattended testing of the software (overnight or over the weekend, for example), it is still possible on a large project for the test suite to grow sufficiently large to cause test execution performance problems. One of the case studies reported the use of an automated test suite that in the worst case could take up to ten days to execute! Under such circumstances, consider implementing the "identify targets of test practice" to reduce the size of the regression testing suite and to allow automated testing to fit into the required project timescales.

▶ *Requirements management tools* – For large agile projects, with increasing team size, high complexity of the system being developed, and potential lack of co-location of key stakeholders, the use of an automated requirements management solution is essential. Bottom line – without formal tool support that provides rigorous traceability, it will become very difficult to ensure that the delivered system does what the customer actually requires of it.

From a development and testing perspective, distributed requirements management tools allow the developers to understand what functionality needs to be implemented to support the customer requirements, and the tester to know what needs to be tested to ensure the implemented code meets the customers needs. In selecting a requirements management solution, ensure the tool integrates and interoperates with existing or planned products (and particularly change management and test management solutions).

Where important stakeholders are unable to be co-located with the development team, ensure that the selected tool provides support for distributed requirements management. A number of such tools provide a web-based interface to allow distributed teams to inspect, use, and modify the requirements (such as [95]); such a facility will be essential for offshore projects.

▶ *Build management tools* – Such tools automate the process of generating a build, bringing together the units and components required to assemble the application under development. A number of the case studies describe the use of build management tools in combination with a continuous integration approach that incorporates automated unit test and functional test, and generates code coverage and complexity metrics. Used as a key component of an integrated tool architecture, automated build management tools can save projects significant time and effort and improve the quality of the delivered software.

▶ *Change management tools* – With large and complex projects of extended duration involving large numbers of stakeholders (many of whom may not be co-located), the role and use of change management tools becomes critical. The role of robust and reliable commercial change management products, and particularly those with a distributed capability, must be considered for use in such projects (such as [95]). As with other tools, any candidates selected must integrate with other tools used on, or in, the process of being acquired for the project and should be selected with regard to possible company guidelines on tool acquisition.

▶ *Defect tracking tools* – For large projects where substantial time, effort, and money are spent on software quality, it is essential that any defects that are found are fixed. Whatever defect tracking solution is employed, it should support a rigorous workflow that ensures that defects are highlighted to the appropriate stakeholders, that defects are fixed in a timely manner and retested, and that the fix is introduced back into the code base only after formal sign-off of the change by an authorized member of the team.

Similarly, it is critical that defects reported by the customer following delivery of the software should be treated in the same manner, ensuring that they are fixed and that they do not appear in the next release (or later releases) of the software.

Investigate the acquisition of a reliable and robust commercial defect tracking solution that integrates with the functional testing, regression testing, and test management tools already being used or planned for use on the project. Ensure that any such tool provides access for any stakeholder that is not co-located with the project team (this is a particularly valuable facility to provide to the customer – allowing defect reports to be submitted by the users, or a user representative, from their own site). Where a change management tool has already been introduced into a project, investigate whether it also supports a defect tracking solution.

▶ *Process enactment tools* – For larger agile projects, particularly those involving new or inexperienced agile practitioners or where project stakeholders are distributed across a number of separate sites or even offshore, it may be a challenge to ensure that all stakeholders follow the same process.

Process enactment tools provide an integrated development environment that embodies and enforces the use of a particular agile best practice (good examples of such tools can be customized to support a particular agile method). In effect, the users are constrained to follow the specific agile practice selected for use on the project.

Such environments typically incorporate sophisticated facilities to promote effective communications across the project (which can include the offsite and offshore team members). Such tools can provide comprehensive support for metrics collection and use, with, for example, developer estimates and actuals that are captured in real time and which can enable the project leader to accurately report on project progress. Consider using process enactment tools in conjunction with solutions for making process advice and guidance available.

Agile Best Practices for Offsite and Offshore Projects

A key agile best practice is that of co-locating all the project stakeholders. While this may be a realistic option on smaller agile projects, what happens to agile projects where key staff cannot be co-located and spend much of their time at a different site, or where significant numbers of the team have to work in different geographies? Under these circumstances, how can effective communication be achieved?

The best practices documented in this section have been shown to have particular value when used on agile projects where a significant number of project stakeholders are offsite or even offshore. The following practices should be used in conjunction with the agile practices documented in the preceding sections to provide a combined set of best practices for use in offsite or offshore agile projects.

Agile Process and Project Management for Offshore Projects

▶ *Progress measurement* – Due to differences in time zones, combined with potential language and cultural differences, obtaining accurate and timely project data is a particularly challenging aspect of offshore projects. Offshore projects significantly increase the likelihood that important project information will be misinterpreted or misunderstood. Wherever possible, consider tool support for estimating individual and overall project progress. (This issue is covered under the section on agile automation for offshore projects.)

▶ *Progress visualization* – Solutions for delivering essential project data to all members of a team that includes offshore assets must address both technical issues (ensuring that the solution can be distributed) and cultural/language issues (the information must be easily understood by the offshore team). Although an Internet-based project portal [103] satisfies the former issue, the latter is more challenging, perhaps involving the assistance of a co-located offshore representative (see the section on non-co-located teams), considering the role of semiotics [105], or through a pilot scheme to explore and address these issues before the full project is launched.

▶ *Availability of process guidance* – It is critical in an offshore project that all team members follow the same process in developing the software, and it is essential that all members have access to guidance on the process that has been adopted for the project. Process guidance should be made available to all members of the team via a distributed solution, such as an Internet-based project portal [103]. Be sensitive to language or cultural differences when setting up such a solution, and ensure that the content and its presentation can be easily understood and used by the offshore team.

▶ *Metrics* – Effective solutions must be found to ensure important project data can be collected, analyzed, and distributed in an accurate and timely manner. The role of distributed process enactment products in offshored projects, which provide a development environment that enforces the use of the agile process selected for the project, and which also automatically collect data on estimates and actuals, provide an effective solution to this requirement. (Further information on this solution is provided in the section that follows on agile automation for offshore projects).

Agile Communication and Meetings for Offshore Projects

▶ *Non-co-located teams* – The analysis of the case studies provides some excellent best practice guidance on specific solutions for improving the quality of offshore communications.

 ▷ Set up and use an effective project communications infrastructure. The facilities could include instant messaging, Internet telephony (potentially involving a webcam for face-to-face communications), and/or full videoconferencing tools. Web 2.0 technologies, such as virtual team meetings in Second Life, may also be of value.

 ▷ Harmonize offshore time zones. Consider adjusting the working day start and end times between the different time zones to improve the working overlap between the zones. Even starting work half an hour earlier in one time zone, while finishing work a half hour later in the other zone, will make an overall difference of one hour. Each week or every other week, consider varying the start and stop time on one particular day by one hour. This overall two-hour difference could be used for the purposes of holding an extended combined project meeting.

 ▷ Co-location of an offshore representative – On an extended or high-value project, consider having one of the members of the offshore team co-located at the primary project site. This can be of significant value in helping to address cultural and language issues associated with offshoring.

▶ *Agile meetings* – Although the more traditional solution of videoconferencing can be used to provide "face-to-face" meeting support, also be receptive to the use of innovative technologies to support meetings with offshore teams. Web 2.0 tools, such as Second Life [64], may provide one practical solution to holding distributed virtual meetings.

▶ *Improving interpersonal communications* – For the success of those agile projects where key stakeholders or larger parts of the team are offsite or offshore, effective good-quality communication becomes critical. In project meetings and other opportunities for contact, all members of the project must be given the opportunity to communicate clearly as well as have an equal opportunity to contribute to the discussion. Be sensitive to cultural differences and language issues, and find opportunities to establish a good rapport with offshore colleagues. Chapters 15 and 19 provide excellent advice on improving the quality of communications under these circumstances.

Agile Automation for Offshore Projects

▶ *General* – Any productivity tool that is planned to be employed by all team members on an offsite and/or agile offshore project must be robust and reliable, and specifically intended for distributed, cross-geography operation. Integration and interoperation issues have to be carefully considered to ensure that any selected products that need to work together can do so successfully in a distributed manner. A formal tool evaluation and selection process (such as that documented in [4]) is essential in selecting the correct products.

▶ *Requirements management tools* – To ensure everyone on the project has up-to-date and accurate requirements information, consider the use of a distributed requirements management tool. Any candidate product should support distributed access for all stakeholders, such as via a web interface, to enable all team members to submit, review, discuss, and use requirements information.

▶ *Build management tools* – Strongly consider using distributed build management tool support to facilitate continuous integration across the whole team, including offsite or offshored resources. Integrate testing tools (including unit test, code analysis, functional and regression test, and code complexity analysis products) within the build management process to automatically execute the tests and flag those builds containing defects or areas of concern.

▶ *Process enactment tools* – The use of such products appears to be of particular value in offsite or offshore projects. A distributed process enactment tool that is capable of operating in a cross-geography manner can be used to ensure all members of the project are following the same agile process in the same way and that the project manager is able to obtain up-to-date and accurate information on the progress of the project (see [63], for example). Consider using a process enactment tool in conjunction with a process guidance tool to ensure all practitioners have access to information on the agile best practices the project has adopted.

25.7 Summary

This chapter has provided guidance and advice on how the agile practices identified in Chapter 24 can be used as the basis of generating your own agile process. For additional information describing the details of the best practices and their context, you can also refer to the case studies.

To assist you in the selection of agile practices to populate your own agile process, Appendix H contains a checklist of agile practices, showing graphically which practices are particularly appropriate for different styles and sizes of agile project that can be used as a visual summary and an *aide memoire* of the information provided in this chapter.

Finally, the best process in the world will only ever be of academic interest unless it is adopted and used by other agile practitioners. Chapter 26 provides you with guidance on how you can manage the roll-out and adoption of your agile process in your own organization.

26 The Roll-out and Adoption of My Agile Process

> As is so often the case, improving quality turns out not to be a
> technology problem, but a people issue and a leadership challenge.
>
> **Nick Denning, MD of Diegesis**

26.1 Introduction

Having selected and documented your agile best practices, even the best agile development and testing process is nothing without the acceptance and consistent use by a community of testers within an organization. Technical issues aside, the introduction and adoption of your agile testing process is likely to be the most difficult step in delivering effective and efficient agile testing within your organization.

In some organizations, the roll-out and adoption of agile best practices may not be an issue. For example, if you work in an enlightened company that is already familiar with the benefits agile can provide, it is likely that agile practices are already in the process of being used. Similarly, if your company already has a pressing need to adopt an agile means of working – perhaps to satisfy the terms and conditions of another organization that has asked them to bid for some development work, and who are looking for responses from companies that will employ agile practices – you may not need to evangelize about agile.

If none of the aforementioned applies to your organization, the following sections describe a tried and tested strategy for the introduction, adoption, and ongoing use of your agile process. This chapter also addresses the issues associated with the subsequent maintenance and update of your testing process.

The strategy is structured under the following phases with their associated tasks:

- Pre-agile Process Roll-out Phase:
  - ▷ Establish the need for agile process.
  - ▷ Establish the likely return on investment of the proposed agile test process.
  - ▷ Gain management commitment and approval.
  - ▷ Gain agreement to run an agile proof of concept (POC)/pilot project.
- Agile Process Roll-out Phase:
  - ▷ Baseline current development and testing practices.
  - ▷ Resource the POC/pilot project (staff, equipment, software, rooms, etc.).
  - ▷ Provide training, mentoring, and process guidance.

▷ Execute agile POC/pilot project.

▷ Review results of POC/pilot project.

▶ Post-Agile Roll-out Phases:

▷ Report on success of POC/pilot project.

▷ Monitor and improve agile test process.

▷ Advertise results.

▷ Continue to evangelize.

26.2 Roll-out and Adoption

The phases and their associated tasks involved in the roll-out and adoption of your agile process include the following.

Pre-Agile Process Roll-out Phase

During this phase, a number of tasks must be completed in preparation for the roll-out and use of your agile process. The tasks in this phase include the following:

▶ *Establish the need for agile process.* To make a major change to the way it currently develops software, your organization needs a compelling need to act; for example:

▷ If your organization is currently developing software using traditional techniques, have there been issues with projects missing their delivery dates, with projects completing over budget, and/or with delivery of software that contains too many defects?

▷ Do your customers complain that the development approach used by your organization is too rigid, that they do not have the opportunity to influence what gets developed, and that delivered software does not match their needs or expectations?

▷ Are your competitors adopting agile practices to make their software development and delivery process more effective and efficient?

▷ Is your organization under significant commercial pressures to deliver software faster, with less effort and cost, and with higher quality?

If one or more of these compelling needs to act apply to your organization, you can use this information to make a compelling business case for agile to your own senior management.

▶ *Establish the likely return on investment of the proposed agile test process.* Before approaching management with your proposal for the adoption of your agile process, spend some time collecting information that you will need to make a compelling business case. Consider the time and effort involved in rolling out and adopting an agile process and the likely returns to your company compared with continuing to use the current approach to developing and testing software.

▶ *Gain management commitment and approval.* In making a business case to management for the adoption and use of your agile process, there are a number of things you might do:

▷ Identify an agile champion – this should be someone in your organization who can communicate at all levels in the company (from management to practitioner level), who is enthusiastic about agile, and who has the communication skills to make the case for agile.

▷ Consider delivering internal agile educational/lunch and learn/workshop/ external speaker sessions to your colleagues and to management to raise the profile of agile methods and their potential benefits to your organization.

▷ Highlight the compelling need(s) to act, which were identified earlier, to appropriate managers (perhaps making use of your agile champion) and discuss the effort and likely benefits of rolling out your agile process.

▷ Look to gain (and document) management support for an agile POC or pilot project to demonstrate the quantitative benefits of your agile process. Ensure that management support for the POC/pilot includes adequate time, budget, and resources to complete it successfully.

Agile Process Roll-out Phase

During this phase, a number of tasks are performed in preparation for the roll-out of your agile process. The tasks in this phase include the following:

▶ *Baseline current development and testing practices.* If you are to convince management of the benefits of adopting an agile approach, you will need to be able to demonstrate quantitatively that agile will save time, effort, and money. To do this, you need to obtain data on how long it typically takes your organization to write software, how much effort is expended, and what the overall cost is. It may also be necessary to show improvements in software quality, in which case you may need to be able to obtain data on defect detection rates as well. If your organization already collects these metrics, that will make the process easier. If not, you may have to rely on estimates obtained in discussion with your colleagues.

▶ *Resource the POC/pilot project.* Ensure you give the agile pilot project the best chance for success; using your documented management approval, recruit the best staff you can, ensure you have dedicated hardware and software, and appropriate rooms to ensure co-location of the team.

▶ *Provide training, mentoring, and process guidance.* Where necessary, make sure that training and mentoring are available to ensure the team members have the right skills and knowledge to be successful, and make agile process guidance available to the team (this could be as simple as the ready reference cards described in Chapter 5).

▶ *Execute agile POC/pilot project.* In setting up and running the POC/pilot project you need to consider the following:

▷ Select an appropriate project. Ensure you pick a project that is appropriate to an agile approach and that is achievable; you must ensure that you show off your use of an agile approach to its best advantage. Don't be overconfident and bite off more than you can chew on the POC.

▷ Underpromise and overachieve. Look for early wins to increase team morale and confidence, try to deliver working software as quickly as possible, involve the agile champion, and demonstrate early progress to your management sponsor and customer.

▷ Collect accurate metrics. At the end of the POC, enthusiastic qualitative claims about the success of the project are unlikely to influence hard-nosed managers. However, if you have collected metrics that show quantitative improvements over the incumbent development process, this can sway even the most stoic of accountants.

▷ Collect useful collateral. Be receptive to, and make notes on, particular highlights from the POC, particularly successful events, or memorable quotes from team members, management, or the customer; these can be reused after the pilot to help promote the success of the project.

▶ *Review results of POC/pilot project.* Take some time at the end of the POC to review the result. Get together with the team and the agile champion to discuss the highlights of the project, to review project metrics, and compare these with the baseline figures for the existing development and testing approach. Begin to document the results and consider how to report this information to the interested parties.

Post-Agile Roll-out Phases

▶ *Report on success of POC/pilot project.* After analyzing the results of the POC, work with your agile champion to determine the best means of reporting the success of the project. The deliverables from this task could include the following:

▷ A management summary document that highlights the key results of the project. This summary will save senior managers the effort of working their way through a larger and more comprehensive report document (which may make the difference in some cases between the results getting read or not).

▷ A full report that formally documents the results of the project in detail, and which could contain an analysis of the project metrics as well as formal return on investment calculations. This document can be used by anyone in the organization who needs a deeper understanding of the results of the project.

▷ A formal presentation that highlights the results of the POC, and which can be delivered to senior management to provide them with a succinct briefing on the results of the project. This presentation could be used as the vehicle for the delivery of the management summary and/or full report to management.

> ▷ An informal presentation (perhaps reusing a customized version of the formal presentation) on the highlights and results of the project, that can be delivered to interested colleagues and other practitioners.

Following a successful pilot project or POC, seek management approval to introduce your agile process on other projects, perhaps as a follow-on from the POC or on new projects that are in the pipeline.

▶ *Monitor and improve your agile test process.* In the best traditions of agile projects, continue to improve your agile process. Learn from projects that were particularly successful, or from agile projects that didn't do so well, and document the lessons learned for use on future projects. Investigate how the process might be customized for different-size or special needs projects (such as offsite and offshore projects).

▶ *Advertise results.* Nothing succeeds like success; ensure agile win-stories are publicized to management, colleagues, and other practitioners in the organization:
  > ▷ Consider using "lunch and learn" sessions, email newsletters, and/or items on the company intranet to promote agile successes.
  > ▷ Continue to make use of your agile champion to promote the case for agile throughout the organization.
  > ▷ Consider passing on your agile best practice knowledge to others in the industry by writing technical papers and looking for opportunities to speak about your agile experiences.

▶ *Continue to evangelize.* Don't make the assumption that agile will simply take off on its own; it may, but continued agile evangelism by you, your colleagues, and your agile champion will all help to promote the cause of agile development and testing. Consider setting up an agile special interest group within the organization, investigate holding monthly meetings (and ensure management representatives are invited), and look to invite interesting external speakers. The key thing to remember is to have stamina!

26.3 Maintenance of Your Agile Process

Almost as soon as it has been rolled out and adopted, your agile process is likely to be out of date; implementation technology changes at a very rapid pace, new agile practices continue to be developed and refined, and new and improved tools become available to be used on agile projects. At the very least, the process will need to change to take account of lessons learned during its use.

You should establish some key points where your agile process should be reviewed and proposals for changes discussed. These could include the following:

▶ At the end of individual projects to identify any lessons learned during the project. If agile retrospectives are a feature of your agile process, define a formal mechanism for documenting the lessons learned from all agile projects, and put a change management process in place to process proposals for change to the process. Consider the value of using tools to support the process of accepting requests for change and for documenting and maintaining the requirements (ensure these are distributed products if you have a number of sites using your agile method).

▶ Following changes in the wider agile community, such as the availability of new or refined agile best practices. You should be receptive to such changes and new agile practices by being aware of the agile literature, registering on agile special interest Web sites and visiting agile blogs, and attending appropriate special interest group meetings.

▶ As a prelude to the adoption/introduction of new or enhanced testing tools or techniques.

▶ Following changes in the management approach of the organization, such as the adoption of a new project management methodology, or some formal process improvement scheme, that impacts your agile process.

▶ At regular dates, such as an annual or biannual review.

▶ As and when requested by the company quality assurance manager (or equivalent).

Following such a review and where changes need to be made to the process, the following actions should be performed:

▶ Update whatever mechanism you have selected to distribute your agile process to your colleagues (ensuring that any changes do not adversely impact agile projects that are still active).

▶ Actively inform key stakeholders in your company that changes have been made and tell them where they can find more information.

▶ If the change is a major one, consider the need for training and mentoring to make sure that your colleagues are able to employ the changes correctly and benefit from them.

▶ Review the success of the change at some point following its introduction and after sufficient time has elapsed to allow an accurate appraisal to be made of its benefits.

26.4   Summary

As fantastic and as valuable as you believe it to be, your agile process will not roll itself out to your colleagues and your organization.

If you want your process to be anything more than just an academic exercise in assembling a collection of agile best practices, then you need to find some means of getting your colleagues and your organization to use them in earnest on projects that have some value to your company.

This chapter has described an effective approach that you can use to drive the successful roll-out and adoption of your agile process and to continue to manage its ongoing success. Use it to spread the agile word and to gain some agile brownie points in your organization.

And as a final thought: as Jon Tilt and David Evans say in their agile case studies – it's okay to be agile about the roll-out and adoption of your agile process in your organization.

The Principles of Rapid Application Development

In certain situations, a usable 80% solution can be produced in 20% of the time that would have been required to produce a total solution.

Walter Maner

A.1 Introduction

This appendix reviews the essential rules and practices of the Rapid Application Development (RAD) agile method, focusing in more detail on the testing aspects of the method.

The guiding principles of RAD are to deliver usable high-quality systems quickly and with low costs. The RAD rules and practices are discussed under the following sections:

- ▶ Overview of the Characteristics of RAD Projects,
- ▶ Joint Application Design,
- ▶ Rapidity of Development, and
- ▶ Incremental Prototyping.

A.2 Overview of the Characteristics of RAD Projects

RAD seeks to avoid the traditional problems associated with large, monolithic waterfall-style projects by breaking the organization and management of the project tasks into smaller, more easily managed increments.

Historically, RAD projects have been most successful when employed to develop relatively small and simple applications, with low complexity and risk. For larger, more complex applications, such as the implementation of a company-wide customer relationship management (CRM) system, for example, organizations typically looked to more mature software project management and development approaches (such as PRINCE [22]). A number of organizations have had success combining both approaches, with PRINCE used for the overall management of the project and RAD employed to develop the comparatively simple and low-complexity applications that run against (using our preceding example) the CRM system.

RAD appears to be particularly well suited to projects where the user community and its use of the delivered software is well defined and highly interactive. Within such projects, the key RAD technique of rapid prototyping can be used to produce simplified models of elements of the system to obtain feedback from the users and to refine the developers' understanding of the requirements of the final system.

RAD projects commonly fall into one of two types; the intensive and the phased RAD project. In an intensive RAD project, a combined team of users and developers work together:

▶ for relatively short periods (perhaps a couple of weeks, for example),
▶ in a controlled environment where external distractions are kept to a minimum (a so-called clean-room environment; see Section A.3), and
▶ to deliver a complete working element of the final system.

In a phased RAD project,

▶ the timescales are slightly more relaxed, and the project can be of several months' duration;
▶ there is less emphasis on continuous co-location between users and developers, with requirements and design information being elicited and refined through intensive workshops involving users and developers (so-called joint application development workshops; see Section A.3); and
▶ the project is planned and managed in terms of the development, demonstration (to the users), and refinement of a series of incremental prototypes, which build toward the final deliverable.

A.3   Joint Application Design

The principles of Joint Application Design (JAD) include

▶ *Dedicated teams* – Developers and users work together in small teams (typically four to eight people) that are empowered to make design decisions. The most successful teams are made up of members with good communications skills, combined with specific domain knowledge; users with detailed business knowledge; and experienced developers with appropriate techniques and tools skills.
▶ *JAD workshops* – A series of JAD workshops are used throughout the development process to elicit and refine requirements and design details. These workshops are attended by customer representatives (including key users); developer representatives (with good requirements elicitation skills); plus a secretary or "scribe," who documents the results of the workshop. The workshop is administered by a facilitator who, in addition to chairing the session, is responsible for ensuring that
   ▷ all project issues are identified, reviewed, and refined;
   ▷ any political issues are identified and resolved; and
   ▷ the views of users and developers are given equal weight.

The deliverables from a JAD workshop are a set of documented business requirements, which may also contain information on priority and timescales of the documented requirements. A key testing output from a JAD is the test plan (or the amended test plan in subsequent JADs).

▶ *Clean rooms* – JAD workshops are convened at locations away from the customer and developer sites to ensure that there are no interruptions or distractions that might compromise the success of the workshop. The location should be selected to encourage good communication and focused problem solving and should be equipped with appropriate support facilities such as whiteboards, notepads and pens, computers, and plentiful supplies of caffeine. Attendees should be strongly encouraged to switch off mobile phones and avoid doing email for the duration of the workshop.

A.4 Rapidity of Development

Completing projects on time, within budget, and to acceptable levels of quality is RAD's *raison d'être*; as such, RAD projects can be characterized as having short timescales (particularly with respect to earlier development methods such as waterfall projects), employing rigorous project management techniques, and ensuring that automated tool support is considered wherever possible:

▶ *RAD timescales* – RAD projects can be characterized as being of relatively short duration, with two to six months considered the norm, and of no more than six person-years' effort in total. The RAD philosophy is that projects taking more than six months to complete are likely to have been overtaken by developments in the business (due perhaps to changes in legislation, competitive pressures, or changes in technology). Smaller, more focused development timescales also mean that projects are less likely to suffer from time and cost overruns, since it is easier to assess progress accurately and to identify risks and mitigate them before they can cause a serious threat to the project success.

▶ *Time boxing* – Time boxing [17] is a project management technique in which a series of development and testing tasks are planned to be completed in a fixed time period or time box; the deadline for the time box is set in stone and cannot be moved – even if it is clear that some aspect of the system functionality planned to be implemented within that time box cannot be completed.

Time boxing relies on the awareness of the priorities documented during the course of the RAD project to work (typically through user and developer discussion in JAD workshops); when timescales are tight, the least important features are sacrificed to ensure that development still meets the deadline. Testing effort and timescales must be included in the time-box planning process to ensure adequate testing is completed.

▶ *Rapid development tools* – RAD encourages the use of automated development tools in projects wherever it is appropriate and whenever they can be shown to save time, reduce effort, and save cost. Such tools can include requirements elicitation and management tools such as [61], development tools such as [7], testing tools such as [62], and configuration and change management tools such as [88]. Where the effort involved in acquiring, rolling out, using, and maintaining such tools outweighs the savings in terms of time and effort, their use must be challenged.

Given the iterative nature of RAD development, testing tools have an important part to play in terms of saving time, effort, and cost through the reuse of automated test scripts created during earlier iterations for continuous regression testing in subsequent iterations.

A.5 Incremental Prototyping

The development of incremental prototypes is core to the success of RAD; simplified working models of the system are constructed and then demonstrated to the customer representatives. The choice of features implemented in the prototype is determined by the priorities agreed in discussion with the customer representatives, and, although built quickly, the prototype is intended to provide the customer with a representative view of the look, feel, and functionality of the features implemented. Once the prototype has been completed, the developers test the prototype using test scripts developed during the earlier design stages.

The customer representatives are able to discuss their perceptions of the prototype with the developers, and agree on and document any changes they may feel necessary. After making any required changes to the prototype, the process is repeated. Within the constraints of project progress and time-box deadlines, this cycle may be repeated a number of times to ensure the customer representatives are satisfied with the prototype and that the developers are confident that they understand what the customer is looking for.

From a quality perspective, prototyping has two key benefits:

▶ Customer representatives are exposed to early versions of the system and can provide immediate feedback on the suitability of the system to the developers.
▶ The prototypes can be used to manage the expectations of the customer in terms of the final delivered system, ensuring that there are no last-minute surprises for the customer that might result in potentially costly rework to the system.

Prototyping can be successfully used throughout the project from requirements elicitation, design, implementation, testing, and on through to delivery.

The Rules and Practices of Extreme Programming

Its OK to be agile about your agile adoption.
David Evans

B.1 Introduction

This appendix reviews the essential rules and practices of Extreme Programming[1] (XP), focusing in more detail on the quality aspects of the method.

The XP rules and practices are grouped into four sections: (1) planning, (2) designing, (3) coding, and (4) testing. It is notable that in virtually every description of the principles of XP you read, you will find that testing is covered last. In this appendix, testing is covered as the first topic.

B.2 Testing

Quality assurance (QA) is considered to be an essential aspect of XP. QA may be performed by a separate group, or it can be integrated into the development team itself. In either case, XP promotes the idea that the developers have a high degree of contact with the QA group; this is very much in line with the XP philosophy of closer communications between the stakeholders in a project.

XP provides some excellent guidance on testing:

▶ XP encourages early and frequent testing.
▶ XP looks to make the process as efficient and effective as possible by promoting the use of test automation.
▶ XP demands that all code have associated tests, and that where code is changed that the tests be rerun (and/or modified where appropriate to reflect the changes).
▶ XP requires test design to be completed before coding has started, with all code having associated unit tests.

---

[1] Extreme verses eXtreme; although both forms can be found in the literature, for consistency, I have opted for Extreme. Sincere apologies to anyone who prefers eXtreme and who is seriously offended by this choice.

There are just two types of test in XP:

▶ Unit tests written by the developers to test their code. These are white box tests [4], which rely on the knowledge of the code and its purpose.
▶ Acceptance tests written with the help of the customer and the user stories, to validate some expected result from the system. These are black box tests [4], which are created using the user stories as well as direct user input where available.

The use of test automation in XP is promoted to help save time, effort, and cost of testing. In addition to finding defects and verifying requirements, the testing tool can be used at both unit and acceptance testing.

The testing rules and practices of XP state the following:

▶ *All code must have unit tests.* All classes in the software under development must have associated tests that are released into the code base alongside the code they test. Code that is found without a corresponding test cannot be released, and the unit test must be created as soon as possible to test the software.

All code must pass unit tests before the code can be released. A unit test framework (such as JUnit [50]) is an essential tool that should be used through-out the development and testing process to help test, as well as be used to formalize requirements, refine architecture, write, debug, integrate, release, and optimize code. It is possible to write your own unit test framework, but this must be balanced against the productivity gains that reusing a commercial or share-ware product can deliver.

In XP, unit tests support the concept of collective code ownership; the unit tests act as a gatekeeper against accidental and deleterious changes to your code functionality. Since all code must pass unit tests before it can be released, there is good confidence that the code satisfies its required functionality, irrespective of who has worked on it.

In principal, this is an excellent agile best practice; implemented properly, it means that all code that resides in the code base has been validated by specific tests written against the specification/requirements/user story[2] for that code. If only this were true for all components found in more traditional software development projects, there would be much higher confidence in the quality of the software components, with a corresponding simplification in the execution of the later testing phases.

▶ *Tests must be designed before coding begins.* This is an excellent best practice that ensures that the developers review the requirements for the software, understand them sufficiently well to have a clear idea of how they will be tested, and then design and implement the unit tests.

It is claimed that the overall time taken to create the unit test and write code is equivalent to the time taken to just code the software from scratch – plus you

---

[2] Analogous to use cases.

have a set of tests ready to run against the code – saving additional time and effort.

As a final thought, it is almost a development and testing cliché that coding always overruns and eats into the time planned for testing; create the tests before coding begins and you have a much higher chance of ensuring that proper testing will take place.

▶ *When a bug is found, tests are created.* In the event that a defect is found in production, tests are created to ensure that, once fixed, the defect remains fixed; the tests can be reused to ensure the defect does not reappear at a later point in the development process.

Working with the customer and the appropriate user story to develop an acceptance test, the programmer gains a better understanding of the nature of the defect as well as of the correct behavior the code should exhibit.

In the event that an acceptance test has failed, the programmer creates a unit test to show the defect from the source-code perspective; once the unit tests are all executed successfully, the corresponding acceptance test is rerun to ensure the defect has been fixed properly.

▶ *Acceptance tests* are created from user stories, the tests are run frequently, and the result is published – the acceptance tests are based on the user stories created in conjunction with the customer representative.

During the iteration planning meeting for each iteration, a number of user stories are selected as the basis of the acceptance tests. A given user story may result in one or more acceptance tests (the number being determined by what is needed to show the system performs as expected); each acceptance test represents some expected result from the system.

The customer is responsible for reviewing the acceptance tests to ensure they are correct. The customer is also responsible for reviewing the test results and test scores to identify which failures of the system are most important and specifying the priority for remedial work, with the developers scheduling the time at each iteration to correct any failed tests.

Any given user story is not considered complete until it has passed all of its acceptance tests.

B.3 Planning

The planning rules and practices of XP include the following:

▶ *User stories* – are written by the customers as descriptions of things that the system needs to do for them. They are also used to create time estimates for release planning and as the basis of creating the acceptance tests.

▶ *Release planning* – a *release planning* meeting is used to create a release plan for the project, with individual iteration plans based on the release plan schedule.

Developer and customer discuss and agree to the order in which the user stories are to be implemented.

▶ *Make frequent small releases* – the development team will release iterative versions of the software to the customers on a frequent basis. These releases are determined by decisions made during the release planning meeting about units of functionality that reflect useful business activities that can be delivered to the customer as early as possible within the project timescales.

▶ *Project velocity* – the project velocity is a measure of how much work is being completed on the project. The metric is easy to calculate – simply add up the estimates of the user stories that were finished during the iteration. Used in conjunction with the sum of the tasks finished in the iteration, this information is used for future iteration planning.

▶ *Iterative development* – an iterative approach to development promotes agility in the development process. By dividing the overall development schedule into about a dozen smaller units of up to three weeks in length (and keeping the duration of each iteration the same), development will follow a regular and predictable rhythm. By following this approach, the task of estimating progress and planning becomes more simple and more reliable.

▶ *Iteration planning* – an iteration planning meeting is called at the beginning of each iteration to produce that iteration's plan of programming tasks. User stories are chosen for this iteration by the customer from the release plan in order of the most valuable to the customer first. Where implemented user stories have failed their acceptance tests in the previous iteration, these can also be selected for rework and retest, as long as the total amount of effort does not exceed the project velocity from the previous iteration.

▶ *Move people around* – to avoid bus-count problems,[3] move people around within the project to avoid serious knowledge bottlenecks. If only one person on your team can work in a given area and that person leaves or you just have too many things waiting to be done in that section, project progress will suffer. Pair programming makes this approach more practical since typically it is possible to swap individuals in a pair out to other tasks (and other staff in) without major impact on productivity.

▶ *Daily stand-up meeting* – ensuring good communication among the entire team is a key aspect of XP. Each morning, the project team stands in a circle to review problems, discuss solutions, and promote team focus. A goal of the stand-up meeting is to reduce the need for other meetings that might take place during the day, helping to focus people's minds on making progress and saving potential lost effort.

---

[3] Heaven forbid, but bus-count refers to the number of staff in your project that could be hit by a bus without there being a significant impact on project success. It is a measure of the amount of key knowledge tied up in too few people in a project. Also known as "truck count" in the United States.

▶ *Fix XP when it breaks* – XP does not assume that it will have the answers to all software development projects; in fact it assumes that it won't. Projects are encouraged to always start by following the XP rules but not to hesitate to change any aspect of the approach that does not seem to be working within a given project. Where deemed necessary, such changes must be fully discussed, agreed on, and communicated before being implemented.

B.4 Designing

The design rules and practices of XP include:

▶ *Simplicity* – complexity is the enemy of progress; a simple design is easier and quicker to complete. XP challenges developers to seek out the most simple (and often most elegant) means of satisfying the needs of the system they are involved in developing. Another guiding principle of simplicity is not to be tempted to add functionality ahead of when it is scheduled.

▶ *Choose a system metaphor* – it is essential that all members of the development team follow a common vision of how the program works, adopting a common naming convention and using a common vocabulary. This can be achieved by adopting and being guided by an appropriate metaphor for the way the system works; for example, a nest of leaf-cutting ants might be employed as a metaphor to represent an agent-based Internet-search program, with individual agents (the ants) sent out to search across the information superhighway (the branches of the tree) for specific information or pages (the leaves).

▶ *Use CRC cards for design sessions* – Class, responsibilities, and collaboration (CRC) cards [106] encourage the project team to avoid thinking in a procedural manner and to enable the team to make full use of the object-oriented development model. CRC cards are also a powerful means of involving as many of the project team to contribute to the design as possible; the more people involved, the more good ideas are incorporated in the design.

▶ *Create spike solutions to manage risk* – a spike solution is a simple program used to investigate possible solutions to a potentially risky aspect of the project. The spike focuses exclusively on the issue under examination, such as a specific technical risk or equivocal user story estimate. Once the spike has served its purpose, it is typically discarded (very few such solutions make it into the released code).

▶ *No functionality is added early* – focus on what is scheduled today; it is always a temptation to elaborate your code, to add extra code, or to make the existing code more intricate. Some metrics suggest that only 10% of this additional code will have any use in the delivered system – ergo, you will have wasted 90% of the time in unnecessary effort.

▶ *Refactor whenever and wherever possible* – refactoring (taken from the title of Martin Fowler's book *Refactoring: Improving the Design of Existing Code*

[56]) is a powerful technique for refining the design and implementation of the system.

B.5 Coding

The coding rules and practices of XP include the following:

▶ *The customer is always available* – this is a key requirement of XP. In practice, the customer should become part of the development team, ideally co-located with the other team members but at least available at all times for communication purposes. The customer is encouraged to actively assign one of their staff members to the XP project who is expert in the business activity the software is being developed to address, and who is able to develop the user stories, agree on timescales, and assign priorities. The customer is also able to review progress on the developed software and see the working code as it becomes available (ensuring the delivered code meets expectations).

▶ *Code must be written to agreed standards* – developed code must meet agreed coding standards. Such standards ensure the developed code is consistent and easy to understand and refactor (see [57], for example).

▶ *Code the unit test first* – creating the unit test before writing the code allows the developer to focus on what the code needs to do and how to show that it does it; requirements are reviewed in detail, identifying any potential misunderstanding or errors in the specification. All of this is essential work that would have had to be done before writing code in any case; having the tests available on completion of the code means tests can be run immediately, allowing bugs to be quickly identified and fixed and ensuring that development keeps in step with the plan. Close contact with the customer ensures the tests are realistic and match what they expect of the software, as well as managing their expectations of what the delivered software will do.

XP practice says that designing unit tests before code development has begun makes it much easier and faster to develop the code. It has been claimed that the additional focus on the requirements and the intended purpose of the code needed to generate good tests, enable the developer to write the code and test it faster than the code that could be developed from scratch without any thought about testing [107].

It is also claimed that there are additional benefits from this approach to the overall system design. Compared with development approaches that lead to tests being designed and executed after the software has been implemented (and often by a separate team of dedicated testers), by developing the tests first as XP advocates, the design is influenced by the goal of testing those aspects of the software that are important to the customer, hence leading to an overall design that is easier to test.

▶ *All production code is pair programmed* – all code is written by two developers working together at the same workstation. Having two developers may seem wasteful in terms of resources, but experience shows that two heads are better than one (or even two separate heads) at producing higher-quality code in equivalent (or even shorter) timescales than two separate developers. This improvement in quality of the developed code also leads to savings toward the end of the project, with reductions in defect detection and reworking of the software.

▶ *Code integration* – where a number of developers are working on separate aspects of the system in parallel, the results of their work should only be integrated sequentially (and where there are more than two parallel threads, in turn). This solves the chaos and uncertainty of bringing multiple parallel development threads together in one go, trying to resolve the inevitable multiple collisions in the code that such activity typically brings. It is essential that the corresponding tests (as embodied in the unit test suite) are treated in exactly the same manner.

Integration should be done on a frequent basis to ensure that all the developers are able to work with the most up-to-date version of the software. As a key principle, the longest period that coding should continue without integration is one day. In parallel, good communications between developers is essential to ensure everyone is aware of what code can be reused or shared.

▶ *Use collective code ownership* – using this approach, everyone involved in the development project is seen as a stakeholder in delivering the system. This means that everyone involved is encouraged to contribute ideas to the development effort at any point in the project. In practice, this means developers are allowed to edit code that they may not have originally written to correct a defect, add functionality, or refactor. Although this sounds haphazard, following any changes, the software must still pass the tests written for that aspect of the system.

▶ *Leave optimization until last* – this is an inevitable consequence of following the aforementioned development rules; with the overall development continuing in parallel, with frequent integration and testing, and with the frequent ad hoc changes to the code that collective code ownership brings, it only makes sense to try to optimize the system once it has begun to achieve some level of stability. A common mantra of XP is "make it work, make it work right, then make it fast."

▶ *No overtime* – it is one of IT's best known clichés that testers end up with no social life – chained to a workstation, probably in a subterranean office with no windows, working on into the evening or weekend trying to play catch-up with the pitiful timescales the late delivery of the code from the developers has left us with! The result? Tired, resentful staff whose concentration, creativity, and motivation is inevitably compromised.

XP advocates the use of a release planning meeting to modify the project timescales and/or the scope of the deliverable to ensure overtime is avoided. Maintaining good communications with the project stakeholders, and particularly with the customer, should make this process more straightforward to achieve.

The Principles of the Dynamic Systems Development Method

We have no plans, therefore nothing can go wrong.

Spike Milligan

C.1 Introduction

This appendix reviews the essential principles and practices of the Dynamic Systems Development Method (DSDM) and focuses in more detail on the quality aspects of the method.

Specifically, this appendix reviews and discusses

▶ the Quality Aspects of DSDM,
▶ the Fundamental Principles and Assumptions of DSDM,
▶ the DSDM Phases and Stages,
▶ DSDM Roles and Responsibilities, and
▶ DSDM Techniques.

C.2 The Quality Aspects of DSDM

One of DSDM's fundamental principles is that testing is integrated throughout the life cycle. Testing is considered to be an integral activity within DSDM, must begin as early in the project as possible, and must continue throughout the project life cycle. Testing is a mandatory part of each increment and is conducted to ensure that the software meets its business needs and is robust and reliable.[1]

"Fitness for business purpose" is another important DSDM fundamental principle and informs one of the key acceptance criteria for the software: delivering a system that addresses the current business needs. In practice, this means that it is better to deliver software that supports critical business functionality than to deliver a more complete, more polished, or more perfect system.

Co-location of users and developers ensures that users are able to continuously evaluate the quality of the software being developed and to provide the developers

---

[1] It is interesting to note that this principle is listed at number eight out of the nine fundamental DSDM principles.

with essential feedback on the suitability of the software. A specific DSDM example of this approach allows for the delivery of "partial solutions" to support urgent business needs, with later versions of the software implemented using the feedback gained from the users.

Another key testing requirement that is enshrined as one of DSDM's fundamental principles is the ability to be able to revert quickly, easily, and accurately to previous versions of the application under test. In practice, this requirement is typically supported through the use of a configuration and change management tool (see [88], for example).

While DSDM has been created to be agile enough to expect and to deal with frequently changing requirements, it also incorporates the need to formally manage those requirements changes, ensuring that the changes are promulgated to all members of the project team that need to know, such as the testers.

In terms of the testing artifacts (i.e., test documents and items created or used during the project), the following are commonly employed in DSDM projects:

▶ *Test plan* – Testing effort is initially considered during the DSDM preproject phase (see later) and refined during the later phases and stages.

▶ *Test record* – A Test Record is created or updated during each iteration of the DSDM project life-cycle phase and is used as part of the process of documenting the implementation strategy for that iteration. The test record incorporates test scripts, test procedures, and test results:

▷ A *test procedure* provides the means of documenting the specification for a test.

▷ A *test script* documents the detailed implementation of a test procedure, describing navigation and verifications, and is used by the tester to execute one or more tests.

▷ *The test results* provide a documented record of the results of executing the test scripts.

Although the quality of the delivered system is considered the responsibility of all members of the team, DSDM identifies a number of roles with specific quality assurance responsibilities:

▶ *Technical coordinator* – The Technical Coordinator has overall responsibility for designing the system architecture as well as responsibility for controlling the technical quality of the project.

▶ *Tester* – The Tester role is responsible for implementing the test plans, writing the test procedures, implementing and executing the test scripts, recording the test results, and reporting on the test results.

▶ *Project manager and team leader* – These management roles have responsibility for the planning and day-to-day implementation of quality within the project, respectively.

C.3   Fundamental Principles and Assumptions of DSDM

An important foundation of DSDM is the recognition that there is no one-size-fits-all solution to developing software and that no development framework can provide all the answers. DSDM addressed this observation by closely following nine fundamental principles and eight additional assumptions, which, if adhered to, provide a higher likelihood of project success.

The nine fundamental principles are as follows:

1. *Active user involvement is imperative* – Co-location and close collaboration between users and developers are vital in running an efficient and effective project, allowing decisions to be made jointly and without ambiguity.
2. *DSDM teams must be empowered to make decisions* – DSDM project teams consist of developers, testers, and users who must be empowered to make decisions that are important to the progress of the project, without waiting for higher-level approval. Testers and developers must be able to rapidly decide on technical solutions, whereas the business users must be able to decide on key requirements for the application.
3. *The focus is on frequent delivery of products* – DSDM projects emphasize frequent delivery of products, with the assumption that to deliver something "good enough" earlier is always better than to deliver something that is "perfect" later. By delivering product frequently from an early stage of the project, the product can be tested and reviewed and the test record and review document can be taken into account at the next iteration or phase.
4. *Fitness for business purpose is the essential criterion for acceptance of deliverables* – The main criterion for acceptance of a "deliverable" is delivering a system that addresses the current business needs. Delivering a perfect system that addresses all possible business needs is less important than focusing on critical functionalities.
5. *Iterative and incremental development is necessary to converge on an accurate business solution* – In DSDM emphasis is put on evolving a system via incremental steps. Within this process, partial solutions may be delivered to fulfill immediate business need, with later versions of a system built upon the lessons learned from users in the feedback process. Only by explicitly reworking a system in this way can an accurate business solution be produced.
6. *All changes during development are reversible* – It must be possible to quickly, easily, and accurately revert to a previous version of the system under development.
7. *Requirements are baselined at a high level* – The high-level requirements for the system should be agreed and in a static state before the project starts. This does not preclude the likelihood that detailed requirements will change as the project proceeds.
8. *Testing is integrated throughout the life cycle* – Testing is not considered to be a separate phase or activity within DSDM and is expected to begin as early in the

project as possible and to continue throughout the project life cycle. Testing is an integral part of each increment and is conducted to ensure that the software meets its business needs and is robust and reliable.

9. *A collaborative and cooperative approach between all stakeholders is essential* – Because the low-level requirements are not fixed at the outset in a DSDM project, there must be continuous cooperation and collaboration between sponsors, developers, and users throughout the life of a project.

The additional eight assumptions are as follows:

1. *No system is built perfectly on the first try* – As a rule of thumb, 80% of the business benefit comes from 20% of the design requirements; therefore, DSDM starts implementing this first 20%, which is sufficient as long as the end users are satisfied with the functionality, and that the missing 80% does not cause any serious business consequences. This mitigates the risk of the project going over deadline and over budget.

2. *Project delivery should be on time, on budget, and of good quality* – DSDM emphasizes the need to meet project timescales and cost, but not at the expense of quality.

3. *Each step of the development only need be completed far enough for the next step to begin* – This practice allows a new iteration of the project to commence without unnecessary delay. Changes in design can coincide with the changes in demand from the end users, because every iteration of the system is improved incrementally.

4. *Both project management and development techniques are incorporated* – DSDM recognizes that technical agile best practices cannot exist successfully in a project management vacuum and acknowledges the need to follow good project management techniques.

5. *DSDM can be applied in new projects and for expanding current systems* – Just because the previous phase of a particular development project was based on another development approach, the adoption of DSDM for future development and enhancements to the system is not precluded.

6. *Risk assessment should focus on business function being delivered, not on the development process nor its artifacts* – Projects can go wrong in spite of following good development practices or having produced very elegant but time-consuming design or requirement documents; DSDM emphasizes the scrutiny of delivered business function as the means of assessing project risk.

7. *Management rewards product delivery rather than task completion* – DSDM considers customer satisfaction and success using the delivered business functionality to be a better measure of project progress than developers reporting the completion of a particular iteration.

8. *Estimation should be based on business functionality instead of lines of code* – As with assumptions 6 and 7, this assumption focuses again on the delivery of successful business functionality to the customer rather on traditional metrics of counting the lines of code or function points.

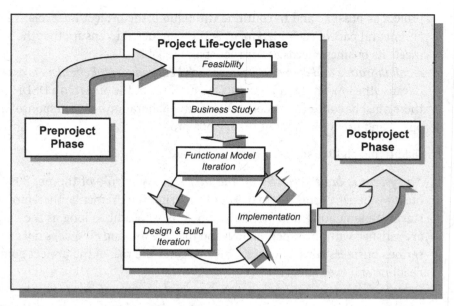

Graphical overview of the DSDM phases and stages.

C.4 The DSDM Phases and Stages

DSDM consists of three phases and a number of substages (Figure C.1 provides a graphical overview of the DSDM phases and stages):

▶ *The preproject phase* sets the context of the project and ensures it is set up correctly from the outset to give the project the best likelihood of success. Key products delivered from this phase include the initial definition of the business problem to be addressed, budget and resourcing, outline scope and plans for the feasibility study, and a decision on whether or not to proceed with the project.

▶ *The project life-cycle phase* combines both sequential and iterative stages, leading to the incremental development of the system. Following initial feasibility and business study stages, the project iterates through the functional model, design and build, and implementation stages:

▷ *Feasibility study* – In this stage, the likelihood of the project meeting the customer's business requirements is evaluated. Other issues that are covered in this stage include assessing the suitability of DSDM in implementing the customer's business requirements, reviewing possible technical solutions to the business problem, and producing initial estimates of costs and timescales. The key products from this stage include
  • a feasibility report,
  • an optional feasibility prototype,
  • an outline plan that also addresses quality issues, and
  • a risk log.

▷ *Business study* – In this stage, the business processes to be supported are scoped out. Other issues that are covered in this stage include outlining the future development in terms of prototyping deliverables; identifying customer representatives to be involved in the prototyping activities; prioritizing the requirements of the proposed system; reviewing the project risks and updating the risk log; establishing the foundation for technical development and test to proceed; and scoping the nonfunctional requirements, including usability, security, performance, and maintainability requirements. The key products from this stage include
  - business area definition,
  - prioritized requirements list,
  - development plan,
  - system architecture definition, and
  - updated risk log.

▷ *Functional model iteration* – In this stage, static models (such as visual class and data models) and working software prototypes are used to animate and explore the required business functionality with the customer. Through early exposure to the software, the customer is able to provide essential feedback to the developers. This stage is also used to discuss, refine, and document those nonfunctional requirements that the prototypes may not be able to demonstrate. The key products from this stage include
  - a functional model plus review records,
  - a list of nonfunctional requirements,
  - any functional prototypes developed during the stage,
  - an implementation plan including time-box plans, and
  - an updated risk log.

▷ *Design and build iteration* – In this stage, the system is developed against the functional model and incorporates any reusable aspects of the prototypes. Nonfunctional requirements are also addressed. Testing is conducted to ensure the software satisfies the customer business requirements. The key products from this stage include
  - time-box plans,
  - design prototypes plus review records, and
  - tested software plus test records.

▷ *Implementation* – In this stage, the tested system is installed in the customers' working environment. As part of this process, the users, operators, and support staff are trained on their specific aspects of the system. This stage is also used to elicit any additional development requirements for future iterations. The key products from this stage include
  - the tested and delivered system;
  - the trained users, operators, and support staff;
  - user documentation; and
  - an increment review document.

Following the implementation stage, the development process either continues with a further functional model iteration or, if development is complete, the project enters the postproject phase.

▷ *The postproject phase* covers postdeliver activities, such as maintenance, enhancements, and fixes, and is used to ensure the ongoing effective and efficient operation of the delivered system.

C.5 DSDM Roles and Responsibilities

Compared with the relatively few roles found in Extreme Programming, DSDM defines a larger number of project roles, each with well-defined responsibilities:

▶ *Executive sponsor* – the executive sponsor is a senior member of staff in the user organization who has the power and influence to commit appropriate user funds and resources as required by the project. This role is also termed the "project champion."

▶ *Visionary* – the visionary role is taken by a user who has the most accurate perception of the business objectives of the system and the project and who has the responsibility to initialize the project by ensuring that essential requirements are found early on. Another visionary task is to supervise and keep the development process on the right track.

▶ *Ambassador user* – The ambassador user is able to communicate with the user community at all levels (from management through to user level) and is able to bring the knowledge of the user community into the project. The ambassador user is able to mobilize the users to ensure that the developers receive enough user feedback during the development process.

▶ *Advisor user* – The advisor user is any user that is able to provide the developers with appropriate depth of knowledge and/or experience about some element of the project, such as a particular aspect of the business needs that are being implemented.

▶ *Project manager* – The project manager provides overall management of the project, including responsibility for planning, resourcing, progress monitoring, reporting to senior stakeholders, tasking the team leader, and so on. Although the project manager is typically drawn from the IT staff, it is also possible for the project manager to be drawn from the user community.

▶ *Technical coordinator* – the technical coordinator is responsible for designing the system architecture and controlling the technical quality of the project.

▶ *Team leader* – the team leader provides day-to-day leadership of the project team, implements the project manager's vision for the running of the project, and works to ensure that the project environment is free of any issues that might impact on the effectiveness and efficiency of the team.

▶ *Developer* – the developer is responsible for interpreting the system requirements, generating the design (through visual modeling, for example), writing the deliverable code, and building the prototypes.

▶ *Tester* – the tester is responsible for implementing the test plans; writing the test cases, procedures, and scripts; executing the tests; and recording the results. The tester is also responsible for updating the test record and reporting on the progress and results of testing.

▶ *Scribe* – the scribe is responsible for documenting the requirements, agreements, and decisions made during a DSDM workshop (see next section).

▶ *Facilitator* – the facilitator is responsible for organizing and facilitating the DSDM workshops (see next section).

▶ *Specialist roles* – A number of specialist roles may be employed within the project as and when needed and dependent on the size and scope of the project. These could include automation engineers, business architects, quality managers, and system integrators, for example.

C.6 DSDM Techniques

DSDM incorporates a number of specific techniques:

▶ *Testing* – As described in the preceding sections, testing is considered an essential and integral aspect of DSDM projects. Through the iterative nature of DSDM projects, testing is mandated to begin as early in the project as possible and to continue throughout the project at each iteration. Testing covers both functional and nonfunctional aspects of the system.

▶ The *MoSCoW Principle* – MoSCoW (must, should, could and, would) provides a means of prioritizing requirements within a DSDM project, by allowing requirements to be identified that
  ▷ *must* be implemented for the software to meet the business needs;
  ▷ *should* be implemented if at all possible, but without which the project can still be successful;
  ▷ *could* be implemented as long as the time and effort involved do not impact the fitness of the business needs of the project; and
  ▷ *would* be implemented if spare time and budget are left at the end of an iteration.

▶ *Time boxing* [17] – It is a technique used to manage the time and cost aspects of tasks within a DSDM project. Using this approach, at each iteration a number of business requirements are selected for implementation according to the MoSCoW principle. As the iteration proceeds, should time and budget allow, further requirements are selected and implemented.

▶ *Prototyping* – The production of animated models and working prototype software is a key technique that DSDM employs in the process of developing the final system. This approach allows the developers to explore the business requirements with the users, to show them working examples of business functionality, and to obtain immediate feedback that isused to refine the final delivered software. Conversely, prototyping can be used to manage the users' expectations of the developed software, ensuring that the delivered system closely matches the user perceptions of how the software should appear and how it should perform.

▶ *Workshops* – A DSDM workshop is a structured meeting attended by user and developer representatives that is convened to gain understanding of a particular project issue (such as business needs, requirements, and/or business functionality). A facilitator manages the agenda and progress of the meeting, while a scribe is responsible for documenting the information gained as a result of the workshop.

▶ *Visual modeling* – The failure of users to successfully communicate business requirements and other domain knowledge to the developers has historically been a major cause of project failure; quite simply, the final delivered system fails to match the user expectations in terms of what they thought they had agreed with the development team. Visual modeling is a powerful technique that helps bridge the knowledge gap between users who are expert in the business aspects of the system and the developers. Techniques such as use cases [8] and notations such as the Unified Modeling Language (UML [33]) allow diagrams to be created that allow users and developers to confirm their understanding of what needs to be developed in a simple and unambiguous manner.

▶ *Configuration management* – Because of the highly dynamic nature of DSDM projects, with changing requirements and rapid development of code, good configuration and change management are essential to the success of a project. Within DSDM projects, the requirement for good configuration and change management is typically supported by means of tools ([88], for example), of which there are many available to choose from.

The Practices of Scrum

A pig and a chicken are walking down a road. The chicken looks at the pig and says, "Hey, why don't we open a restaurant?" The pig looks back at the chicken and says, "Good idea, what do you want to call it?" The chicken thinks about it and says, "Why don't we call it 'Ham and Eggs'?" "I don't think so," says the pig, "I'd be committed but you'd only be involved!"

D.1 Introduction

This appendix reviews the essential rules and practices of Scrum,[1] focusing in more detail on the testing aspects of the method.

The Scrum rules and practices are discussed under the following sections:

- ▶ Scrum General Practices,
- ▶ Scrum Roles and Responsibilities,
- ▶ The Sprint,
- ▶ Scrum Meetings, and
- ▶ Scrum Artifacts.

D.2 Scrum General Practices

- ▶ Customers must become a part of the development team; it is essential that the customer is genuinely interested in the success of the project.
- ▶ There should be frequent intermediate deliveries with working functionality; this enables the customer to get exposure to working software earlier and enables the project to change its requirements according to changing needs.
- ▶ The development team should be alert to project risks and develop appropriate mitigation strategies; valid risk mitigation, monitoring, and management should be actively performed throughout the project.
- ▶ Problems, issues, and risks must not be swept under the carpet; no one should be penalized for identifying or highlighting any unforeseen problem.
- ▶ There should be transparency in planning and module development; everyone must be aware of who is accountable for what and by when.

---

[1] Scrum versus SCRUM: although Scrum is often shown in the uppercase form – SCRUM – it was not originally employed as an acronym, which is why my preference throughout this book is for Scrum. Sincere apologies to anyone who prefers SCRUM, and who is seriously offended by this choice.

- ▶ Frequent stakeholder meetings should be held to monitor progress, with dashboard/stakeholders' updates; procedures must be put in place to ensure visibility of potential slippage or deviation in a timely manner to allow it to be corrected.
- ▶ The project environment and work time must be energized; "working more hours" does not necessarily mean "producing more output."

D.3 Scrum Roles and Responsibilities

The roles that are defined in Scrum are divided into two high-level groups: pigs and chickens, based on the joke presented at the beginning of this appendix.

The implication is that the pigs represent those roles that are committed to building software regularly and frequently, while all other roles in the project are considered to be chickens, who, although interested in the project, are effectively irrelevant because if the project fails they weren't the ones that committed to doing it. The needs, desires, ideas, and influences of the chicken roles are taken into account but should not be allowed to affect, distort, or get in the way of the actual Scrum project.

The "Pig" Roles

Pigs are the ones committed to the project and the Scrum process; they are the ones with "their bacon on the line!" The pig roles include

- ▶ *The product owner* – The product owner represents the voice of the customer and ensures that the Scrum team is focused on the right issues from a business perspective. The product owner writes user stories, prioritizes them, then places them in the product backlog.
- ▶ *The ScrumMaster (or Facilitator)* – Scrum is facilitated by a ScrumMaster, whose primary job is to remove impediments to the ability of the team to deliver the sprint goal. The ScrumMaster is not the leader of the team (as they are self-organizing) but acts as a buffer between the team and any distracting influences. The ScrumMaster ensures that the Scrum process is used as intended. The ScrumMaster is the enforcer of rules and sprints of practice.
- ▶ *The Scrum team* – A small team of five to nine people with cross-functional skills to do the actual work (tester, developer, designer, etc.).

The "Chicken" Roles

Chicken roles are not part of the actual Scrum process but must be taken into account. An important aspect of this agile approach is the practice of involving users, business people, and other stakeholders into the process; it is important for these people to be engaged and provide feedback against the outputs for review and planning of each sprint. The chicken roles include the following:

- ▶ *The users* – The software is being built for someone! There is a Scrum mantra that says, "Never forget that software that is not used is like a tree falling in the forest – was it ever written?"

▶ *Stakeholders* – The people who enable the project but are not directly involved in the process. This includes executives.

▶ *Consulting experts* – The people who provide expertise that is not required on every sprint. It is possible for a chicken to become a pig as part of the Scrum team during some sprints.

D.4 The Sprint

Scrum follows an incremental development approach, whose increments are termed *sprints*. During each sprint, a 15–30-day period (length decided by the team), the team creates an increment of shippable software, or deliverable.

The set of features that go into each sprint come from the *product backlog*, which is a prioritized set of high-level requirements of work to be done. The choice of which backlog items go into the sprint is determined during the *sprint planning meeting*. During this meeting the product owner identifies the items in the product backlog that she or he wants completed. The team then determines how much of this they can commit to complete during the next sprint.

During the sprint, the team works to complete the fixed set of items (termed backlog items). During the sprint no one is able to change the backlog, which means that the requirements are frozen for a particular sprint.

D.5 Scrum Meetings

In line with its goals of promoting good communications, proactively highlighting project risks and issues, transparency in planning and development, and stakeholder involvement, meetings are a key aspect of a successful Scrum project. The different types of Scrum meetings include the following:

▶ *The sprint planning meeting.* Prior to each sprint, a sprint planning meeting is convened and attended by the product owner, ScrumMaster, the entire Scrum team, and any interested and appropriate management or customer representatives. The purpose of the meeting is threefold:

▷ The product owner outlines the highest priority features that need to be developed and tested to the Scrum team members, who ask sufficient questions to allow them to determine which tasks they will move from the product backlog into the sprint backlog.

▷ The Scrum team members discuss and agree how they will convert the selected sprint backlog into an increment of potentially shippable product functionality. The output from this activity is a list of tasks, task estimates, and assignments that will start the team on the work of developing the functionality.

▷ Together, the Scrum team and the product owner agree on a sprint goal that succinctly describes what the sprint will achieve, and which will be used during a sprint review meeting to assess the success of the sprint.

▶ *The Scrum.* Each day during a sprint, a project status meeting is arranged. This is called a Scrum. The Scrum has specific guidelines:

▷ The meeting starts precisely on time with team-decided punishments for tardiness (e.g., money, push-ups, hanging a rubber chicken around your neck).

▷ All are welcome, but only "pigs" may speak.

▷ The meeting is time-boxed at fifteen minutes irrespective of the size of the team.

▷ Where practically possible, all attendees should stand.

▷ The meeting should happen at the same location and same time every day.

▷ During the meeting, each team member answers three questions:

1. What have you done since yesterday?
2. What are you planning to do by tomorrow?
3. Do you have any issues or impediments preventing you from accomplishing your goal? (It is the role of the ScrumMaster to remember these issues.)

On a larger Scrum project, which potentially has a number of distinct teams, it may become impractical for all the stakeholders to get together for a single meeting. Under these circumstances, a Scrum of Scrums may be employed. This is a meeting attended by one or more representatives from each of the team Scrums, and can be used as an opportunity to obtain information on areas of integration and overlap between the teams.

▶ *Sprint retrospectives.* After each sprint a brief sprint retrospective is held, at which all team members reflect about the past sprint. The purpose of the retrospective is to make continuous process improvement. This meeting is time-boxed at four hours.

D.6 Scrum Artifacts

The following artifacts (things that are created, used, and/or delivered) are employed during a Scrum project:

▶ *User stories* – Originally borrowed from Extreme Programming (see Appendix B), user stories provide the means of capturing user requirements throughout the project. Written in simple, nontechnical, jargon-free language, a user story is a simple statement of what a user wants some feature of the system to do. They should focus on documenting the who, the what, and the why of the requirement rather than specifying the "how" aspects of the required feature; a very basic template for a user story could be written as, "As a ⟨User Role⟩, I want to ⟨Goal⟩, so that I can ⟨Reason⟩."

▶ *Product backlog* – The product backlog is a high-level document for the entire project. It contains broad descriptions of all required features, wish-list items, and so on. It is the "what" that will be built. It is open and editable by anyone. It contains rough estimates, usually in days. This estimate helps the product owner to gauge the timeline and, to a limited extent, priority (e.g., if "add search" feature is estimated at three days rather than three months, that may affect the product owner's decision on what to do next).

▶ *Sprint backlog* – The sprint backlog is a detailed document containing information about how the team is going to implement the requirements for the upcoming sprint. Tasks are broken down into hours with no task being more than sixteen hours. If a task is greater than sixteen hours, it should be broken down further. Tasks on the sprint backlog are never assigned; rather tasks are signed up for by the team members as they like.

▶ *Burndown* – The burndown chart is a publicly displayed chart showing the effort remaining over time. A burndown chart presents a graph of effort versus time and is updated daily (and/or as required). Typically, there are two types of burndown charts:

▷ a sprint burndown chart, recording the daily progress of a sprint, and

▷ a product burndown chart, showing overall monthly progress.

▶ *Dashboard* – It is possible to drown in too much project information; information overload prevents team members from being able to focus on key metrics and indicators. A dashboard is a tool intended to provide all members of the team with a concise view of key project metrics, such as tasks, impediments, and bugs. Typically, an automated tool is used to implement the dashboard, either developed in-house, obtained from a number of shareware sources, or purchased from one of the suppliers producing such tools.

▶ *Increment of shippable software* – The deliverable from a sprint is a software product termed an increment of shippable software. Once this software deliverable is transitioned into routine use by the customer, it becomes a release.

Agile Test Script Template

E.1 Introduction

The following pages of this appendix contain a test script template (Figure E.1) that may be copied and used within your own testing task or project.[1]

The test script template contains the following sections:

► **Project ID** – the unique project identifier;
► **AUT Name** – the definitive name of the Application Under Test (front sheet only);
► **AUT Version** – the definitive version information for the Application Under Test (front sheet only);
► **Iteration ID** – the unique identifier for the iteration this test is being conducted in (front sheet only);
► **Date of Test** – the planned start date of testing (front sheet only);
► **Test ID** – the unique identifier for the test;
► **Purpose of Test** – a brief description of the purpose of the test including a reference, where appropriate, to the requirement that is to be tested (consider providing references to the requirements specification, design specification, user guide, operations guide, and/or installation guide), as well as any dependencies from or to other test scripts/test cases;
► **Test Environment** – a brief description of the environment under which the test is to be conducted (may include a description of the state of the AUT at the start of this test, details regarding the platform or operating system, as well as specific information about data used in this test);
► **Test Steps** – concise, accurate, and unambiguous instructions describing the precise steps the tester must take to execute the test, including navigation through the AUT as well as any inputs and outputs; and
► **Expected Result** – a brief and unambiguous description of the expected result of executing the test.

---

[1] Where the test script template provided in this appendix does not exactly match your needs, an electronic version of the template can be obtained at the following URL for you to customize: http://www.cambridge .org/9780521191814 (Cambridge University Press Web Site / Agile Script Template)

Text appearing in angle brackets ($\langle\,\rangle$) denotes a place marker, which must be replaced with the appropriate information for a particular testing phase. For example, $\langle$Client$\rangle$ should be replaced by the name of your own company or organization.

Figure E.2 provides an example of how the test script template provided in this appendix might be completed in practice.

(Client) Test Script			(*front sheet*)
Project ID			
AUT Name		Version	
Iteration ID		Date of Test	

Test ID	
Purpose of Test	
Test Environment	

E.1 Test script template.

Test Steps	
Expected Result	
	Page 1 of Pages

E.1 *(continued)*

	(Client) Test Script	*(continuation sheet)*
Project ID		

Test ID	
Purpose of Test	
Test Environment	

E.1 *(continued)*

Test Steps	
Expected Result	
	Page of Pages

E.1 *(continued)*

CTS Wiki Test Script			*(front sheet)*
Project ID	CTS Group News Wiki and Process Framework		
AUT Title	CTS Wiki	Version	v1.0
Iteration	02	Date of Test	07/07/2008

Test ID	02-Team-Org-Chart-01
Purpose of Test	To ensure that: • It is possible to navigate to the screen showing the Team Org Chart • It is possible to view the whole Team Org Chart, and that it is legible
Test Environment	The test environment is as follows: • Client Hardware: IBM T60 Laptop • Server: Company Intranet system • No other applications should be running on the laptop • The Wiki should be running and at the top level intro page, with the login dialog box visible • Hand-rafted "login data" is held in C:\test-dir\login.dat

E.2 Specimen completed test script for the CTS Company Wiki project.

Test Steps	In the login dialog box, the tester should: • Left-click into the "User Name" field and enter "testuser" • Left-click into the "Password" field and enter "password" • Left-click on the "OK" button • Once the next screen appears, left click on the **CTS Org Chart** link in the left hand navigation pane
Expected Result	On completing the above steps, the CTS Team Org Chart should be displayed. • Verify that the whole org chart is visible on the screen • Verify that the contents of the org chart is legible
	Page 1 of 1 Page

E.2 *(continued)*

Agile Test Result Record Form Template

Introduction

The following pages of this appendix contain a test result record form template (Figure F.1) that may be copied and used within your own testing task or project.[1]
The test result record form template contains the following sections:

- **Project ID** – the unique project identifier;
- **AUT Title** – the definitive title of the Application Under Test (front sheet only);
- **AUT Version** – the definitive version information for the AUT (front sheet only);
- **Iteration ID** – the unique identifier for the iteration this test is being conducted in (front sheet only);
- **Date of Test** – the date on which the test was performed (front sheet only);
- **Test ID** – the unique identifier for the test;
- **Time of Test** – the time at which each individual test case was started;
- **Observed Test Result** – a brief textual description of the result of the test;
- **Test Result Category** – the test result category assigned to this test (as specified from the Test Specification document for this testing phase; see Appendix D);
- **Test Error Description** – a brief textual description (if appropriate) of the observed test error;
- **Name of the Tester;**
- **Tester Signature** – the signature of the tester, recording their participation in the test, their observation of the result of the test, and their agreement to the documented test result;
- **Name of the Test Observer** – this might be the user/customer representative, or somebody from the quality assurance group (if your organization has one); and
- **Test Observer Signature** – the signature of the test observer, recording their observation of the result of the test, and their agreement to the documented test result.

---

[1] Where the test result record template provided in this appendix does not exactly match your needs, an electronic version of the template can be obtained at the following URL for you to customize: http://www.cambridge.org/9780521191814 (Cambridge University Press Web Site / Agile Script Template).

With the exception of the last item, these sections of the test result record form are completed by the tester in consultation with the independent test observer and any other staff attending the testing phase in an official capacity (such as the user representative in User Acceptance Testing).

Text appearing in angle brackets (⟨ ⟩) denotes a place marker, which must be replaced with the appropriate information for a particular testing phase. For example, ⟨Client⟩ should be replaced by the name of your own company or organization.

Figure F.2 provides an example of how the test result record form template provided in this appendix might be completed in practice.

(Client) Test Result Record From			*(front sheet)*
Project ID			
AUT Title		AUT Version	
Iteration ID		Date of Test	

Test ID		Time of Test	
Observed Test Result			

F.1 Test result record form template.

Test Result Category	
Test Error Description	

Tester Name		Tester Signature	
Test Observer Name		Observer Signature	

F.1 *(continued)*

(Client) Test Result Record Form				*(continuation sheet)*
Project ID				

Test ID			Time of Test		
Observed Test Result					
Test Result Category					

F.1   *(continued)*

Test Error Description			
Tester Name		Tester Signature	
Test Observer Name		Observer Signature	
			Page of Pages

F.1 *(continued)*

CTS Wiki Test Reset Record Form			*(front sheet)*
Project ID	CTS Group News Wiki and Process Framework		
AUT Title	CTS Wiki	AUT Version	v1 .0
Iteration ID	02	Date of Test	07/07/2008

Test ID		Time of Test	
Observed Test Result	Having – • Left-clicked into the "User Name" field and entered "testuser" • Left-clicked into the "Password" field and entered "password" • Left-clicked on the "OK" button • And having left-clicked on the **CTS Org Chart** link in the left hand navigation pane of the window that was displayed, the CTS Team Org Chart was to be displayed. I was able to verify that: • The whole org chart is visible on the screen. • The complete content of the org chart was legible.		

F.2 Specimen completed test result record form for the CTS Company Wiki project.

Test Result Category	Pass
Test Error Description	N/A

Tester Name	Dass Chana	**Tester Signature**	*D Chana*
Test Observer Name	Andy Nigel Other	**Observer Signature**	*A N Other*
			Page 1 of 1 Page

F.2 *(continued)*

Agile Test Summary Report Template

G.1 Introduction

The following pages of this appendix contain a test summary report template, which may be copied and used as the basis of a test summary report for a particular iteration or phase of the test project.[1]

Text appearing within the body of this template in angle brackets ($\langle\ \rangle$) denotes a place marker, which must be replaced with the appropriate information for a particular testing phase.

Text that appears in italic is provided for information only (such as illustrative examples) and should not appear in the final test summary report.

---

[1] Where the test summary report template provided in this appendix does not exactly match your needs, an electronic version of the template can be obtained at the following URL for you to customize: http://www.cambridge.org/9780521191814 (Cambridge University Press Web Site / Agile Script Template).

Test Summary Report

Document Information {to (Client) Doc Standard}	
Project ID:	(Project ID) *the unique ID for this testing project*
Document Ref:	(Doc Ref) *a unique document reference for this document*
Iteration ID:	(Iteration ID) *the unique iteration ID*
AUT Title:	(AUT Title) *the definitive title of the application under test*
Date:	(Date) *the date this document was completed*

Distribution	
Copy Number	Recipient
1.	(recipient 1)
2.	(recipient 2)
3.	(recipient 3)
	etc.
N.	Project File

Contents

1. Introduction
2. Overview
3. Variances
4. Assessment
5. Results
6. Evaluation
7. Summary of Activities

1 Introduction

1.1 Background

This document provides the Test Summary for the testing activities within iteration ⟨Iteration ID⟩ for the ⟨AUT Title⟩.

This section should contain a brief background and history to this testing project which should include a brief description of the purpose of the AUT, definitive version information for the AUT, any other relevant supporting information.

1.2 Structure of the Report

This report is structured in the following manner:

▶ Section 2, Overview, provides an overview of the significant events and activities documented within the ⟨Iteration ID⟩ testing of the ⟨AUT Title⟩.

▶ Section 3, Variances, records any variances of the artifacts from those areas agreed on previously, especially in areas that may cause concern to the group accepting the test results, including any references to supporting documentation that covers the reasons for the deviations.

▶ Section 4, Assessment, provides a brief assessment of the comprehensiveness of the testing process for the ⟨Iteration ID⟩ testing of the ⟨AUT Title⟩.

▶ Section 5, Results, provides a summary of the results of the ⟨Iteration ID⟩ testing of the ⟨AUT Title⟩.

▶ Section 6, Evaluation, provides an overall evaluation of the testing process, including any observed problems and/or limitations.

▶ Section 7 provides a summary of the major testing activities and events for the ⟨Iteration ID⟩ testing of the ⟨AUT Title⟩.

1.3 References

A list of documents referenced within this test summary report document.

2 Overview

This section provides a high-level overview of the significant events and activities documented during the ⟨Iteration ID⟩ testing of the ⟨AUT Title⟩.

This section also specifies the scope of the testing (what was and what was not tested), and specifies the test environment details (including the hardware, software, and data used in the testing).

For example:

The Iteration 02-Team-Org-Chart-01 Test for the CTS Wiki (v1.0, 2008) was begun on July 7, 2008, and completed on July 8, 2008. During this testing only the CTS Org Chart section of the Wiki was considered.

The testing was conducted on an IBM T60 Laptop with 4Gbytes of memory running Microsoft Windows XP Professional V2002 SP2.

3 Variances

This section is used to record any variances of the artifacts from those areas agreed on previously, especially in areas that may cause concern to the group accepting the test results and including any references to supporting documentation that covers the reasons for the deviations.

For example:

Conditions observed during the course of testing resulted in the design of additional test cases to explore concerns regarding the CTS Wiki Org Chart legibility. A number of additional defects were identified as a result, which were subsequently corrected and successfully retested.

4 Assessment

This section provides a brief assessment of the comprehensiveness of the testing process for the completed testing phase against the test objectives and constraints specified in the test plan document.

Where code coverage measurements have been made, the results should also be included in this section.

This section also identifies any aspects of the AUT that were not tested as thoroughly as planned (due to insufficient time or resources).

For example:

All test cases were executed with the exception of Test Cases 02-Team-Org-Chart-04 and 02-Team-Org-Chart-05 (testing the CTS Wiki Org Chart Navigation), which were omitted due to challenging testing timescales combined with the need to further investigate concerns associated with the CTS Wiki Org Chart legibility.

5 Results

This section provides a summary of the results of the ⟨Iteration ID⟩ testing of the ⟨AUT Title⟩, identifies all resolved issues, and summarizes the details of their resolution and lists any outstanding issues.

For example:

Test Case 02-Team-Org-Chart-03 revealed problems with the legibility of the CT Wiki Org Chart (and in particular potential issues with Red–Green perceptually challenged users). The developers corrected the observed defects and the amended code passed the retest. However, it was not possible within the timescales of the testing task to regression-test the associated navigation requirements. This issue remains outstanding and should be observed following installation and use in the live environment.

6 Evaluation

This section provides an overall evaluation of the testing process including problems and limitations.

For example:

The Org Chart section of the CTS Wiki (v1.0, 2008) underwent comprehensive testing, with only two defects being observed.

Additional test cases were designed and executed to explore the CTS Wiki Org Chart legibility, and following correction and retesting it is believed that legibility will be acceptable in use.

Since a number of problems were observed with navigation, and only perfunctory retesting was possible due to challenging testing timescales, it is thought that there will be a medium likelihood of navigation failure in use.

7 Summary of Activities

This section provides a summary of the major testing activities and events for the ⟨Iteration ID⟩ testing of the ⟨AUT Title⟩. This section also summarizes testing resource information, such as total staffing levels and total testing time.

For example:
Test Start Date: July 7th 2008   Test End Date: July 8th 2008

Item	Planned	Actual
Staff Levels	*3*	*2*
Test Design Effort	*1.5*	*2.0*
Test Execution Effort	*2*	*2*
Re-Test Effort	*0.5*	*0.75*
Test Management and Reporting	*0.5*	*0.5*
Etc.		

My Agile Process Checklist

H.1 Introduction

To assist you in the selection of agile practices to populate your own agile process, this appendix contains a checklist of agile practices that show graphically which practices are particularly appropriate for different styles and sizes of agile project. This information can be used as a visual summary and *aide memoire* of the information provided in Chapter 25.

To help you understand the format and contents of the checklist, refer to Figure H.1.

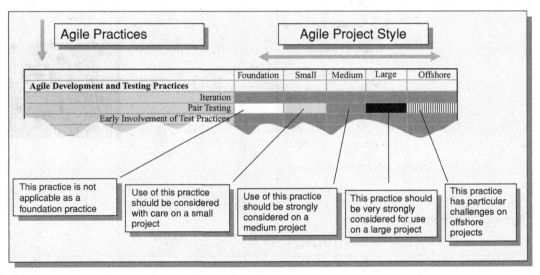

H.1 Explanation of the format and content of the agile practices checklist.

	Foundation	Small	Medium	Large	Offshore
Agile Development and Testing Practices					
Iteration					
Pair Testing					
Early Involvement of Test Resources					
Test-Driven Design					
All Defects Fixed Immediately					
Continuous Integration					
Test Refactoring					
Identify Targets of Test					
Code Coverage Metrics					
Rapid Prototyping					
Collective Code & Test Ownership					
Every Day Is Test Day					
Agile Exploratory Testing					
Agile Process and Project Management Practices					
Co-Location of Project Stakeholders					
Be Sensitive to the Reuse of Traditional Test Techniques					
Well-Bounded Iterations					
Progress Measurement					
Progress Visualization					
Availability of Agile Process Guidance					
Metrics					
Process Improvement					
Everyone Is a Software Engineer					
Agile Estimation					
Agile Requirements Management Practices					
Use Cases / User Stories					

Reduce Requirements Documentation Overload

Look Beyond Requirements to Customer Needs

Ensure all Requirements have Tests

Agile Meetings and Communications Practices

Improve Interpersonal Communications

Agile Project Start-up Meeting

Agile Iteration Start-up Meeting

Daily Stand-up Meeting

Interim Iteration Meeting

Agile Retrospectives

Agile Workshop Meetings

Agile Closedown Meeting

Agile Automation Practices

Tool Selection Process

Static Analysis Tools

Automated Unit Test

Test Harness Tools

Functional Test Tools

Requirements Management Tool

Build Management Tools

Automated Configuration Management

Change Management Tools

Defect Tracking Tools

Process Enactment Tools

References

1. National Institute of Standards and Technology (NIST), U.S. Dept. of Commerce, *The Economic Impacts of Inadequate Infrastructure for Software Testing*, May 2002.
2. Miller, P., *An SEI Process Improvement Path to Software Quality*, Presented at Quality of Information and Communications Technology, 2007.
3. Object Management Group, *Software Process Engineering Metamodel (SPEM) 2.0 Request for Proposal*, May 2005.
4. Watkins, J., *Testing IT: An Off-the-Shelf Software Testing Process*, Cambridge University Press, 2001.
5. Royce, W. *Managing the Development of Large Software Systems*, Proceedings of IEEE WESCON, August 1970.
6. Boehm, B., A Spiral Model of Software Development and Enhancement, *IEEE Computer*, May 1988.
7. Krushten, P, *The Rational Unified Process*, 2nd ed., Reading, MA: Addison-Wesley, 2000.
8. Jacobson, I., et al., *Object-Oriented Software Engineering: A Use Case Driven Approach*, Wokingham, UK: Addison-Wesley, 1992.
9. Rentsch, T., Object-Oriented Programming, *SIGPLAN Notices*, Vol. 17, No. 18, p. 9, September 1982.
10. Carroll, J., and Long, D., *Theory of Finite Automata with an Introduction to Formal Languages*. Englewood Cliffs, NJ: Prentice Hall, 1989.
11. Booch, G. *Object-Oriented Analysis and Design with Applications*, 2nd ed., Redwood City, CA, 1994.
12. Rumbaugh, J., et al., *Object-Oriented Modelling and Design*, Englewood Cliffs, NJ: Prentice Hall, 1991.
13. http://www.stickyminds.com/sitewide.asp?Function=edetail&ObjectType=ART&ObjectId=3572&tth=DYN&tt=siteemail&iDyn=2
14. IBM Rational Purify Plus Documentation, International Business Machines, 2008.
15. Graham, D. and Fewster, M., *Automating Software Testing*, Reading, MA: Addison-Wesley, 1999.
16. Martin, J., *RAD, Rapid Application Development*, New York: MacMillan, 1990.
17. http://blogs.msdn.com/jmeier/archive/2007/10/21/how-to-use-time-boxing-for-getting-results.aspx

18. Benyon-Davies, P., et al., Rapid Application Development (RAD): An Empirical Review, *European Journal of Information Systems*, Vol. 8, 1999.

19. Crinnion, J., *Exploitation of the 4GL, Software Development '92 – Management Track*, Blenheim Online Publications, London, 1992.

20. Kent, B., *Extreme Programming Explained: Embrace Change*, Addison-Wesley, 2000.

21. DSDM Consortium, *The DSDM Framework*, v1.0, 1995.

22. CCTA, *PRINCE 2: Project Management for Business*, 4th ed., 1996.

23. Takeuchi, H., and Nonaka, I., The New New Product Development Game, *Harvard Business Review*, Jan.–Feb. 1986.

24. DeGrace, P., and Stahl, L. H., *Wicked Problems, Righteous Solutions: A Catalogue of Modern Software Engineering Paradigms*, Prentice-Hall, 1990.

25. Sutherland, J., and Schwaber, K., *Agile Development Lessons Learnt from the First Scrum*, OOPSLA '96, Austin, TX, 1996.

26. Schwaber, K., and Beedle, M., *Agile Software Development with SCRUM*, Pearson Education, 2008.

27. http://agile.csc.ncsu.edu/

28. Larman, C., *Agile and Iterative Development: A Manager's Guide*, Addison-Wesley Professional, 2003.

29. Fernandez, O., *The Rails Way*, Addison-Wesley, 2007.

30. Thomas, D., et al., *Agile Web Development with Rails*, 2nd ed., Pragmatic Bookshelf, 2006.

31. Greenfield, J., et al., *Software Factories: Assembling Applications with Patterns, Models, Frameworks, and Tools*, Wiley, 2004.

32. Gilb, K., *Evolutionary Project Management and Product Development*, prepublication draft, May, 2007. http://www.gilb.com/

33. Booch, G., et al., *UML Users Guide*, Addison Wesley Longman, 1998.

34. www.ivarjacobson.com/products/essup.cfm

35. Garcia, S., and Turner, R., *CMMI(R) Survival Guide: Just Enough Process Improvement (The SEI Series in Software Engineering)*, Addison-Wesley Professional, 2006.

36. http://www.wikipedia.org/

37. Paulk, M. C., et al., *Key Practices of the Capabilty Maturity Model – V1.1*, Pittsburgh, PA: Software Engineering Institute, Carnegie-Mellon University.

38. Bittner, K., and Spence, I., *Use Case Modelling*, Addison-Wesley, 2002.

39. Reeser, T., et al., *Citrix XenApp Platinum Edition for Windows: The Official Guide*, Mc-Graw Hill Osbourne, 2009.

40. Lowe, W., *VMware Infrastructure 3 for Dummies*, John Wiley & Sons, 2008.

41. Lipp, P., et al., *Trusted Computing Challenges and Applications*, Springer, 2008.

42. Graham, D., Evans, I., and Van Veenendaal, E., *Foundations of Software Testing: ISTQB Certification*, Cengage, 2008.

43. http://www.nunit.org

44. http://www.artinsoft.com/

45. http://en.wikipedia.org/wiki/Adapter_pattern

46. http://en.wikipedia.org/wiki/Sed

47. http://nant.sourceforge.net/

48. Morrison, M., *Sams Teach Yourself XML in 24 Hours: Complete Starter Kit (Sams Teach Yourself)*, SAMS, 2005.

49. http://xjb.codehaus.org/

50. Beck, K., *JUnit Pocket Guide*, O'Reilly Media, Inc., 2004; http://www.easymock.org/

51. http://www.sevenmock.org/

52. Buckley, C., et al., *Implementing IBM Rational ClearQuest*, IBM Press, 2006.

53. Bach, J., *Exploratory Testing*, http://www.satisfice.com/articles.shtml

54. Gloger, B., *The Six Step Approach to Perform Heartbeat Retrospectives*, http://www.glogerconsulting.de/downloads/Gloger-heartbeat-retros-V11.pdf, 2006.

55. http://www.panopticode.org

56. Fowler, M., et al., *Refactoring: Improving the Design of Existing Code*, Addison-Wesley Professional, June 1999.

57. Ambler, Scott W., Vermeulen, Allan, Bumgardner, Greg, and Metz, Eldon, *The Elements of Java Style*, Cambridge University Press, 2000.

58. Holzner, S., *Eclipse: A Java Developer's Guide*, O'Reilly Media, 2004.

59. Dick, J., Hull, E., and Jackson, K., *Requirements Engineering*, 2nd ed., London: Springer-Verlag, 2004.

60. Wiegand, J., and Gamma, E., *The Eclipse Way: Processes That Adapt*, Presented at EclipseCon, 2005.

61. Zielczynski, P., *Requirements Management Using IBM Rational RequisitePro*, IBM Press, 2007.

62. IBM Corporation, *IBM Rational Functional Tester Documentation v7.0*, 2007.

63. Gamma, E., *Collaborative Software Development – Developing Software Like a Band Plays Jazz*, Presented at EclipseCon, 2008.

64. Robbins, S., and Bell, M., *Second Life for Dummies*, John Wiley & Sons, 2008.

65. Meatzel, Kai-Uwe, *What If Your Tools Knew Your Team? – Bringing Processes to Life*, Presented at EclipseCon, 2008.

66. http://www.iconixsw.com

67. http://www.bloomberg.com

68. Nissen, C. F., *Passing Your ITIL Foundation Exam*, TSO – The Stationary Office, 2007.

69. http://emma.sourceforge.net/

70. http://portal.acm.org/citation.cfm?id=1158776

71. Wagner, A., *The Transactional Manager- How to Solve People Problems with Transactional Analysis*, Denver: T.A. Communications, 1981.

72. Evans, I., *Achieving Software Quality Through Teamwork*, Artech, 2004.

73. Brookes, F. P., *The Mythical Man Month and Other Essays on Software Engineering*, 2nd ed., Addison-Wesley, 1995.

74. Busco, C., et al., *When Crisis Arises and the Need for Change Confronts Individuals: Trust for Accounting and Accounting for Trust*, http://www.cimaglobal.com/downloads/research_enroac_busco.pdf, November 2003.

75. de Bono, E., *Six Thinking Hats*, London: Penguin Books, 1999.

76. Pas, J., *Emotional Intelligence as the Key to Software Quality*, EuroSTAR, Stockholm, 2001.

77. de Bono, E., *Edward De Bono's Web*, http://www.edwdebono.com/, October 2003.

78. TQMI, *Problem Solving – Tools and Techniques*, TQMI, 2001.

79. Robson, M., *Problem Solving in Groups*, Gower, 1995.

80. Belbin, R. M., *Management Teams – Why They Succeed or Fail*, Butterworth Heinemann, 1981.

81. Belbin, R. M., *Team Roles at Work*, Butterworth Heinemann, 1995.

82. Belbin Associates, *Belbin Team Roles*, http://www.belbin.com/belbin-team-roles.htm, October 2003.

83. Kroeger, O., Thuesen, J. M., and Rutledge, H., *Type Talk at Work: How the 16 Personality Types Determine Your Success on the Job*, Bantam Doubleday Dell Publishing Group, 2002.

84. Team Technology Web site, *Working Out Your Myers Briggs Type*, http://www.teamtechnology.co.uk/tt/t-articl/mb-simpl.htm, October 2003.

85. Team Technology Web site, *The Mother of Strategic Systems Issues: Personality*, http://www.teamtechnology.co.uk/tt/t-articl/news1.htm, October 2003.

86. Kirton, M. J., *Adaptors and Innovators defined*, see KAI Web site, http://www.kaicentre.com/, July 2003.

87. Honey, P., *Learning Styles*, http://www.peterhoney.co.uk/product/learningstyles, October 2003.

88. White, B., *Software Configuration Management Strategies and Rational ClearCase: A Practical Introduction (Object Technology)*, Addison-Wesley, 2000.

89. Bell, M., *Service-Oriented Modeling (SOA): Service Analysis, Design, and Architecture*, John Wiley & Sons, 2008.

90. http://en.wikipedia.org/wiki/System_of_systems

91. From the *RUP for Large Projects* Rational Method Composer Documentation, version 7.2., IBM Rational.

92. Young, R., *Effective Requirements Practices*, Boston: Addison-Wesley, 2001.

93. http://www.ibm.com/developerworks/rational/library/05/510_svc/

94. http://www.ambysoft.com/surveys/agileFebruary2008.html

95. Lee, K. A., *IBM Rational ClearCase, Ant, and Cruisecontrol: The Java Developer's Guide to Accelerating and Automating the Build Process*, IBM Press, 2006.

96. Preece, J., et al., *Human Computer Interaction*, Addison-Wesley, 1994.

97. Schein, E., *Organizational Psychology*, 2nd ed., Prentice-Hall, 1970.

98. Standish Group, *Chaos Report*, Boston: The Standish Group, 1995.

99. Derby, E., et al., *Agile Retrospectives: Making Good Teams Great*, Pragmatic Bookshelf, 2006.

100. MacDonah, M., *Implementing EssUP within Rational Team Concert*, Proceedings of the Rational Software Developer Conference, U.K., 2008.

101. IBM Corporation, *IBM Rational Team Concert Documentation v7.0*, 2008.

102. http://www.pmcomplete.com/BPM/HTML/bpm2f1v.asp

103. Watt, D., *E-Business Implementation*, Butterworth-Heinemann, 2002.

104. http://www.scrumalliance.org/articles/46-advice-on-conducting-the-scrum-of-scrums-meeting

105. Andersen, P. B., *A Theory of Computer Semiotics: Semiotic Approaches to Construction and Assessment of Computer Systems*, Cambridge University Press, 1997.

106. Belin, D., and Simone, S. S., *The CRC Card Book*, Addison-Wesley, 1997.

107. http://www.extremeprogramming.org/index.html

(Old Ref 29) Object Management Group, *Software & Systems Process Engineering Meta-Model*, v2.0, April, 2008.

(Old Ref 80) Ahern, D. M., *CMMI Distilled: A Practical Introduction to Integrated Process Improvement (SEI Series in Software Engineering)*, Addison-Wesley, 2008.

(Old Ref 107) Beck, K., *Test-Driven Development by Example*, Pearson, 2004.

Index

Printed in the United States
by Baker & Taylor Publisher Services